Also by Monty Don

The Prickotty Bush
The Weekend Gardener
The Sensuous Garden
Gardening Mad
Urban Jungle
Fork to Fork, with Sarah Don
The Complete Gardener
The Jewel Garden, with Sarah Don
Gardening from Berryfields
Growing Out of Trouble
My Roots: A Decade in the Garden
Around the World in 80 Gardens
The Ivington Diaries
The Home Cookbook, with Sarah Don
Great Gardens of Italy
Gardening at Longmeadow
The Road to Le Tholonet: A French Garden Journey
Down to Earth
Nigel: My family and other dogs
American Gardens
Paradise Gardens, with Derry Moore
Japanese Gardens, with Derry Moore
American Gardens, with Derry Moore

My Garden World

THE NATURAL YEAR

Monty Don

First published in Great Britain in 2020 by Two Roads
An Imprint of John Murray Press
An Hachette UK company

This paperback edition published in 2021

1

Copyright © Monty Don 2020

A CIP catalogue record for this title is available from the British Library

Paperback ISBN 978 1 473 66658 0
eBook ISBN 978 1 473 66657 3
Audio Digital Download ISBN 978 1 473 67438 7

Typeset in Minion Pro by Palimpsest Book Production Ltd, Falkirk, Stirlingshire

Printed and bound in Great Britain by Clays Ltd, Elcograf S.p.A.

John Murray policy is to use papers that are natural, renewable
and recyclable products and made from wood grown in sustainable forests.
The logging and manufacturing processes are expected to conform to the
environmental regulations of the country of origin.

Two Roads
Carmelite House
50 Victoria Embankment
London EC4Y 0DZ

www.tworoadsbooks.com

In memory of Nigel, 2008–2020.

When the Present has latched its postern behind my tremulous stay,
And the May month flaps its glad green leaves like wings,
Delicate-filmed as new-spun silk, will the neighbours say,
'He was a man who used to notice such things'?

'Afterwards', Thomas Hardy

CONTENTS

INTRODUCTION

This book is a celebration of the extraordinary diversity and richness of life that I share my garden with, much of which can be observed and enjoyed from any garden or even in the sky from the window of a garden-less flat.

I have written millions of words about my garden over the past 30-odd years but the subject matter has nearly always been plants and gardens and how to grow, control and nurture them for maximum beauty or productivity. However, from a very early age I loved the countryside as much as any garden and was fascinated by the life that I saw all around me, whether that was trees, wild flowers, birds, insects or mammals.

My sky is never empty. At dawn there may be just a lone crow beating a steady path north or at dusk, the curiously undulating, huge wings of a heron heading to roost in a willow above the ditch. Ducks in pairs race headlong and straight, and thin skeins of geese breast the morning air. Until about ten years ago, spring was rich with the sad warbling call of the curlew but here, as in so many places, it is now just a haunting memory. Then in late spring and summer, our sky is positively chaotic with martins and swallows by the hundred, cutting wheeling curves like sky skaters.

One of the reasons for so much bird activity is that we do everything we can to encourage insects in the garden and they too have their own fascinating stories. We all inevitably romanticise 'wildlife' to some extent, but every creature that we can share our gardens with, including slugs, rats, mice, ants, worms, caterpillars and aphids – all the so-called 'pests' that gardeners have spent far too much time and trouble trying to eliminate – is part of the rich, interlocking web of life.

––––––

I am not a trained naturalist but when I become fascinated by something I want to know every tiny detail, to accumulate every fact that has any possible relevance to the subject. I know that it is no substitute for observation and the slow accretion of wisdom, but having the kind of mind where facts lodge and are easily retrieved, I am inevitably drawn down this road.

However, you can know every fact about a creature – or a plant – and yet never understand it at all. But watching even the most common sparrow at a bird table in your back garden teaches so much. Familiarity breeds not so much contempt as a shift in perception. This is also true of the more dramatic elements of nature that occasionally visit – the birds of prey or the polecats or badgers. Instead of being purely theatrical, there is almost an insouciance to them. A peregrine swoops on a pigeon in the Cottage Garden with murderous and terrifying intensity – and the robin still sings and the roses still flower. You realise that this is not a single dramatic event put on to entertain and thrill you, but a daily part of life.

Spend a little time observing the natural world in your garden and you quickly learn that, unlike the sanitised version of nature put out there via films, television and stories, there are no good guys and no bad guys. Nature knows no moral hierarchy. The spider traps and eats the honey bee, the wren catches a spider to feed its young, the hedgehog finds and munches the nest of baby wrens, and the badger delights in nothing more than eviscerating a hedgehog for dinner. But from this brutally raw reality also come the song of a blackbird at dusk, the rainbow glint from a dragon-fly's wings and the mystery of a hare crossing the road in the snow. They are all part of the same story.

———

There is another element to this book that goes beyond my garden boundary. Some years ago we bought a small, derelict farm 30 miles west of here across the border in the Black Mountains of Wales, intending to move on from this garden to tackle a completely new project. But life – and not least *Gardeners' World* – intervened and the move has been delayed. However, I spend as much time there as I can.

The two places could not be more different. The flat, lowland garden is a sharp contrast to the very steep, wooded slopes of the farm. One has heavy but very fertile soil, whereas on the farm the soil is light, acidic and poor. One is tame and the other wild. The actual garden at the farm is just a small yard but the meadows, streams and woods are as beautiful as any garden could ever aspire to be. This means that the range of wildlife that I share my life with has been greatly enlarged. There are different plants, different birds, different mammals and different weather – all within 30 miles of each other, and throughout this book, I move easily from one to the other because both are an integral part of my own personal experience.

The one thing that they have in common is that both are very wet. And when the weather is very wet, the two places, under the same rain – after all, they are only an hour apart – react completely differently. The garden is set on the edge of a flood plain that has had seasonal and regular floods since the last Ice Age. The flooding comes from a river that passes within 50 yards of our boundary. This means that the flood meadows are often under water for weeks on end and we are privileged to live in that liminal space where earth becomes water and returns to dry land again. The fields around the garden slowly fill, the water rising as a brown sheet until it laps against the borders and paths of the garden.

On the farm, all water moves constantly. It rushes and tumbles in the dingles and bubbles up from the open fields on its journey down to the river that runs along the valley bottom to join the Wye and on out to the sea. Whereas around the garden water sits and becomes the landscape for weeks at a time, around the farm it is constantly shaping and moulding it, wearing the hills down to their ancient bones.

———

In a sense, this book has been over 60 years in gestation. I have kept notebooks and journals ever since I could write and I have drawn upon these as well as on the events of the past year. But in March 2020, the world changed. Covid-19 swept across the globe and put us all into confinement in our own homes. I must confess that there were far worse places to be locked down in than in this garden. However, spring was blessed with exceptionally good weather so those of us with gardens spent more time in them than perhaps we had ever done before.

The result of this enforced horticultural confinement has resulted in a much closer awareness not just of plants but of all the other living elements of our gardens. The natural world is all around us, wherever we are. Wildlife is not something that we watch happening in remote and exotic parts of the world on our screens, but is right here in our own back yards, and the more that we encourage it and learn to live with it, the more rewarding it becomes. Gardens have become the front line of animal conservation and climate change. In the last few years, awareness of the importance of the natural world on human health and wellbeing has grown enormously, and the small but significant changes that gardeners can make – like having a small pond, allowing grass to grow long and growing plants for pollinators – have become main-stream.

_____

This book is personal, selective and based on my own particular interests rather than trying to be a reference book of any kind. I have used the calendar months because these fit in with the rhythm of my gardening year – I always begin each January with a sense of hope and optimism because the garden is starting to wake up after the slow descent down to the end of the year. Some creatures are present in this book on a number of occasions, whilst others fail to appear at all, although they might be the stars of somebody else's garden.

But that is the point. All our gardens, streets and patches of sky are part of our own perception of the world. We are all individually enlarged by our connection to them. If, in our own modest back yards, we can help preserve and treasure our natural world, then we will make this planet a better place – not just for ourselves but for every living creature.

JANUARY

Robin Orangebreast

On Twelfth Night, 6 January, I gather up the holly decorating the house and take it outside, leaving it in a pile on the path in the dark to take to the bonfire in the morning. Next morning a robin is hopping about the prickly pile, feeding on the berries. Against the bright red of these fruit, I realise that it is not so much a robin redbreast as a robin orangebreast.

Oranges were not introduced to Britain until the Middle Ages and the word 'orange' was not coined until the 1570s. By then the 'redbreast' was firmly ensconced in the language and in our gardens. Language is fixed by familiarity as much as by accuracy.

Well into the nineteenth century, the most common name for a robin was ruddock, which comes from the Saxon for ruddy or red. Redbreast was a kind of modernisation of that and 'robin', which came much later, was a nickname that shows a particular level of affection and familiarity with birds that we have especially close daily contact to – Robin Redbreast, Tom Tit, Jenny wren, Mag (short for Margaret) Pie, or Jack Daw. In fact, the robin was not habitually known as just robin until the twentieth century.

———

Goshawk

Walking the dogs at 4.30 p.m. – getting dark but noticeably lighter than even two weeks ago – I noticed a large bird flying towards the house from across the fields. It looked black so I thought at first that it was a crow – but all the birds looked black in that light, silhouetted against the sky and I quickly realised it was too big for a crow. Probably a buzzard then, but there was something about it that was not buzzard-like in its shape and the way that it was flying. The tail was longer and its head stuck out a little more. I realised with a flush of excitement and triumph that it was a goshawk.

Although they have become much more common over the last 20 years, I still think of goshawks as our rarest raptor and something that I would be lucky to see just once in my life. So, although I now see them once or twice a year and sometimes more, every time is like that first time, that moment fulfilling my dreams. Ever since I read TH White's *The Goshawk* when I was seventeen, I have been obsessed with birds of prey of all kinds and goshawks became totemic, representing all that was untameable, pure and exquisitely beautiful, yet honed to kill.

This gos flew quite slowly and casually but in a dead straight line, perhaps 100ft up. Its wings had an almost deliberate flap that rose as high above its back as below, quite unlike a buzzard. It passed directly over the house, and then was swallowed up by the dark sky. But my day was made.

————

Great Spotted Woodpecker

The great spotted woodpecker is one of the most dramatic and spectacular of garden birds, with its black-and-white wings, long beak with yellow pad at its base and, most flamboyantly of all, its startling crimson bottom and, in the male, crimson head. Just to see one at all is a thrill. It is much more often heard than seen as it drums for insects on a tree trunk. Yet its numbers have been steadily increasing since the 1970s.

I see 'our' woodpeckers most often when they are right outside the kitchen window, feeding off the caged peanuts or slabs of fat. They will approach with extreme wariness, starting in the big ash tree in the Spring Garden and moving slowly onto the fig, moving by degrees, checking all around them until they reach the bird food and busily hammer away at it.

But if they sense any movement, even from within the kitchen, they are gone, retreating to the safety of the big ash tree. The female – recognisable through her lack of red cap – seems to be less wary than the male, who can almost sense a shadow moving within the building. It is apparently unusual to see more than one woodpecker at any one bird feeding station but our male and female visit equally regularly.

The young have a red-flecked head which, given their slightly smaller size, makes it possible for them to be confused with lesser spotted woodpeckers but the latter are much smaller – sparrow-sized – and much, much rarer. I watch birds all the time and have yet to see one.

Great spotted woodpeckers are woodland birds and need trees of a certain size, so are most likely to be seen in gardens and parks with large trees. They drum on rotten wood to extract invertebrates and this is their main source of food. However, when they have young, they will take chicks and eggs, especially from tits, drilling into the nest or nest box to get at the young. Then in autumn and winter, when protein is more scarce, like many carnivorous birds, they eat a lot of tree seeds.

The drumming is not only to extract insects and beetles from the wood but also to mark territory. It has been established that the frequency of their blows – five to 20 strikes per half-second – is exactly the best number for maximum resonance, with the timber becoming a sounding board that spreads the sound through even dense woodland.

The birds have a pad of tissue between their beak and skull that absorbs the percussive effect of the drumming and means that they can hammer into hard as well as softer, rotten wood. It is not just their skulls and beaks that have evolved to drill into wood, but their feet are zygodactylous, with two toes pointing forwards and the other two facing back. This, along with the tail feathers being able to press stiffly against the trunk – and acting like a vice on a wire tube of peanuts – makes an exceptionally firm and secure base from which to hammer. They have an exceptionally long, barbed tongue that can reach into the tunnels that insects make under bark and prise them out.

Their nests are dug into tree trunks, and often involve both sexes taking turns nest-digging for a fortnight or more. Whilst the entrance hole is small, the real work takes place inside as the nesting space will be large – in fact, roomy enough for birds as large as ducks to use. However, this mammoth effort is an investment because great spotted woodpeckers will keep the same nest for years.

I have never seen nor heard (and as well as their drumming, their repeated, alarmed single note call is very recognisable) a great spotted on the farm although I found the body of a fully fledged dead young bird – so they must be there. However, we are right on the margin of their comfortable breeding zone and our patches of woodland are perhaps not big enough for them.

———

House Mice

'The thing about your mouse', Ron said, 'is that he does his business everywhere. Pees on the run. Rats are bad but mice are worse 'cos your rat at least has some control, not like your mouse what does it everywhere.'

Ron had a point. Mice are, compared to rats at least, quite sweet and seemingly unthreatening but house mice, as well as defecating around 50 times a day, constantly mark their territory with urine – and this includes kitchen surfaces, bathrooms, cupboards and almost anywhere they go. Therefore they should be taken seriously as a pest. Yet few houses do not have them at some time and if you live in an old house, like we do, then you can share it with a lot of *Mus musculus domesticus*.

They have superb night sight and hearing so are active mostly at night. I remember when we moved into our last house the nights were marked by endless, thunderous scamperings. I quickly worked out that the 1950s heating pipes, fuelled by an enormous solid-fuel boiler in the cellar, were the mouse highway because they were boxed in. I removed all the boxing around every pipe and although I don't think it did anything to lessen the mouse population, at least it was quieter.

Old houses are perfect for house mice. They live in the walls, under the floorboards and in the roof space. If you have a lot of mice in the house you will know by the smell – they leave a very distinctive, rank musty odour – although this is not nearly as bad as the smell of a decomposing mouse under the floorboards.

They are noisy at night because they scurry about a lot. They will visit up to 30 different feeding locations or, if they have found a really good food supply, go back and forwards hundreds of times in the course of a single night. They eat almost anything including meat, soap, plastic, cardboard, wiring insulation and plaster, but they like grain best of all. Although cheese is the archetypal bait of a mousetrap, they find chocolate or peanut butter much more enticing.

House mice in fact are extraordinarily resilient creatures. They can climb, jump and swim, and there are many house mice that live in hedgerows, gardens and fields. They can also reproduce with truly astonishing fecundity, with one female having up to ten litters of about six young a year. In theory, that will result in tens, if not hundreds of thousands, of mice by the end of the year although the mortality rate is high and they have many predators such as owls, stoats and weasels.

Mice infestations and population explosions occur when there is a limitless supply of food – such as a grain store – and mice predators are reduced, such as a house without cats. In fact they can live in a very limited range, keeping to part of a house or just one room or even, in some extreme cases, spending their entire life inside one sack of grain.

But house mice have lived with people for at least the past 15,000 years – before the advent of farming – and should there be people, buildings and food in 15,000 years' time, there will also surely be mice.

———

Butterflies

My workroom is full of red admiral and peacock butterflies. They flutter weakly against the windows and high up on the sloping roof of the hop kiln, sometimes reaching the oculus at the top, 30ft above me, where they vainly circle and flap, unable to reach the sky that is the other side of the dome. They have obviously come indoors to hibernate and there are dozens of them around the house.

Modern, insulated and centrally heated houses are mostly too warm for them but our ramshackle, timber-framed Tudor house, with its stone floors and endless dark nooks and crannies, suits them well. Sometimes I manage to catch them and throw them up and out into the air through the open window, but I am not sure that I am doing them any favours. The warmth of the house might be a safer bet than the cold garden full of hungry birds.

———

Goldfinches

I get letters asking why we lay fake birdsong over filming in the garden because – I assume – viewers cannot believe that it could ever be that present or loud.

Yet there are lots of birds that are a hidden, constant presence that I largely take for granted. But putting out feed in the winter months changes all this. I get to see close up and for extended periods birds that disappear into the fabric of the garden from mid-spring.

My favourite of all these are the goldfinches. They are not remotely rare or unusual but as striking as any bird in the field. They specialise in eating the seeds of thistles and can pluck the seeds from the downy seedheads and from the otherwise prickly teasels – which have self-seeded all over the garden. Like all finches, they have thick, powerful beaks that seem unnecessarily over-geared for eating these small, quite delicate seeds but the beaks are designed to break open hard seed cases and get at the intensely nutritious interior. Their beak is not just a large, wedge-shaped crushing machine but has evolved so that on each side of the upper mandible is a groove where the bird can wedge the seed before using the lower mandible to do the actual crushing. The seed is then held in place by the groove whilst the bird peels the husk with its tongue and spits it out before consuming the seed itself.

Goldfinches get their name from the yellow undersides to their wings that show as a golden band, edged and accentuated by black feathers in flight. But their greatest distinction is the clown-like make-up of their bright crimson faces banded by a white aureola topped with a Mohican of coal-black feathers on their scalp. They arrive at the feeding table in clusters, jerky and bold. A group or flock of goldfinches is, delightfully, known as a 'charm', which derives not from their attractiveness or good manners but from their song, which is sibilant and sweetly tuneful.

Their regular appearance in gardens only began on a large scale very recently, in the early 1990s. This has been put down to the huge increase in bird food – and in particular sunflower and niger seeds – that people now regularly put out in their gardens.

Not all British goldfinches remain over winter and many will migrate to France, Spain and Portugal, returning to breed in April. They can have two clutches a year, with the white eggs, speckled with brown dots, laid in a lovely, neat, deeply cupped nest. These are usually found on the outer reaches of branches rather than near the trunk or tucked within a climber or other hiding place. The nests are made entirely by the female (the male apparently watches) from moss lined with thistledown and cobwebs. Although goldfinches are essentially seed-eaters, the chicks are fed mostly a diet of caterpillars and aphids, so are useful as part of a balanced control of garden pests.

———

Mist

Another very misty day – the garden deep in the clouds. Trees smudge the horizon like lichen on bark. A crow is a dark shadow, flapping indistinctly, then vanishing into thick air.

———

Robin

There is a robin waiting for me each morning when I come out to the larder to get the bird food. The larder is in an old hop kiln that looks over the herb garden and the only access is via a short garden path. This excursion is fine for most of the time but a little less enticing when it is really rainy or we have thick snow. However, the occasional slip is worth it because the brick walls, brick floor and three external walls make it cool and dark, and perfect for storing onions, garlic, pumpkins, all tinned and dry food – and the bird food that I mix and store in two dustbins just by the door.

Perhaps he – for it is a bright red-breasted he – sits there for hours waiting for me but I suspect he has worked out when I come and that I am sure both to spill some from the scoop as I walk and that I always leave the door open so he can nip inside and have a quick feed from the uncovered dustbin. Some days he sits patiently on the shelf with the jars of jam and pickle just inches from me, whilst I fill the scoop.

I often wonder how robins' confidence with mankind evolved. They must be subject to predation from sparrowhawks in the same way that similar-sized garden birds such as sparrows, finches and tits are, so standing alone and exposed with an air of swaggering confidence seems a trifle risky. Perhaps it is exactly that terrier-like confidence – after all, few birds are as aggressive or territorial as robins – that protects it. My sweet robin, gracing me with his attendance every morning, is probably less the sweet creature bonding with me but more like a pumped-up terrier bullying for scraps.

———

Polypody

Down at the bottom of the dingle on the farm, the water has rolled, split and smoothed large boulders and striated others into layers of fissured seams. Since we have been there, two huge stones, each the size of a small car, have been turned on their sides by the power of the water that hurls down the slopes after heavy rain. But the biggest rock of all is now slightly up above the water and stands about 7ft tall, a rectangle, sheer on three of its sides but on the fourth, the flattened trunk and roots of an ash tree all but cover it.

From any viewpoint other than that third, stream side, it looks as though the substantial tree is growing directly out of stone. It is a circus trick, a piece of performance art and, rather like watching someone balancing on a pole inside the Big Top, there is a frisson of anxiety every time I visit it that it will have overbalanced and been blown over by the winds. But so far, nearly 20 years in, it has stood strong.

Around its base, spilling out of the inevitable layer of moss, like a green display with the stone as its vase, is a mass of common polypody (*Polypodium vulgare*). Although this fingered fern looks feathery and soft, it has surprisingly leathery, ladder-like fronds held on stiff stems. The new fronds appear in June and stay green and fresh right through winter. Its natural home is on acid rocks and banks and – given sufficient rainfall – epiphytically on the level surfaces of branches. Rain-sodden, rocky, acidic and yet with nowhere for the water to sit and pool, this particular clump has found its ideal home and completes the strange picture of the tree growing out of a rock.

———

Rooks

I walk Nigel and Nell on a greying afternoon to what we call the Long Field. This is because it is very long. The oldest maps show the Long Field with an unchanged outline, although on one side are two medieval open fields that were subdivided in the early nineteenth century, and on the other, another field that is also long and slim. The hedge between them is the parish boundary.

I have never been able to work out whether the hedge marks the boundary or the boundary was chosen because of the hedge but in any event, hedge and boundary are at least 500 years old and quite possibly twice that.

Before it reaches the hedge, the boundary diverts through a little wood, used as cover for pheasants. Like half the Long Field, the wood often floods and the pheasants' pens get washed away. But up in the tops of the trees, safe and dry, is a rookery with scores of great twiggy nests, and one of the pleasures of walking through the Long Field is not just musing about the history of parish boundaries, but seeing the rooks gathering ready to return for the night. If they are on the ground still feeding with their stiff-legged walk, the presence of the dogs will set them up in the hundreds from the field in a cawing, heavy flurry.

The flock swirls and streams back to roost in a noisy gaggle but with outliers, and invariably quite a sizeable division breaking off and swinging away, making a deal of noise as they do so. It all seems a slightly chaotic, disorderly process. That communal cawing increases as the light falls, leeching into the darkness, settling slowly as the flock fidgets and grumbles itself down for the night. Then it starts up again before the first light, and in the pre-dawn of a January morning their calls echo around the garden and fields and into the open bedroom window, black birds against a charcoal sky smudged with a line of light on the horizon.

For the first few months of the year I see them ferrying to and fro across the garden with beakfuls of twigs, making and mending their untidy nests with material they have gathered and stolen. The flooding makes this easy work because as the water drains away it leaves tidemarks of twiggy debris for them to gather.

But although rooks are often part of our garden sky, they rarely visit us, preferring the surrounding fields. They are most present in the garden through sound alone, in the last darkness before a winter dawn, as the rookery wakes and gathers itself for the day ahead, chattering, squabbling, calling, marshalling the troops.

The choice of that patch of trees for the rookery is connected, I suspect, to the flooding, which limits what the Long Field can be used for. Although the really lucrative crops around here are potatoes and wheat, and the soil is suitable for both, it has not been ploughed in the past 25 years and, I suspect, hardly ever. It is even too wet to be reliably used for hay and certainly not for silage, so it remains exclusively a pasture, used only for grazing cattle and sheep. This is ideal for the rooks that are essentially birds of steppe and prairie, and need short grassland on relatively soft, moist soil so they can feed on worms and whatever invertebrates they can find, although they will also take almost anything they can find, including young birds, carrion and small rodents.

Rooks have a good press with their sociability, waddling walk and great grey pickaxe beaks emerging from a bare face, giving them a slightly comical, clownish appearance, unlike the feathered sinisterness of crows or the massive heads of ravens. But in the air, rooks and crows look pretty similar save for quantity. What is the old saying – 'If you see a rook then 'tis a crow and if you see crows then 'tis rooks'? Something like that. The point being that you almost never see a rook on its own and, equally, crows hardly ever go about in more than twos and then in a semi-detached, not-really-talking-to-each-other, sort of manner. Rooks on the other hand are always social and descend upon a field like a busload of holidaymakers heading for the beach.

———

Not Fox

Sometimes the wildlife in and around the garden is not so much wild as just badly behaved.

I was in the orchard pruning apples when I saw a particularly large fox three fields away, almost on the horizon. It seemed to be working the hedgerow, dipping down into the ditch that separated it from the field, absolutely intent on its business. Although foxes are now common in cities, it is rare to see them here in the middle of the day, especially in winter.

So I watched, at first enthralled and then, with mounting suspicion that grew into certainty that my 'fox' was in fact Nellie. I called from the top of the tree, she heard, looked up and charged back across the fields, barely breaking stride to slide snake-like under the gate and arrive back happy and entirely guilt-free.

We are surrounded by fields and although in two directions these fields run for miles until you reach a road, in the third, the main road is just half a mile away as the crow flies – and Nell runs as fast as any crow. Even in rural Herefordshire the traffic is desperately dangerous for a very unstreetwise dog. Nigel is hefted to the garden and although he will stand at the gate looking at the fields with longing, he has never taken himself off for a walk. Not Nell. She can wriggle and squeeze through the tightest fence and the smallest gap, and when bored thinks it completely reasonable to go off on a long cross-country ramble. And sooner or later that rambling will take her right up to the main road.

I wondered how often she had made these jaunts when I assumed she was merely pottering around the garden. I habitually open the door and push the dogs out into the garden and assume that they spend most of the time pottering around or lying in the sun. And 99 times out of a 100 they are out there or come quickly when I call them. But perhaps Nell has a secret life, slipping off for a quick roam on a regular basis.

———

Wren

A wren in the larder all day. Scarcely bigger than a butterfly, flitting about and dodging behind pots and boxes. Sharp, curved beak and beady eye, and white stripe above the eyes. A feathery thimble of a bird.

———

Long-tailed Tit

The bird table brings me birds I hardly ever otherwise see and yet I know they are here in the garden the year round. One of my favourites are the long-tailed tits. They are always in the plural, with as many as a dozen or more suddenly appearing in a flurry of pink and grey feathers and tails twice as long as their tiny bodies, all clinging to the same fat ball or wire tube of peanuts. Then when they go, they all shoot off as one.

These are family groups – parents with a large gaggle of offspring and aunts and uncles of the young in one extended family – that stick together from fledging, with the solitary aunts and uncles helping to raise the young in late spring until the following March, when the young mostly disperse. But from November to February we see them almost daily, descending all at once, taking over the fat and peanuts.

They have round heads with tiny bills and bright little eyes almost lost in feather, and are the prettiest of birds, as though spun from candied sugar. Their nests are the stuff of fairy tales – long and almost gourd-shaped and made from moss and lichen lined with thousands of tiny feathers all bound together by cobwebs. The clutch can be as many as a dozen or more eggs, and as the young grow the nest expands and stretches – but held together by its cobweb ties.

———

Foxes

There are no reliable figures for British foxes although in 2016 it was estimated that the urban population was 150,000, with another 300,000 spread across the rest of the British Isles. The life expectancy of most foxes is one to three years but their mortality rate is high. About 400,000 cubs are born each year but as many foxes, young and old, die with up to 100,000 killed on roads. But the evidence seems to be that numbers have declined overall by about one-third since the hunting ban, and a much greater proportion of the total population is now urban.

I was brought up in a world that viewed foxes as sport or vermin. The sport was fox hunting, which was as much part of rural life as the local cricket or football teams. But fox hunting has always been about horses and hounds much more than foxes. What mattered was the chase and without that the kill was meaningless.

I have been hunting three times in my life and found each occasion to be a mixture of excitement, uncertainty and intense, crippling boredom. The excitement came from the few moments when we all galloped along, with the odd jump thrown in, the uncertainty was based on my ignorance of what exactly was going on at any given time, and the boredom quickly kicked in as most of the day was spent sitting on my horse in the rain waiting to be told what was happening, where the hounds were and what I was supposed to be doing. All in all, it seemed to me to be a poor way to spend a day and after the third outing I stopped and was never remotely tempted to do it again – although I loved the hounds.

But I cannot pretend I ever had particular pity for the fox.

I also know that fox hunting preserved the lives of many more foxes than it ended. The hounds tended to catch the old, ill or injured and, despite the graphic sensationalism of the foxes being 'torn apart', death was quick and no worse than the death of a rabbit hunted by a fox or a mouse caught by a cat.

It preserved foxes because wherever you had a hunt, you had to have foxes, so farmers and gamekeepers refrained from shooting or gassing them. The minute the hunting ban was enacted, foxes started to be killed by the thousand since most farmers and gamekeepers regard them simply as vermin to be eradicated. I remember one neighbouring farmer proudly telling me he had shot fourteen foxes the night before, 'now that the bloody hunt was out the way'.

A fox's earth is a tunnel about 15ft to 40ft long and 3ft to 10ft deep, dug down at 45 degrees to the surface – although foxes like to use a slope, so the tunnel is often more horizontal than this. It ends in a chamber where the foxes can sleep and raise a litter, and there is usually at least one emergency entrance and often more. The thing is very subterranean. It is a very long, very deep lair. But where possible, foxes will occupy holes that have already been dug – often by badgers and often with the badger still occupying part of the sett.

I have a skull on my desk in front of me, taken from a badger's sett, which I was given over 30 years ago. For years I assumed it belonged to a Jack Russell terrier and built a story around it in which brutal badger baiters sent the poor dog down after the badger – which was at least three times its size – and instead of flushing Brock out to be battered by the slavering farmhands, the terrier was killed instead, and no doubt devoured.

It was a good, bloodthirsty tale but completely inaccurate. In time I discovered that the skull once belonged not to a Jack Russell but to a fox. It is surprisingly small and probably came from a half-grown cub – but then all foxes, beyond the bushy tail and fur, are surprisingly slight. With a little imagination, it was not hard to see the long, vulpine face fleshing out the skull. Either the badger objected to the fox's presence in its sett or the fox died down there of unknown causes.

Unlike a badger's sett, a fox's earth is not used all the time. They are primarily for rearing cubs and once these have grown and moved out – which takes about four months – they are used only sporadically, mainly in bad winter weather or to hide. The rest of the time, foxes will lie above ground, often in a dense patch of weeds such as nettles or brambles.

They do not use any bedding material so, unlike badgers that will clean out their leaves and dried grass bedding periodically and leave it accumulating outside the entrance, the only likely sign of an occupied fox's earth is a pile of black poo or 'scat'.

Unless chickens are kept in a fox-proof pen and locked up at night, they will certainly be caught and eaten in weeks, and foxes have eaten half of all the chickens we have kept in this garden over the past 30 years. This is especially bad in late spring and early summer, when the parents are feeding growing cubs, and then when the cubs leave the earth and have to learn to fend for themselves – and a fat chicken is easy prey and good eating.

But whilst anyone living in central London is almost certain to see a fox in broad daylight and sometimes nosing around their back garden, here in the middle of the most rural county in England we see foxes very rarely. The most likely sightings are from our bedroom window at dawn as one heads home across the field, always completely ignored by the grazing cattle. Occasionally, it will stop to snuffle after an earthworm, or even, if lucky, a vole. Although they will eat anything they can find, voles and rabbits are their best prey and fox numbers in the countryside are determined by the prevalence of both.

It has been pointed out that because foxes are so territorial, frequency of sightings is no indication of the local population. In other words, if you repeatedly see foxes in a certain place, you are almost certainly seeing the same ones each time.

But much more often than seeing them, I smell our foxes. Scent for foxes, as for all dogs, is much the most important sense. They spray urine to mark territory and the scent of this – particularly in the February and March mating season – is still very strong hours later and immediately recognisable for its musty odour. There are times when the aroma of fox is right outside the back door as well as at points all round the garden.

———

Snowdrops

When we first came to live here there was no garden at all. The part that had once been the vegetable plot – which is now the Walled Garden – was filled with building rubble. Everything other than the little brick yard outside the back door was scrubby grass that had not been cut or grazed for three or four years. Nowadays we would call this rewilding but back then it was just derelict, abandoned land. Unloved and neglected. Good for voles but not a lot else.

Gradually I began to clear and make the garden, starting with the area nearest to the back door. I began planting it in spring, based around a large batch of hellebores I bought very cheaply, and then added bulbs the following autumn and so, by default, it became the Spring Garden. The very first flowers to go in were a bundle of snowdrops wrapped up in newspaper brought to us by a friend who had dug them up from her garden that bordered onto a church. These snowdrops had seeded themselves from the churchyard and were gradually spreading out across her garden.

Snowdrops do that, reappearing and slowly spreading by seed year after year when they have the right, slightly damp, slightly shady, conditions so, in time, a small clump can become a large swathe of white flowers.

One of the most endearing characteristics of snowdrops is their longevity. They will reappear year after year for generations – even centuries. In some cases, this is long after the garden that they were planted in has been taken over by scrub and woodland. I once visited a wild hillside in mid-Wales. There, up in a clearing in a little blasted wood, was the outline of a small house, long since disappeared but marked out in snowdrops that had been planted outside the front door and had slowly spread right around the building, liking the dampness caused by the dripping of rain from the long-vanished, gutterless stone roof. It was as if a whole world of domesticity was measured out for a few winter weeks in ghostly white flowers.

Our snowdrops are hardly a swathe yet but from that one little clump we now have snowdrops all over the garden and they certainly number by the thousand. I am frankly bored by the hundred minute variations that delight galanthophiles. I am completely happy to have just these single, unnamed *Galanthus nivalis* that could be spawned from a very rare type only found in that one Herefordshire churchyard or could be as common as – well, ordinary, everyday snowdrops. It does not alter or lessen their beauty one bit.

The essence of snowdrops in the garden is that they combine a domesticated, comforting familiarity with the untrammelled freedom of a wild flower. But no one seems to know whether snowdrops are a native or not. They certainly grow freely in the wild, but equally certainly nearly all 'wild' snowdrops are garden escapees. There is apparently no reference to snowdrops growing wild before 1770, and the first garden reference is in Gerard's

The Herball, or Generall Historie of Plantes of 1597. It is strange to think that a flower we think of as native as a bluebell or primrose could have been an exotic introduction from the Continent in the sixteenth century – like a floral muntjac or a grey squirrel.

But we want to believe that snowdrops have always grown here, always been a better part of our better selves. The fragile beauty of their nodding white bells is imbued with a sense that all is fundamentally well with the world and all we really have to do is to aspire to be as good as a snowdrop. Perhaps that is as challenging a motto as anything more grandiose.

Sparrows

Sparrows are so ubiquitous, so small and brown, so chirpily buoyant that they have become a kind of collective avian wallpaper. They are there but not noticeable. They are noisy, too, rushing around this garden, squealing and cheeping and squabbling in a high-pitched cacophony, dashing through the hedges and along the paths in gangs, like children bowling along the streets.

However, although sparrows are still present in large numbers their decline has been little short of catastrophic, with numbers falling by over 70 per cent since 1977. Whilst rural sparrow populations have been affected, that reduction has been fastest and most recent in cities. No one quite knows why although there have been many suggestions, including lack of insect prey for chicks, air pollution, parasites, fewer suitable nesting sites in new buildings as well as lack of gardens and the reduction in autumn stubble.

However, one constant has come through the study of this decline and that is that house sparrows thrive most where there are gardens. Allotments, suburban gardens and inner-city streets with gardens are all stocked with higher densities of sparrows than anywhere else.

There are two types of sparrow here in this garden although one of them, the tree sparrow (*Passer montanus*), is increasingly rare. The house sparrow (*P. domesticus*) has long been associated with people and buildings – indeed with any kind of man-made structure from machinery to ships – where it will nest. It will always be present at any bird-feeding table and is the first to appear here whenever I put out food. It also seems to frequent every street cafe and bar, hopping around tables eating crumbs or, more boldly, from your plate. Although wary and quick to flee, they seem fearless. But people have long slaughtered them by the hundreds of thousands, partly to protect grain from being eaten and partly to eat the birds themselves – although each one must produce a pitifully tiny slither of meat.

The tree sparrow was only differentiated from the house sparrow as recently as 1720, not least because it coexists with its house sparrow cousin and will be part of the same flock. The house sparrow is bigger and the male has a grey cap that looks like a toupee that has slipped, whereas the tree sparrow is smaller and has a rich chestnut-coloured head with white cheeks with a black spot in the middle, and a white collar. It often cocks its tail and is more flighty and mouse-like. Whereas the male and female tree sparrows look very similar, the female house sparrow differs from her mate in having a brown head with a distinct ochre stripe running from the eye round the back of her head, and her wing and back feathers are noticeably striped and streaked, whereas the male gives the overall impression of a much richer, chestnut-brown colour.

The tree sparrow is even more catastrophically in decline, with the population falling by over 95 per cent since 1970. This is in line with, albeit an extreme example of, the general decline of farmland birds as a result of agricultural intensification, with the use of pesticides and herbicides, thousands of miles of hedgerows ripped out and the obsession with cutting those that remain into neat, low blocks rather than allowing them to grow taller and to include mature trees.

The shift to sowing crops in early autumn rather than spring also means that there is much less stubble in the fields over the winter months and this has had a profound effect on the availability of food for many birds. It has been shown that tree sparrows rarely feed further than half a mile from their nests and prefer to stay within a few hundred yards. Making field sizes larger by removing hedges is thus destroying their available nesting sites and feeding range.

The tree sparrow is a rare bird in upland areas and we never see them on the farm. Here in the garden, just 30 miles to the east, we are right on the edge of its territory and it is almost absent from the whole of the south-west of the country and most of Scotland. That we see them at all is because the garden provides them with cover, nesting sites and food, and it is situated next to reasonably unintensive farming country. The conjunction of these two things is becoming increasingly rare so the future of the charming little tree sparrow does not look good. That is the gloomy picture. But the better news is that where they do live, they will nest and produce up to three broods a year between April and August, with each clutch having five to six eggs, so their ability to increase is good. Pairs mate for life but this love match is pathetically short, extending, if they are lucky, to a life expectancy of two or at most three years.

———

Cocker Spaniels

Cocker spaniels were so named because they were bred to flush out woodcock. My father had one before I was born, called Barney. I remember the pictures of him and his great judge's-wig ears. A friend has three and they are the busiest, most energetic dogs imaginable. Utterly charming – unless I suppose, you happen to be a woodcock.

Dunnocks

Dunnocks tend to get lumped in with sparrows – indeed, they used to be known as hedge sparrows – but although they are often seen together and mingle freely, they are quite different in many ways. For a start, dunnocks are the only British representative of the Accentor family that is spread across Siberia, the Himalayas and the damp hillsides of Japan. So for all their little brown anonymity, they come from exotic stock.

Their numbers, like those of sparrows, suffered a dramatic decline in the 1970s and 1980s but, unlike sparrows, have seen a recovery so are now modestly – cautiously – successful. They have a very different beak to the sparrow's, which is surprisingly thick and powerful, whereas a dunnock's is thin and pointed and better adapted for eating flies and beetles than cracking open large seeds. They also stand more horizontally, leaning over their chest, than the more upright tree sparrow.

They tend to creep around under the cover of hedges and shrubs, and are predominantly ground-feeders. This makes a garden with plenty of woody shrubs an ideal nesting site for them, although because they tend to make their nests low down and spend so much time on the ground, they are particularly prone to being predated by domestic cats.

In agricultural countryside, woodland edges and occasionally the lucky garden, dunnocks are a very common host for cuckoo eggs. There is an irony in this because dunnocks have an interesting, not to say racy, sex life, involving fairly drastic changes to the physiology of the male, whose testicles will swell until they account for nearly eight per cent of its body weight – the equivalent of over 15lb for a 200lb man. Meanwhile the female, who initiates mating, may copulate 30 times a day and with every male dunnock around and the males aim to do likewise with every local female. It is quite a set-up. What this means is that in every nest – which is then cared for by a steady pair – there is likely to be a number of different fathers. After all this frantic action it seems deeply ironic that the cuckoo, once hatched, will ditch the eggs and hatchlings of the dunnocks over the side of the nest – often with the parent dunnock present and seemingly unconcerned.

One of the fascinating aspects of the cuckoo's choice of foster parents for its eggs is that it seems the choice is never arbitrary. Certain cuckoos choose only certain species. One that selects a dunnock's nest would never choose a meadow pipit and vice versa. A reason for the choice of dunnock seems to be that they are one of the few birds that fail to recognise the difference between their own small, beautiful, turquoise blue eggs and the much bigger, greyish-white cuckoo eggs with their russet brown spots.

In other nests the cuckoo makes a much more effective effort to produce an egg that is like the host. For example, there are cuckoos in Finland that lay their eggs in redstarts' nests, which have blue eggs very similar to a dunnock's, so the cuckoo also lays a blue egg – but because of the dunnock's total lack of discrimination, it has not needed to develop that masking technique, just as it seems the dunnock – which is only used parasitically by cuckoos in about two per cent of nests – has not had time or need as a species to evolve a rejection response. So the single cuckoo chick grows to be a monster weighing five or six times as much as its tiny foster parents, who at no stage seem to resent or even recognise this disparity.

_____

Moss

One of the most frequent horticultural questions sent to me is how to eradicate moss from a lawn. I could not care less if there is moss in my own lawn – not that we have a lawn as such but we do have areas of grass that we mow, and almost every square foot of this has as much moss as grass. But there is – or at least used to be – a generation of gardeners who regarded anything less than the 'perfect' lawn (one that definitely did not contain any moss) to be a failure of horticultural duty and skill. As it happens, moss in grass is a symptom, indicating that the ground is either too wet, too shaded or too compacted – and probably a combination of all three – for grass to grow well, whereas all three conditions are ideal for moss. So moss wins out.

Our hillside farm is a completely mossy place and away from recalcitrant lawns, on stumps, rocks, walls and stones, moss is simply beautiful. Great swathes of the fields are moss, the trunks and branches of trees wear a fur coat of velvety moss and every rock and stone not constantly washed by the streams that tumble down the hillside are mossy. The dry-stone walls neither rock nor roll and gather moss accordingly. The great oak near the house is a giant green woodland deity, limbs shining, emerald-green in the deep starkness of winter. And what may look to the untutored eye – mine, for example – to be a single mossy species is very likely to be a subtle tapestry of mosses, each precisely adapted to the slightly different conditions they prefer. So mosses on the north side of a tree trunk are unlikely to be the same as those on the south, and mosses growing near the base of a wall or tree will not be the same as those that have adapted to the drier, more exposed positions higher up – and the difference may only be a few feet.

Our farm was once part of a much larger estate and in the estate records for 1912, there is an entry reading '4 shillings for boy to collect mosses for roof'. There is a similar entry for the next year. I think it refers to moss that was gathered from the stones and used to wedge between the roof tiles to keep the wind and rain out. Moss was also collected in large quantities and dried and then used to pack around anything fragile, from eggs to porcelain.

Mosses are bryophytes, which are small, green plants that do not produce flowers, seeds or fruit. Moisture is the key to healthy mosses and in this western side of the country there is never a shortage of that. The life cycle of bryophytes consists of a generation of the familiar green plant which photosynthesises, alternating with a generation that does not photosynthesise but which produces spores. This produces a much smaller plant, often attached to the green one and living for a shorter time, yet it is the dominant part of a moss's life cycle.

Many bryophytes also reproduce vegetatively, often cloning themselves. The spores are absolutely minute and blow in the wind till they land on a tree or rock surface, where they will start to grow. Mosses do not have feeding roots but can absorb moisture and nutrients through any part of themselves, with the 'roots' acting as an anchor – which is why they can grow quite happily on a vertical surface.

But although mosses can spread very rapidly in the right conditions of damp shade, the ultimate size of each plant is severely limited by its inability to produce wood or vascular tissue, so rather than growing up and out, it spreads laterally. Some mosses are minute and can barely be seen by the naked eye but may grow by the million to form an unbroken carpet. Others are surprisingly big, with the largest British moss being hair moss, which can reach eighteen to 24in tall.

I often bemoan our wetness, especially in winter, when we can have weeks of rain, but the lovely mosses, spreading out over every hard, horizontal surface, from the slanting stems of old laid hedges to the stones edging the pond and the green lane running under the trees, prove that every rain cloud has a mossy lining.

Magpies

One for sorrow, two for joy, three for a girl, four for a boy. Actually there are five magpies – for silver – outside our bedroom window, noisily courting and cajoling and bickering. They hop and half-jump, half-fly from hawthorn to ash, taking a stance, throwing a shape whilst another mocks or petulantly admires. It is a busy, argumentative, rackety show – and all at six in the morning.

Their feathers are unbelievably clean and clearly defined – white, blue, black and grey touched with iridescent green. If I did not know how ruthlessly cruel they were, it would be easy to think them simply ravishingly beautiful creatures.

But magpies have a reputation as thieves and collectors of all things bright and sparkly, as well as being ruthless predators of other birds' eggs and their chicks. They are always the boldest and first onto any carrion – usually roadkill – and their powerful corvid beaks are menacing. They are beautiful and striking but their chattering cries are harsh and aggressive, and their body language is cocky and dominant to the point of bullying. They are clever and funny and easy to admire, but perhaps harder to love.

Magpies always featured heavily on gamekeepers' gibbets but

since they became protected under the Wildlife and Countryside Act 1981 (save for a special licence which ceased to be available in April 2019), numbers have risen greatly and in the past 20 years have levelled out – arguably to a sustainable equilibrium. However, people have attributed the reduction in the number of songbirds such as skylarks almost entirely to the increase in magpies.

However, the evidence for this is thin to the point of non-existent. They certainly do predate on songbird eggs and chicks but songbird numbers have dropped regardless of the local magpie populations, and in many cases, have increased where there were numerous magpies. In other words, the loss of habitat and insects for songbirds far outweighed any loss of their eggs or chicks.

The truth is that magpies, like most members of the crow family, are very smart and will always take the lowest-hanging fruit, which mostly means invertebrates like beetles, although they will quickly find any carrion and they do a huge amount of tidying up of roadkill, but they will also take food from a bird table or a nest of unfledged chicks in exactly the same spirit that a thrush will take a worm or a snail.

They are supremely successful survivors and their only natural predators other than humans are goshawks, peregrines and perhaps an exceptionally bold female sparrowhawk.

Each breeding pair needs about twelve acres, so up to half of all magpies in any area do not breed but instead form a non-breeding flock. Their nests – and we have two currently in the garden – are bulky, twiggy affairs, high up in a tree, often domed with an entrance on the side and lined with mud. The young stay with the parents within their breeding territory until autumn, when they will leave to join other young birds and form over-wintering flocks. Despite their adaptability and wide diet, many die in their first winter although some can live to be 20 years old.

———

Roe Deer

Many years ago I used to go deer-catching. It is a long story and an honourable and fascinating enterprise that was started in an attempt to reduce the fatalities incurred when darting deer to move them or take samples. For the tranquilliser to be strong enough to knock the animal out quickly, yet not so strong as to harm or kill it, you needed a pretty precise dose, which meant knowing the deer's weight and state of health. That was almost impossible in a park herd and completely impossible for wild deer, and many died before they could be caught in time to give the antidote. But by catching them with nets, blindfolding them and securing them firmly but harmlessly, the injury and fatality rate dropped to almost zero.

So back in the 1970s, a team of between eight and 20 of us would catch red deer, sika, fallow, roe, muntjac and Chinese water deer. It involved going off all over the British Isles and Ireland and tackling large animals before bundling them into nets without doing them any harm – and trying not to do too much to ourselves. This still continues with great success but is not ideal for an old codger with crocked knees.

However, deer do not play much of a part in my life here. There is no evidence of them ever visiting the garden and we do not often see them in nearby fields. When we do, it is invariably roe deer.

Nor was there any sign of deer on the farm. But my son gave me a fixed camera for Christmas and we set it up in various places, recording foxes, badgers, buzzards and crows all visiting the corpse of a dead ewe.

Then we moved the camera to a glade in a wood and the next day found that we had been visited by a roe deer and a fawn. It was nervous and barely crossed the lens for more than a few seconds, but was unmistakable. It was tremendously exciting, although mysterious that I had scoured every inch of our very small farm obsessively for sixteen years, yet never found any trace of deer before. It is no wonder that the Spanish call them *el fantasma del bosque* – the ghost of the forest. If they were out on the hillside, we would see them sooner or later because everything becomes silhouetted against the sky. It must mean that they stay in the valley bottom, near the river, keeping to the woods and well away from people.

Roe and red deer are the only British natives and whereas red deer roam in large herds on upland moors and large tracts of semi-wooded land like the New Forest, roe are woodland animals. The males are solitary and the females live in small family groups.

Although they are so secretive and thus not seen a great deal, there are reckoned to be as many as a million roe deer in the British Isles, making them by far the most common British deer. They rut in summer but the fertilised eggs do not start to develop into embryos until the new year and the doe does not give birth until the following June. Triplets are not unusual and twins are common.

Seeing deer on our land is wonderful and cause for celebration but we know if they make a habit of visiting, the trees we have planted and are planning to plant will be the first thing they will eat. Deer of all kinds, but especially roe, do great damage to forests and especially to young plants as they eat the new leading shoots. They also eat the understorey of established woods, which has a knock-on effect on bird nesting and feeding habitats.

Another problem is not so much what deer naturally do, but that they have no predator, so where they breed, numbers quickly shoot up and the population exceeds its natural balance. The solution seems to be culling on a large scale – around 50 per cent annually. This is often impractical and bound to be extremely unpopular, so for the moment numbers look set to increase.

———

FEBRUARY

Foxes' Yowl

Woken at 4 a.m. by yowling foxes. It is mating season and the vixen's curious rasping, strangled scream cuts eerily through the silence. Going to the window I can just make her out in the moonlight, trotting across the field, stopping every ten yards or so to call and advertise herself to the local dog foxes before she slips under the fence into the turnip field.

Next morning I walk across and see just a few strands of her orange coat caught on the barbed wire.

––––––

Ducks

Ducks are a permanent feature of the sky and fields above and around the garden and on four separate occasions we have kept ducks here, along with the chickens and, for a few years, guinea fowl. I have never known a wild duck land, let alone nest, in the garden and I don't think I have even seen one in the sky above the farm. Our water there is too fast and rocky for them to feel at home.

We normally see them in pairs, flying straight and fast, using the sky as an express route, sometimes doing laps three or four times around the same aerial circuit. There is none of the sense of using the three dimensions or of the playfulness that so many birds have in flight. Clearly our seemingly benign rural sky is a dangerous place for them.

In winter they burst out of the ditches and streams in a flurry when the dogs disturb them (and Nell chases them for hundreds of yards as they skim the ground) but in spring and early summer they spend a lot of time out in the open, walking the fields to find a place to make a nest in the wet grassland. Unlike urban ducks, they seem to spend very little time paddling about in the water of either the river or the streams that lead into it. Their lives seem busy and fretful, and restricted to pairs sticking together, watching each other's back.

Although I see ducks daily and am aware of variations from mallard to wigeon, teal, goldeneye and smew – sounding like a firm of country solicitors – I have not really taken the same sort of interest in them as I unthinkingly do about songbirds or raptors, or even the little brown jobs that so easily merge into anonymity.

When we kept ducks I adored their charm as they waddled around the garden or came running to greet me, and was heart-broken every time they got eaten by fox, mink or polecat. That is the reason why we do not keep ducks any longer – not because we don't want to but because they are too much like pets. I get too attached to them, so the subsequent and almost inevitable loss is unbearable. We could, of course, build a fortress pen with sunken wire netting, and a covering to stop them flying out or anything coming down in, but that destroys the point. Ducks waddling round the garden are a joy (whereas chickens are like a gang of bored vandalistic teenagers looking for trouble) and I would not want to coop them up. So I get my hit of ducks from the sky, racing across with none of the easy curiosity of their domestic counterparts.

―――

Moles

I am confused about moles. On the one hand they are charming, appetising little creatures, with their black, velvety bodies and enormous, alarmingly hand-like front feet. Our cats would occasionally catch one and present it proudly to us in the kitchen and

I always mourned this with a real pang of sadness. Yet moles are also immensely destructive and do their damage in almost every corner of my garden, tunnelling under borders, lawns, and even in the greenhouse. That damage is compounded by Nellie's curiosity at underground movement and her subsequent enlarging of the holes. At least she does not do what Poppy, an erstwhile Jack Russell of ours, used to do, which was to follow the line of the tunnels with ferocious concentration, resulting in long trenches running through the garden and a very happy, muddy-nosed little terrier.

A mole can dig at a rate of about 15ft an hour and as it digs it pushes the soil behind it and when sufficient soil has accumulated, it turns and pushes the soil back down the tunnel until it reaches the surface, which makes a molehill. When moles are really active, molehills can appear all over the garden and some of our nearby fields have hundreds. But however many molehills you have at any one time, they are, in anything other than the largest garden, likely to be the work of a small handful of moles, as their average density is about four per acre.

If your garden is occupied by moles it is an indicator that you have healthy soil with plenty of earthworms – which are the mole's favourite food, although they also eat slugs and insects. Moles have an ingenious – although distinctly macabre – way of dealing with worms. Once they are caught the mole nibbles off an end and rolls the rest into a ball that it then tucks into a crevice or wall of its tunnel. The worm stays alive but paralysed and immobile until the mole returns and decides to eat it.

Moles live for about four to five years and are solitary, only meeting up in the breeding season between the end of February and May, when they will make long tunnels just below the surface of the soil in search of a mate. They are beautifully adapted to their curious lives, with huge lungs that can extract enough oxygen from the stale air underground, whilst the amount of blood and haemoglobin that carries that oxygen around their body is twice that of other animals their size.

_____

Blackbird – Early Challenge

The liquid insistence of the blackbird at the 6.30 a.m. first light is staking territory, challenging all comers, as well as an act of seduction. He might as well be flexing bronzed muscles on a Californian beach.

_____

Coltsfoot

The coltsfoot is leaping out in bright yellow stargazies, the round, flattened-dandelion flowers unseasonably bright in the chill of a February morning. The stems, rising leafless, are scaly and stained crimson. They are a plant of disturbed soil and waste heaps that appeared suddenly in a new bed we made in the Wildlife Garden.

The leaves do not start to grow until the flowers have died back. Then they appear, rather larger than the flowers might suggest and shaped like a fan or hoof, which gives the plant its name, a muted green on top but pale felted silver underneath. These leaves were widely used as a cough medicine and curative against all diseases of the lung, either smoked like tobacco – which sounds a little counter-intuitive – or soaked in water or milk to make a drink.

But for now, leafless, coltsfoot serves to brighten a cold winter's day, both in the garden and in a little vase on the kitchen table.

_____

Curlews

I miss the curlew call growing out of the dark with a pang. For the first ten years or so that we lived here, the curlews were as regular seasonal visitors as swallows or fieldfares. The first call would come bubbling out of the pre-dawn sky around the time of Sarah's birthday on 15 February, as the birds came inland to nest and raise their young. Then again that haunting cry would accompany the fading March light as darkness fell, and I associate the early years of making this garden, staying outside until the last glimmer of light was gone, with their call.

In fact, they had two distinctive calls. One was the famous 'curl-oo' which is long and fluting and sonorous, and the other is a bubbling, swelling, whistling 'tu tu tu tu tu', which the male sang whilst gliding with his wings held high in a V-shape above the proposed nesting site in order to show any attendant females what a fine and irresistible mate he would make. They are big birds, the largest of the UK's waders, the size of a pheasant but infinitely more graceful flyers, with long wings and a slightly portly but gracefully curved midriff and, of course, that long curved bill.

They nested and fed in the wet fields around us, making a scrape in the grass on a dry patch in an open spot where they could have a good view of predators such as foxes, crows and stoats, and stayed until the young were fledged, which was around the end of May. Their sorrowful song gradually diminished throughout spring and early summer until by mid-July it was gone and the birds were heading to the coasts of Europe for the autumn and winter.

I have not seen or heard one here for ten years. I feel guilty now that I did not really take their decline seriously enough, nor really notice it until suddenly they were not here at all. But their decline has been countrywide and catastrophic with breeding pairs down by nearly 70 per cent since 1970. The reason seems to be the gradual loss of suitable breeding grounds due to the draining of meadows and, more precisely, the increase in silage making over hay.

To the town-dweller such niceties might seem bafflingly arcane, but they are really significant. Silage is cut when the grass is very green and wet and full of nutrients. As long as it is immediately stored in an anaerobic environment – either in covered clamps or bales wrapped in heavy black plastic – it will store well and make highly nutritious food for cattle and sheep – although horses do not like it.

The big advantage for farmers, other than the nutritional one, is that they can make at least two cuts a year and often three, giving a huge increase in winter fodder compared with the traditional hay harvest. But the first cut is made some time between the end of April and the middle of May, which is exactly when ground-nesting birds such as curlews, lapwings, skylarks and yellow wagtails are rearing their young. To compound this, a farmer going for maximum silage production will manure or add nitrogen to the fields in early April as well as rolling and harrowing them. All of which amounts to disturbance for the birds.

So the curlews have gone. At least I have the clear memory of their thrillingly evocative call rising out of the pre-dawn dark.

———

Violets

The first violets start peeking coyly from the base of hedges in autumn but by mid-February they are resplendent – albeit modestly so. They do not leap out at you but invite you in. A little clump of violets is, if the ground were not so damn wet, something to get down on your knees for and enter into their microscopic, bejewelled world.

The sweet violet (*Viola odorata*) is a woodland plant and in this garden they grow in the coppice and run along the base of the bare hawthorn hedges in little splatters of colour. On the farm, as well as tucked into the mossy banks of the dingles, they also pop up in surprisingly open spots, underneath bracken and exposed in winter and spring but when I check those precise locations against the old maps, it is always where woods once were.

Look closely at individual flowers and they vary quite a bit in their shades of purple, violet, mauve and blue – with the occasional pure white one. But hold a bunch of any shade to your nose and you will be suffused with their gentle yet persuasive fragrance. It has been imitated in toilet water, sweets and soaps but nothing can compare to the scent of a few flowers on stems as fine as those of a cress seedling. The flowers rise from heart-shaped green leaves that remain in a modest form all winter but have lovely fresh leaves in spring.

They spread by seed and runners, with the seed pollinated by bees, although I have never come across pure violet honey. There are probably never enough flowers around for a hive to gorge on.

_____

Valentine's Day

Blackbirds chinking into the dusk like two porcelain cups being tapped against each other – 'chink chink chink chink' – part alarm and part territorial as the night settles at 5.30 p.m. It has been a windy and wet Valentine's Day – the Feast of the Birds. I hope they have chosen their mates well.

_____

Blue Tits

Blue tits are easily the most common of the tits in this garden and the bravest, too – busily taking peanuts and swooping off with them, one at a time. At times it is like Heathrow, with two or three coming in to land as each one takes off. It is hard to know if you are seeing the same birds coming back time and again or if there really are a lot of them, but it does seem that the latter is the most likely.

Blue tits rarely travel far from where they hatched and grew up, and there can be hundreds in any reasonable-sized garden. Certainly, recent surveys have them as one of the most commonly observed British garden birds after blackbirds and robins.

Much of that is down to the way they go about their business. They are not lurkers, hiding in the undergrowth. They flit and dart to the feeding table, taking a peanut or a sunflower seed and always zipping away to eat it in the privacy of a nearby branch. They are jerky and cocky and clever, working out how to get the peanuts from a container, managing the system, cracking the code.

Anyone who grew up before the 1970s will remember blue tits pecking open the foil milk-bottle tops on cold days. This has largely stopped along with the almost universal delivery of milk in bottles to people's dawn doorsteps. But in fact, it was not milk that the birds were after but the cream, and until the 1980s almost everyone drank full-cream milk, with the yellow cream, especially when cold, forming a plug at the neck of the bottle, just below the foil, perfectly placed for a hungry blue tit.

In summer they are less visible because of the leaves but always vocal, with their high, thin repetitive trill. And if you can see them they are instantly distinctive, standing out of a crowd of little brown jobs, with their white face, black eye-band, sky-blue crest, powder-blue wings and yellow chest.

For many years we have had a blue tit's nest inside the wall of the front of the house at the back of the Dry Garden. Their entrance is a gap in the mortar where the tits constantly pop out and in, disappearing into the inner depths of the wall to feed their brood. The female builds the nest single-handed, starting around the beginning of April in this garden, although it will be a few weeks earlier in the south and later further north. She gathers dry grass and roots for the framework, then lines this with moss, swivelling her body to form it into a cup, adding some feathers and perhaps wisps of fine grass. Then she will start to lay an egg a day for up to two weeks, with birds breeding in woodland laying the biggest clutches. She then retreats to the nest for another two weeks, leaving only briefly to feed and drink.

The life cycle of the blue tit is dependent on the very limited availability of caterpillars with which to feed their young. They raise just one large brood and feed the young almost entirely on invertebrates, so aim to coincide hatching with the maximum availability of prey which happens later in spring. Although these charming little birds are ubiquitous and seemingly very successful, only a fraction of them make it past the first few weeks and months, let alone through the next winter.

Mice, woodpeckers and squirrels can take up to a third of all blue-tit eggs. The surviving eggs will all hatch on the same day between mid and late May, and then the male bird's work begins, constantly ferrying caterpillars to the ravening brood. Each chick will consume around 100 a day, which means a parental pair having to catch and bring to the nest up to 1000 caterpillars daily, going to and fro every few minutes during the daylight hours. This is why woodland clutches tend to be bigger as the availability of caterpillars in mature trees is much greater. It is, for example, reckoned that each mature oak will host around 100,000 caterpillars, so blue tits nesting in or near one will not have far to travel to feed the growing family.

Around the second week in June, when the young are about three weeks old, they leave the nest. For all the burgeoning beauty of the early-summer garden, it is a harsh world that they are entering. With their bumbling, fluttering flight they are desperately vulnerable to predators of all kinds and a huge number are taken in their first week out of the nest. A cold, wet spell will also account for many. Those that do survive the first few days are identifiable by the greenish tinge to their caps and the yellow cast to their cheeks that are yet to turn white.

Summer can be surprisingly hard for them as the caterpillar population starts to fall. The adults now need all their energies to both recover from the rigours of feeding the brood and to see them through the annual summer moult. The young do not have a full moult until their second summer, so do not take on full adult plumage until at least fifteen months old. As up to 90 per cent die before they reach their first birthday, it means that these newly fledged adults are a tiny minority of the large clutch laid a year earlier. So for all the seemingly innumerable blue tits swarming round the winter feeding table, they represent the lucky few.

In late summer the surviving tits, adults and young alike, merge to form flocks, often including other tits and even other species of small birds. These are the birds that come to the bird table outside the kitchen, and this is why there are so many of them and why I never see tits feeding there alone.

However, as it gets dark, the blue tits go off alone to find a solitary roost, often tucked away in a nook or cranny. A few will spend the night in an empty peg-hole in the timber framing of the house, and one often darts out of the brass bell that hangs outside the back door – put up years ago to call the children in for lunch – where, if not warm under freezing metal, it is at least dry.

———

Peregrine

A peregrine circling above the farm. A pair of crows divert to escort it away like fighter jets scrambled to see off a plane that has crossed a national frontier. The peregrine – I cannot tell if it is male or female in the rain and gloom – is lazy, unhurried, but rippling with latent power. Then it picks up a gear and skims across the face of the hillside at tree height, disappearing from view. The crows turn away, the threat over.

Butterbur

There is a patch of pale pink eruptions on a verge by the side of a track that is covered with ghostly flowers that look as much like toadstools as flowers. They are butterburs, emerging from the grassy soil before any sign of leaf. Butterbur is a relative of coltsfoot, sharing the way in which the flowers arrive, do their thing and depart before the first sign of any leaf.

The male and female plants are very different and rarely grow together. Females are much more likely to be found in the north, whilst the males are more widespread. It has been suggested that this is a result of deliberate planting, with male flowers preferred because they do not set seed so their leaves tend to be bigger. These leaves, like those of coltsfoot, are large and a felted grey colour underneath. Because they are soft and flexible they were used to wrap butter in to take to market – hence the name 'butterbur' – and male plants, with their bigger leaves, provided better butter holders. I don't know the truth of this but I do know that quite a few different types of large leaves were used to transport butter.

The presence of butterbur in this particular spot by the lane indicates that it is damp because butterbur thrives in wet places, spreading by rhizomes to make a very localised but dense patch. Bees love it because each flower spike carries a mass of tiny flowers radiating out from the central stem so they can, in very bee-like fashion, gorge themselves on this one source of nectar.

———

Starlings

Back in the 1990s, when we had lots of starlings and no mobile phone reception here, no email and no internet, as a freelancer working from home the landline was my essential link and I had – very grandly – a dedicated phone on my desk with its own special ring tone. This was 'Dad's work phone'. One year, a starling tormented me for months by exactly mimicking that ring tone, usually when I was as far away from my desk as possible. I would rush in to answer it to find it dead – and a very pleased bird preening itself outside my window.

Starlings used to be considered as barely a notch above vermin, descending on buildings like feathered rodents and making a huge amount of mess. I remember in 1980s London people went to elaborate lengths with nets and spikes to stop flocks roosting on buildings. But then three things happened to make me – and most other people – feel differently.

The first event was deeply personal. It would have been about 1970. Summer. I was fourteen or fifteen. I had an air rifle – a .177, not at all powerful – the sort of thing we shot indoors at school at targets in the gym. Almost a toy. Almost, but not. I was in an attic bedroom whose opened dormer window almost disappeared into the branches of the large copper beech by the house. A starling landed perhaps 20ft from me, high in the canopy, unaware of my presence. I took aim and shot. From that range it would have been hard to miss and it dropped straight to the ground some 40ft below. Elated at my marksmanship I ran downstairs to collect my trophy. When I reached the bird it was sitting on the ground flat on its belly, legs tucked beneath it, head up, beak gaping. As I came closer its wings tried to flap but failed. I noticed that its feathers, which I had always considered a muddy, uniform brown, were indescribably beautiful, all golds and purples, sea-greens and touches of iridescent blue. And then I felt a deep, abiding shame. I had tried to kill something beautiful with a life force as developed and vital as my own. Not only had I attempted that murder but had merely succeeded in mortally wounding it. I put it out of its misery and have never killed anything for pleasure since.

The second event was technological. The easy availability of cheap video cameras followed by phone cameras and computer screens, not to say the internet, means that most of us have now seen murmurations of tens of thousands of starlings wheeling and interweaving across the sky in a synchronised display as though one integral organism. But until the 1980s or even the 1990s, that was a rare sight. For most of us, starlings squabbled and scrabbled in our back gardens and under the eaves rather than danced across the setting sky.

The third event was disastrous. From being ubiquitous in town and country, starling numbers plummeted. One of the most common garden and street birds suddenly became rare. When we moved here in the early 1990s they nested in the roof and were a noisy nuisance. Then one year they didn't. At first it was wonderful. No more endless scratching and rustling at night in the roof space. No more droppings or the constant flurry of coming and going. No more ugly fledglings furiously flapping round the rooms as they mistakenly came in through the open windows. But be careful what you wish for. They quickly became an absence, an uncomfortably empty starling-space. In just a few years, starling numbers dropped so fast that you were more likely to see a murmuration of 100,000 birds on a screen than a single starling in your back garden.

In fact, the decline had been steady and much slower than I had been aware of. Breeding populations declined by 89 per cent between 1967 and 2015, with the major drop happening from the early 1980s. No one knows for sure what caused it but changes in agriculture were the most likely reason. Farmers started sowing wheat almost immediately after harvest so whereas formerly there were months of stubble for the birds to pick over for invertebrates, this was all ploughed out.

Widespread changes in grass management meant that the short grass that is so important to starlings in spring and summer for feeding on invertebrates became less common, and pastures are now grazed more intensively or used for silage. Hedges were ruthlessly ripped out throughout the 1970s and 1980s, resulting in prairies controlled by pesticides, where once there had been a network of small fields divided by hedges and all the complex range of life that they supported. On top of that, the reduction in damp grassland through drainage has reduced the cranefly population, which is a vital part of the starling's diet. Even such a robust population as starlings is affected by these seemingly small shifts in human land management.

But they are now coming back, at least to this garden. The winter bird table has a bunch of perhaps a dozen starlings, their sharp yellow beaks chiselling great mouthfuls of fat or pecking up seeds. I am not aware of them nesting here again, certainly not in the eaves of the house as they once did, but they are around. They gather in the tops of the trees by the river, making a fuss about it, quarrelsome, fidgety and then suddenly, as one, they all take off in that fast, direct flight of theirs.

Catkins

The Naples-yellow hazel pollen is drifting across the valley. It passes the sap-filled lavender stems of the alder in a soft cloud backlit by the thin sun, creating an unexpected leaching of spring into the otherwise bleak, wintry landscape.

Catkins are the male flowers. The female hazel flowers look little more than a tiny red bud. The pollen produced by the male catkin is dispersed by the wind and the female flower catches it, is pollinated, and the result is a seed formed inside a hard casing – a hazelnut.

Quite a few other trees, including oaks, alders, birches, poplars, beeches, hornbeams and sweet chestnuts, reproduce via catkins. They have not needed to evolve large, bright or fragrant flowers to attract pollinators because the slightest breeze will do the job, sending puffs of pollen through the woodland to the waiting female flowers.

———

Chaffinch

Sparrows and female chaffinches are easy to confuse, especially if your idea of a chaffinch is of the male's bright pink feathers, black-and-white striped wings and grey summer toupee.

But he is a popinjay whilst the female is altogether drabber. She doesn't need to dress up to catch her mate, whereas he has to out-strut all the other local chaffinches, who are also dressed up in their spring finery. He not only tries to impress with his sparky outfit but is one of the first birds to start singing in spring, and his slightly repetitive burst of rising, trilling song that finishes with a flourish, is always there, coming from the hedgerow in the lane outside our bedroom window.

The young bird learns the basic structure of the song from the parent, masters and slightly embellishes it, then sticks to those variations for the rest of its life. So although chaffinch song is superficially all the same, each bird sings with enough differences to make it recognisable to other chaffinches, and chaffinch 'dialects', varying from region to region, have been identified. The song's limitations are an illustration of our own crudeness of hearing and interpretation rather than the bird's repetitiveness.

Chaffinches come to the bird table but are out-muscled by the tits and tend to stick to the margins. They seem to much prefer seeds to the hanging nuts or fat balls but in the breeding season are almost completely insectivorous, taking caterpillars, flies and spiders from trees and shrubs, so any garden with lots of woody cover will always be better for them than an open space.

Lesser Celandine

As weeds go, a little lesser celandine goes a long way. It has loveliness but those that extol it most are usually those that live with it least.

But its loveliness first. The tiny yellow flowers shine out on a sunny early spring day with a radiance that seems to beam up into the darkness. However, that is wholly against their nature because they respond powerfully to the sun, closing tight at night and on dull days, then opening wide and bright in sunlight, making a speckled carpet of brilliant yellow flowers hugging the ground. The heart-shaped leaves have a polished sheen and it has a creeping, wren-like charm as well as intensity of colour.

So far, so good. But it is incredibly invasive and almost impossible to weed out. It likes dampness and light shade, being particularly happy growing along the base of hedges – and we supply all that in generous measure. Even if we painstakingly hand-weed it out of the beds, it has established itself all along the base of the hornbeam hedges and is embedded amongst their roots.

It can also be spread by bits of root and the bulbils clinging to both animal and human feet. There is the story of celandine flowers appearing along the edges of the trenches in the First World War where, amongst the mud and horror of no-man's-land, soldiers brought back scraps of root on their boots.

It will also grow in grass but I can tolerate and even welcome that. In any event, its spread is much less voracious in grass than in cultivated ground because any kind of digging will break the roots and spread it further. But insects, including queen bumble-bees, like it because it is an early source of pollen and nectar. The leaves are rich in vitamin C and, as a clincher, it is said to be a good cure for piles.

———

Finches

The finch family, rather like tits, tends to mix and match until they blur a little, becoming a thick-billed, dumpy, indeterminate bird, be it chaff, haw, gold, green or bullfinch. But that is unfair and wastes the opportunity to enjoy and celebrate their differences, which are real.

The one thing they all share is a powerful bill, from the relatively delicate beak of the brambling up to the enormous crushing device of the hawfinch. The reason why finches have exceptionally strong beaks is that they eat plants not insects, and the most nutritious part of any plant is the seed. To give themselves a chance to get at seeds with hard outer shells, finches need a beak that is strong and deft enough to open them without losing or damaging the goodness inside.

Chaffinches are easy in their pink and grey finery, albeit the female is a monochromatic brown. Bullfinches leap out at you with their coal-black heads that give them the impression of having a flattened boxer's nose. Their song is modest but I am told they are excellent mimics and can be trained to sing. However, neither their presence nor their mimicry is much in evidence in this garden.

But we do get a lot of very visible greenfinches. This bucks the national trend which is seeing a decline in their numbers, mainly as a result of finch trichomonosis. This inhibits swallowing, so the bird cannot feed and dies. It was first noticed in greenfinches in 2006 and the number of birds has been falling since then. The parasite that causes the infection cannot live long outside the host but it will survive for a day or two in damp bird food, so hygiene at feeding stations is paramount. Old bird food, particularly in wet weather, should be cleaned up regularly – preferably daily.

Greenfinches are an olivey-green with a rather pugnacious appearance and they can be quite dominant, bossing other small birds out of their way. They are a woodland bird and only became common in gardens at the beginning of the twentieth century, which is probably as much to do with the increase in suburban gardens as with any change in the birds' habits. They like large seeds and will eat elm, yew, hawthorn, brambles and rosehips.

Dead Fox

Found a freshly killed dog fox inside a gateway, under a hedge. He was a big, impressive animal – about half the size of Nell – with a large bushy tail and healthy teeth showing under a grimace. Clearly someone had put it there. It was rather like seeing dogs laid out by butchers in Asia. Shocking and revolting and also morally complicated.

I suspect this was the large dog fox that we would see quite often. It had been shot – on our land – by 'lampers', who drive around at night in pickups, shooting foxes caught in the glare of powerful lamps they fix to the truck. For them it is sport and most farmers encourage it as a way of killing vermin, but this made me angry and sad.

Since the hunting ban many more foxes are shot as vermin – and instead of the old and the weak being taken, fine creatures like this, which would probably have got away from the hounds, are shot for sport. That is not necessarily a good reason to reinstate hunting – but it is an added layer of complication to what many see as a black-and-white issue.

———

Goldcrest

Flitting inside the hornbeam hedge flanking the Cricket Pitch is a tiny scrap of a bird, wren-small but unlike the brown, round shape of a wren with its cocked tail, this has a greyish-greenish, yellowy body and a flaming yellow Mohican stripe edged in black running from its bill to the crown of its head. It is a goldcrest, Britain's smallest bird. It is so small, and its song so thin and ghostly and its habit of working the inside of hedges so concealing, that it is the most easily overlooked of birds.

Their lives are lived in miniature. Their nests are exquisite, made from moss, spiders' webs and feathers, and the eggs – up to a dozen at a time amounting to more than the weight of the female laying them – are barely bigger than peas. The underside of a spruce or fir branch is their ideal nesting site but any conifer, including yew and occasionally ivy, can be used.

They prefer conifers to deciduous trees and shrubs, and their thin beaks have evolved to pick out insects from between pine needles. This garden is a very unconiferous place so we see them as visitors rather than nesting birds. They migrate by the tens of thousands from Scandinavia in autumn, the tiny birds crossing the North Sea when the weather is often foul, and as the leaves thin and fall is when you are most likely to see one.

But winter is tough for a bird this tiny and in a really hard winter up to 90 per cent can die of cold. However, they recover well due to the large size of their broods and their ability to have two clutches each summer. It is likely that climate change will be kind to them, so perhaps we might see them more often.

———

Bumblebees

At the first glimmer of February sun the bumblebees appear, fuzzily bumbling around the early hellebore flowers. Bumblebees have a benign, almost cuddly quality, although they can sting and, unlike honeybees, do not die in the process.

There are 22 species of bumblebee in the UK although only six are common and widespread. Unlike honeybees, who have short tongues and need open, simple flowers to access the pollen, bumblebees have long tongues so can get into more funnel-shaped flowers like foxgloves. They are also less temperature-sensitive so start work much earlier in the year and spring-flowering plants such as hellebores rely upon them for pollination.

Whereas honeybees are happiest with a monoculture, gorging themselves on one preferred plant until the supply is exhausted, bumblebees need different types of vegetation for nesting, foraging, mating and hibernating. Even if all four are available in the same small area, the bees will use them at different times. They are powerful fliers and will travel over a mile to a prime foraging site. Pollen must be available throughout the breeding cycle as, again unlike honeybees, bumblebees do not store much food in their nest.

The queen bumblebee hibernates from the first frosts and is the big bee that you see in early spring. They will breed a small colony of workers, drones and young queens, all of whom, save the mated new queens, will die in autumn.

Bumblebees often use abandoned mammal nests such as those of mice or voles and for suitable nesting areas there must be some uncut, tussocky grass, hedge banks, bits of scrub or just an undisturbed corner of the garden. But if you bury an old clay flowerpot upside down beneath a shrub, hedge or in a bank with the drainage hole visible, and stuff it full of straw or shredded paper, it will almost certainly be used by a queen bumblebee for her overwintering nest.

———

Egrets

My only connection to egrets had been through pictures of the Serengeti in East Africa and they were birds of exotic remoteness. My first sighting of one – through the kitchen window out onto the fields as I was doing the washing-up 28 years ago – was surreal, like seeing a dolphin in the stream or a lioness stalking the cattle. My eyes snagged at a splash of pure white in an otherwise dull green, brown and grey winter landscape.

I wanted to ring the papers or the local radio and report the event as a major news story. Only very gradually did I realise that other people were also seeing them, although I assumed at first that it was the same egret – probably an escapee from a zoo – that we were all getting glimpses of.

In fact, these were little egrets (*Egretta garzetta*). They were first noted at the end of the 1980s, a few years before I saw the first one here and they started to breed in the UK in the mid-1990s. To confuse things, there are a very few great white egrets (*Ardea alba*) overwintering in the UK, but the little egret has a black bill whereas its larger cousin has a yellow one.

Gradually, over the course of 20 years, the little egret went from being extraordinary to unusual to familiar, which is as vivid and concrete a measure of climate change as anything.

But I had never seen two together in or around this garden until this morning, when six flew over in formation, looking half-swan, half-heron against a bruised purple sky, and that jolt of wonder I first felt over a quarter of a century ago came back. It was as though they had flown in from another continent, as exotic and glamorous as anything in these skies.

———

Wild Daffodils

The wild daffodils and the crocus are now probably all at their best, flowering in the orchard, the Cricket Pitch and on the banks of the Mound. The bees have found them but I am not sure how much the wind is affecting this early pollen hunt. What is certain is that the miserable wet weather is not affecting the plants at all – if anything, they look very healthy and happy.

———

Spring

Spring needs no justification or explanation. It rises in the blood, arrives on the wind and streams in with the dawn light.

The first hints and clues are laid soon after Christmas with the snowdrops, aconites and hazel catkins, and the gardener in me becomes presumptuous, sowing seeds that will be ready far too soon, planting when the ground is still too frozen or too wet, trying to get winter jobs done and finished, and generally behaving as though spring is racing up upon me.

But the natural world is not fooled. Although Valentine's Day, the Feast of the Birds, is in February, it is not until March that the birds start pairing off, building nests, laying eggs and defending territories with astonishing zeal.

The wild flowers in March begin with the woodland primroses, anemones, violets and wood sorrel, and are quickly followed by wild daffodils in the fields, frog spawn in the ponds and above all, the dawn chorus as the morning light arrives earlier and earlier.

Climate change has meant that April is now the month of blossom, tulips and cow parsley, having prised them from May as in my lifetime, spring has slid forward by at least ten days. The first cuckoo, swallows and house martins give spring the stamp of veracity and by the end of April, there are young blackbirds and thrushes, fully grown but demanding, hopping round the garden with attendant parents desperately trying to keep up with their food demands. The bees – of every kind – are desperately busy, snatching at every burst of sunshine and gorging on the blossom.

On the farm, the bluebells emerge along with the unfurling bracken but, just 30 miles away and 1000ft higher, we have a second spring there weeks later and the leaves of the ash trees high on the hillside are bare well into May. But the ravens tumble in the sky and for some reason, the cuckoo always announces his arrival there days before we hear one in the garden.

Nature is not always cosy or kind. Nettles romp, lesser celandine reaches new parts every year, the chickens have to be more carefully shut up at night as the foxes have young mouths to feed, and slugs start to rip into the lovely soft new shoots of lettuce seedlings emerging in the Vegetable Garden. But above all, in the spring season, life in every shape and form sings and courses through the veins.

MARCH

St David's Day

On 1 March, the orchard is touched, just slightly, with yellow, the hundreds of wild daffodils (*Narcissus pseudonarcissus*) still some way from opening but their buds just hinting at the flower within. Their moment of glory will come two or three weeks later but they, like all the bulbs breaking the surface of the soil or poking through the grass, if not yet flowering, are growing and moving towards spring as part of that surge that is now irreversible, whatever the weather might do.

Frogs

The two ponds are bubbling with the mechanical rumble of croaking frogs and the surface is shimmying with frog spawn.

Having spent winter submerged in mud and hidden amongst piles of wood and leaves, frogs head to ponds to mate, drawn by the smell of the glycolic acid that is produced by algae. They need still, fresh water, so garden ponds without a fountain are ideal. But the water does need to be permanent. There is a particular rut on a track on the farm that becomes a puddle that lasts all winter long. Every year it has frog spawn and every spring it dries up before the tadpoles can develop enough for the froglets to survive.

Make a pond in your garden and the common frog (*Rana temporaria*) is bound to find and use it. In return, the frogs will eat slugs, caterpillars, mosquitoes and flies, and are also a very useful indicator of the environmental health of your garden. They breathe through their skins and are thus extra-sensitive to toxins, so are amongst the first creatures to suffer from pollution of any kind and especially the use of chemicals in a garden.

Frogs can be differentiated from toads by their smooth, olive-coloured skin and their longer back legs. The female will lay up to 3000 eggs, usually at the shallow edge of a pond, where the water will be warmer and receive more light. Each seed-sized egg is wrapped in a globule of jelly and the spawn of several frogs will join to form a gelatinous raft on the surface of the water. About three weeks later, these hatch into tadpoles, which will live in the pond as they develop into young frogs over the summer. They leave the water about twelve weeks after hatching, some time between midsummer and early autumn – you will find that your garden is suddenly full of small froglets, seeking out cool, shady spots. They will not return to the water until they are old enough to breed, which is usually after about two years.

Although so many tadpoles hatch out, only a tiny percentage make it to adulthood because frogs are predated by many fish, newts, birds and mammals. As well as hopping with extraordinary dynamism, to deter predators, they can and will also let out a high-pitched scream when attacked.

In autumn, most amphibians leave the water and hibernate on land in log piles, compost heaps and in piles of stones and leaves – which reinforces the need for gardeners to avoid too much tidiness. However, some male frogs hibernate at the bottom of ponds amongst the mud and sunken vegetation, which is a very good reason not to clean your pond out or dredge it.

———

Alder

Winter still has plenty left in its locker. The hillside is dusted with snow and up at 2000ft the wind has a brutal edge to it. But now, at the beginning of March, the alder and hazel pollen drifts in a yellow haze, a first gentle powdering of spring.

Along the valley bottom, the river is hidden in the alders that run all along its flanks and looking down on them, their twiggy crowns are lavender in the soft light. Hazel grows everywhere here up to about 1300ft and then stops almost dead. The alders (*Alnus glutinosa*) are more particular, needing water, be it wet patches of ground or along the dingles that rush down the slopes. But it is happiest of all along the edge of the river, growing up on the banks with its roots down in the running water. These roots entwine and tangle, and act as a revetment to the water's edges. They have nodules, sometimes quite large, like an apple, that house bacteria that take sugars from the tree and create fertiliser, which is the reason alder survives and thrives in swampy, waterlogged conditions that would kill most other tree species.

Its tiny, air-light seeds are spread by wind and by water, drifting down into the water, germinating downstream and then lodging in the bank, which accounts for the ribbon-like spread of the tree all along the edges of rivers and streams. Whereas the female catkins are yellow and pendulous, so the wind can catch the dust-like seed, the alder is the only deciduous tree to develop male catkins in the form of woody cones about the size of a walnut that stand upright on the branches.

Like their cousins, birches and willows, alder is a pioneering species and crops up in wet, scrubby ground. We have a grove – or alder carr – on a particularly wet patch of ground that I remember clearing of rushes and tussock grass in 2006. Then we put a fence up just below it, enclosing the dry ground for grazing. Alders moved in and it is now a 30ft-high dense little alder wood.

On the steeper banks of the dingle, the alders grow straight and strong up towards the light and are 60ft or 70ft tall, with buzzards and ravens nesting in their branches, but where they are more accessible, the older alders were pollarded and coppiced for years, so are now great stumpy boles sprouting a mass of much thinner branches.

Until the middle of the twentieth century, trees were a major resource for making a thousand menial objects. Alder, for example, used to be harvested regularly to make broom heads and clogs. The latter were not just the archetypal footwear of northern industrial towns, clattering over cobbles down t'mill, but well into the last century, many farm workers wore them as a light, water-resistant, hard-wearing way of keeping out of the worst of the mud. Alder was also the preferred wood to make charcoal for gunpowder which, given that every single shot fired in war or peace between the fourteenth and mid-nineteenth centuries needed gunpowder, was a major industry.

Almost as soon as alder wood is exposed to air, it turns a bright orange that then dulls to a rust colour. But if you do not expose the wood to air but keep it submerged in water or wet ground, it will last almost indefinitely. After all, Venice is still supported by alder piles driven into the lagoon.

―――

Three Swans Flying

Three swans fly over the garden, silhouetted against the cloudless blue sky. Heard the curious whirring vocal sound the wings make long before I saw them. They seem to fly at a cant, inclining to the diagonal as though leaning into a crosswind, but keeping perfect formation and space between them. Perhaps there is a layer of wind up there, blowing like a hidden seam across the sky.

Thirty minutes later a male peregrine flies over, wings seeming very pointed, bird stocky and surprisingly small. This tiercel was nuggety. His wings flapped fast. He was going somewhere with a purpose.

―――

Primroses

There are those that have a deep love of plants. These are the plantsmen and women whose knowledge is full fathoms deep and whose curiosity and hunger for more knowledge is never fully satisfied. I have regular dealings with many of them and each time merely increases my admiration. But I am no plantsman.

I love plants for their setting as much as for themselves. I can love a garden made up of very ordinary plants just as easily as one that contains a treasure trove of rare or interesting specimens.

And I love primroses. Really love them. But it is the association that I love – the memories, the smells of the woods in spring, the emotion of those first late-winter days, when the sun has just a little warmth and the light falls gently on the tiny, delicate little flowers. I love primroses because they fill me with hope and the knowledge that spring will surely come and winter will be over and light will break into my own darkness that can, at times, become very deep. I love primroses because they can feel like salvation.

When I was a child, it was an annual ritual to collect baskets of primroses to decorate the church and graveyard at Easter. Perhaps half a dozen adults and as many children would go up to the woods and coppices, and gather flowers from the clumps that grew there. They would be tied into posies of varying generosity, depending on how good a year it was. If it was very early or very late, the primroses would be fewer. Around the first week in April was the sweet spot although climate change means that this is now more like the middle of March.

But whatever the size of the bunch, the primroses were always tied with coloured wool and always included three or four leaves. These would be carried up to the church on Easter Saturday in a container of water before we went round with a dibber to each grave, planting the bunches into the ground. Quite a few graves in that tiny churchyard were unmarked grassy mounds and for a few days over Easter, the little bunches of pale yellow flowers gave them a floral headstone.

In truth, although even back then I liked the flowers, I rather disliked the picking of them – too slow and fiddly – but I love coppice woodland and primroses grow best in coppices or along the banks of hedgerows.

I regard the common primrose (*Primula vulgaris*) as unimprovable. Primulas hybridise very easily and all kinds of sports pop up, especially in a garden, where the opportunities for promiscuity are greater. The true wild primrose varies from cream to dark yellow – with the occasional patch of pink – but the idea of 'improving' a primrose is like 'improving' an oak or a swallow. It is itself in all its completeness and glory, and not one of the hundreds of garden hybrids is equal to the radiant charm of the wild primrose.

As if making my heart sing was not enough, primroses are also very good for bees, bumblebees, butterflies and moths, all of which find it a rich and very accessible source of nectar whilst pollinating the plant in the process. And the seeds are coated with oils that attract ants and mice, which means that primroses will pop up in cracks in paving, around the base of walls or in amongst the roots of shrubs.

―――

Magpie Moment

Magpies chattering in the early light. Low key, almost as though they have been asked to keep their voices down.

―――

Blackbirds

This garden is dominated by blackbirds. They are dashers – dashing in or out of cover, perpetually alarmed and yet not particularly reticent or shy about humans. Their biggest threat comes from cats and sparrowhawks – I would never begrudge the latter the odd meal of blackbird.

They only seem to be still when singing or limbering up to sing, when they will find their favoured perch – on top of the big ash tree in the coppice or the hazel in the Spring Garden, or amongst the pleached limes, where they cross the entrance into the Cottage Garden. All have their adherents. There they stay for 20 minutes or so as the light falls in March, singing challenges to each other, picking up and answering one another's melody, daring other males to stay away and females to come on in.

Theirs is the song that cuts through all others. It is rich and deep with a low frequency that has evolved to be heard in thick woodland rather than across open spaces.

They are also a bird likely to benefit from any tree planting. Certainly, the population in our garden has increased greatly as the hedges and trees have matured. Surveys have revealed that the taller and thicker the hedge, the more birds like it and the greater a variety of species will use it. I would say that allowing hedges to grow just a couple of feet higher and wider makes a really significant difference to the bird population, to the ecological balance of a garden and thus to the health of your plants. Thicker hedges make a healthy garden.

That there are a lot of blackbirds is not surprising – they are apparently the third most common bird in the country after wrens and chaffinches, and you are far more likely to see a blackbird than either of those two. It seems that their spread and population increased almost in line with the growth and spread of gardens – especially suburban ones – from the early nineteenth century, when there was a growth in interest in horticulture amongst the middle classes. In fact, gardens are their perfect habitat and they can occur at ten times the density there than in our increasingly open agricultural countryside or in big, open landscapes.

I remember visiting a garden in New South Wales, Australia that was achingly nostalgic for a long-departed England, with its Victorian garden of roses and lawns and shrubs – and with blackbirds brought all the way from the other side of the world so that their song could complete the scene.

Another reason for their spread and ubiquity is their adaptability. They will famously nest anywhere, from the inside of a garaged car to an old hat, and will eat almost anything. Their diet includes baby birds, frogs, snakes, mice and fish as well as fruit, insects, seeds, caterpillars and berries, and, unusually, ivy berries. We have also found that newly fledged blackbirds have a particular liking for raspberries, an appetite that develops to coincide exactly with the ripening of the summer-fruiting kinds in late June and July. But they never strip the plants and, by the time the autumn-fruiting raspberries are ready to harvest, from the beginning of August, the blackbirds have had their fill and leave them alone.

Blackbirds are also very easy to see. No one is going to overlook one in the way that the multitude of small brown birds can pass unnoticed. The archetypal male with its jet-black feathers, bright orange beak and yellow-irised eye is only one of the blackbird's various manifestations. The females are a rufous brown, sometimes with an almost thrush-like speckled chest, and immatures from the previous spring's brood are a warm chocolate-speckled brown. You might see visiting males at the winter bird table that have duller beaks and drabber plumage, and that lack the bright egg-yolk yellow circle of the iris. These will not develop their mating plumage until they return to their Scandinavian homes in March. British blackbirds do sometimes migrate from their garden homes but rarely travel abroad, going only in search of a better food supply as they seek to feed up after their autumn moult. They will return to base later in winter.

They have two calls, apart from their song, both of which are very distinctive. One is the repeated 'dink dink dink', when they suspect danger or spot something they are not sure of, like a cat appearing or the discovery of a roosting owl. The other is the shrieking, shrill alarm call, invariably screeched as they dash off to find cover.

Toothwort

In a few of the shadiest pieces of bank by the streams, where the soil is almost vertical and overhung with hazels and alders, curious columns of flowers with bells of petal stacked on top of each other appear each March. They emerge naked, leafless, seemingly colourless, although in fact hued with ivory tinged with pink. It is like a plant more fungus than flower, an excrescence bubbling out of the earth. This is toothwort (*Lathraea squamaria*), one of the few plants that grows without any chlorophyll, so there is no advantage to it in being exposed to light other than to flower. These flowers are then pollinated by bumblebees. The resulting seeds germinate and the roots find their way down to the roots of the hazel to which they attach themselves to get the nourishment they need.

Hazel is its preferred host and when the tree dies, so too will the toothwort, although it can also be found growing out of the roots of alder, beech, elm or willow.

Mason Bees

Sitting outside with a cup of coffee in the March sunshine, the skies are completely silenced by coronavirus. The distant drone of traffic that normally hums away in the background is replaced by the low-level chatter of small birds in the hedge behind me, buzzards calling in the cloudless sky and the busy buzz of mason bees going to and fro from the stone wall of the house.

Osmia bicornis (also known as *O. rufa*) loves the south-facing stone walls of the old barns that we use as our workrooms. These are mortared with lime, which is soft and easy for them to excavate for making their cells. They scrape out the mortar, make their nest cavity out of mud in the space this creates and then render it over with the mortar again. One particular section of wall is honeycombed with their holes made over centuries – it shows that their cell-building skills are more highly developed than their rendering ones. The wall does look as though it is about to fall apart but I like it and am sure it will last a lot longer than I will.

People tend to think of bees only as honeybees, living in colonies and honeycombs, but most bees, like the mason bee, are solitary and there are around 200 different species of them in the UK. Mason bees raise their offspring on pollen rather than the nectar that honey and bumblebees need, and this makes them especially important as pollinators.

They rarely sting and if they do, it is not as painful as the sting of a honeybee. Nor do they make honey or beeswax and they are completely unaggressive, happily making their nests from mud or regurgitated lime in the gaps in walls, then collecting pollen to feed their larvae. It is a harmless and intensely useful life.

———

Pussy Willow/Purple Emperors

Pussy willow – or goat willow – is a weed tree *par excellence*, springing up largely unbidden but not unwelcome. It does not intrude or displace, and life would be diminished without it.

It gets its 'pussy' name from the catkins that are idiosyncratically soft and hairy and – so someone once decided – like cats' paws. These start out silvery white but become yellow as they fill with pollen. This was the 'palm' that we would collect for the church when I was a child for Palm Sunday – the Sunday before Easter, which invariably falls either at the end of March or in the first half of April. The female catkins start out green but as the seeds form, they turn white and wispy until the wind blows them away. Male and female catkins grow on separate trees so both trees look noticeably different in flower. Their leaves are the least prepossessing of almost any British tree – dully green and devoid of any character.

Around us, it tends to be a smallish, untidy, unremarkable tree, never planted and living on ditches and damp margins. But it can live for centuries and will grow to 30ft. It makes a mass of untidy branches but has often been pollarded and gradually develops a thick trunk from which a regular crop of branches can be cut. Pussy willow used to be a universal feature, along with other kinds of pollarded willow, along all damp areas.

Although the least important of all the willows to farmer, forester, woodworker or gardener, pussy willow is an important early source of pollen and nectar for honeybees and the most important food for the caterpillars of purple emperor butterflies.

I rarely see purple emperor butterflies nowadays but I remember seeing a host of them about 40 years ago on newly growing scrub that had been cleared a year or two before. There were hundreds of them. They are huge – the size of a sparrow – and the males have this extraordinary sheen, as blue as it is purple, despite their name. The male will patrol a favoured oak tree, fighting off all comers – even birds – and woo the female into his love nest. She then finds a pussy willow to lay her eggs, not depositing them just anywhere but carefully choosing thin leaves halfway to two-thirds up the tree on the shady side. The caterpillars hatch and feed on the leaves and overwinter on the trees, changing colour as the season progresses, from bright green to dark brown. Then they pupate the following summer. So, it turns out that the biggest threat to purple emperor butterflies is the modern habit of cutting down and grubbing out pussy willows.

––––––

Owls at Dawn

Just as the first thread of light appears where the hillside meets the darkness of the sky, a male owl calls with a rather strangulated series of hoots and another answers in the distance. A third, with a much deeper, more manly hoot, joins in close by. Sounds as though he could be on the chimney just above my head. Finally, a female answers with her 'ker wick' somewhere in the sycamore – where she has probably been all the while, the centre of all this male attention. Even owls get frisky in spring.

––––––

Stinging Nettles

I did not wear long trousers until I was into double figures – nobody of my generation did. Your first proper pair of jeans or suit trousers was a rite of passage, a coming of age and I remember strutting around in mine, inordinately proud and assuming that everyone else was sharing my long-trousered joy. From then on, shorts were only for sports and even today I still find grown men wearing shorts to be a strange denial of adulthood.

Despite long woollen socks held up by garters, my bare knees and thighs were not just exposed to snow and rain and wind, but also to stinging nettles. However high I tried to jump over or skip round them, they always got you and that burning sting followed by the white goose-bump rash would stay with you for the rest of the day. But everybody knew that the first thing to do was to find a dock leaf, spit on it copiously and rub it on the sting. It worked well although I am assured that there is no scientific evidence for why. Perhaps it was just the combination of spit and cool leaf.

Nettles are still with me but now, having eschewed shorts from the garden on all but the very hottest days, it is not my legs that get stung but my hands and forearms, usually when I am pulling them out. I either grasp the stem firmly (my childhood belief was that the stems did not have any stinging hairs but in fact their firmness matters more than where you grasp – the expression 'grasping the nettle' refers to crushing the fine stinging hairs before they can do their work) and try to bend the leaves away from me, or get my fork under the whole plant to ease out the yellow roots. The stem invariably rebounds and swipes me across my arms or, truly annoyingly, my face. And every gardener knows those middle-of-the-night moments in spring, when your hands are burning with nettle. But for all that, I like nettles and they are important to any garden.

We harvest the young leaves in spring – they make excellent soup and nettle pesto, and can be eaten as a vegetable, like spinach. They taste a bit like spinach but more of iron and, for many communities, they were an important source of iron in early spring, when very few vegetables were growing.

We also make nettle tea, not to drink but as a feed for plants.

This involves collecting as many nettles as can be crammed into a bucket, topping up with water and leaving the mixture for a few weeks before straining it and diluting the resulting concentrate with water.

Nettles are always a sign of soil that is dampish and fertile and especially rich in phosphates. It often means that the area has been used by humans or their grazing animals. When we came here in 1991, there was a very rotten section of tree trunk at the edge of what is now the Damp Garden. It lay amongst a large patch of nettles and although the rotten wood soon disappeared, breaking into pieces as I tried to move it, the nettles persisted for years. Then I saw an old photo of the garden and there was a large elm with cattle sheltering in its shade. It must have succumbed to Dutch Elm disease in the mid-1970s and been cut down and left to rot. However, years of cattle seeking shelter beneath it meant that the circle of nettles was a living shadow of the elm's canopy, the nettles thriving in the manure that generations of cattle had generously deposited.

Nettle stings are the plant's defence against grazing animals – only goats, alpacas or a very hungry sheep will brave them. Every dog I have ever owned has, as a small puppy, had their unfortunate brush with nettles, charging through them only to pathetically lift their paws as the stings do their work on their as yet unhardened pads.

The stings retain their power, too, long after the plant has died. I like the story of the photographer in the Second World War, who was sent to photograph the dried and mounted plants of Carl Linnaeus in case the originals were damaged. As he adjusted the nettle that Linnaeus had handled almost 200 years before, it stung him on the arm, causing a rash exactly as though the plant were still growing.

Every garden should have a patch or two of nettles if only to provide food for the caterpillars of peacock and small tortoiseshell butterflies, both of which feed almost exclusively on stinging nettles. But it is not just these two butterflies – though that would be reason enough. Stinging nettles are also an important food for the larvae of many moths – the less glamorous cousins of butterflies but just as important in the chain of creatures in any garden. Thus, nettles are a fulcrum for a whole cycle of garden wildlife. Young ladybirds feed off them in spring before going off to eat aphids when they mature. Then, in late summer, when the nettles have grown tall, sparrows and chaffinches move in to eat the seed.

———

A Spring Dawn

One of the great luxuries of spring – of life – is lying in bed at dawn listening to the wood pigeons. The soft waves of their call sifting through the morning light is the most evocative and *safest* of all sounds.

———

Hedgehogs

I was cutting back in the grass borders when I uncovered a ball of slowly heaving prickles. It was a hedgehog that had chosen that particular clump of *Miscanthus sinensis* to hibernate in. There was a time when this would have been charming but unremarkable. Hedgehogs were a common sight in this garden, usually bumbling along at night as I walked round with the dogs and shut up the chickens.

But over the past decade or so, hedgehogs have become catastrophically endangered. They have all but disappeared from the agricultural countryside and the only habitat where they still have a foothold is in suburban and rural gardens. To someone of my generation, this is almost unthinkable. Hedgehogs were as much part of life as hares or skylarks – both of which are also desperately under threat.

When I was seven, I raised a baby hedgehog with a pipette and, sent away to boarding school, I would say my prayers every night, asking God to bless all my family, the dogs and Harry the hedgehog. It wasn't until I came home for the summer holidays twelve weeks later that I discovered he had died within days of my leaving home.

Then for years we had a labrador that often returned from a walk carrying a tightly curled adult hedgehog in her mouth. She wished it no harm, treating it as rather an unusual ball or toy. It never seemed to prick her although it invariably shared its fleas.

In the 1980s, squashed hedgehogs were horribly common on country roads but this was a measure of their ubiquity – roadkill is nearly always a sign of the abundance of a creature. The reason for hedgehogs' decline now seems simply lack of habitat both for them and their preferred food, and like so many apparently sudden declines, the loss has actually been gradual.

A hedgehog's preferred diet is essentially carnivorous – a lot of worms, beetles and slugs, with additional caterpillars, millipedes and earwigs. An adult will eat about 100 such invertebrates every night. Obviously, this makes them the gardener's friend but it has to be said that they will also eat birds' eggs, young birds, mice, voles and even baby rabbits.

Hedgehogs will typically travel up to two miles a night looking for food and can climb – there are stories of them hibernating in thatched roofs – and swim and squeeze through seemingly tiny holes.

So, what can we gardeners do to encourage and support them? First and foremost, provide cover. Piles of wood, leaves and compost heaps are all good news for hedgehogs. Never use slug pellets as hedgehogs will eat the slugs that have been poisoned by them – and will sometimes eat the pellets themselves. Go steady when tidying long grass or weeds with a strimmer – it can cause awful wounds to a sleeping hedgehog. And above all, resist tidiness, especially over winter. There may be a hedgehog sleeping in that scruffy corner.

———

Cuckoo Flower

At the end of March, there is a wide strip of ground at the top of the field above the farmhouse bedecked with little pale pink flowers, touched with mauve and hanging like modest bells from curving stems carried on tall stems. These are cuckoo flowers or lady's smock (*Cardamine pratense*). They like damp but pop up in curious patches that, superficially at least, don't seem to be any damper than others nearby. Nor do they necessarily appear where it is really damp and rushes compete with the grass. In fact, cuckoo flowers appear most at the top of slopes, where you expect the drainage to be better, rather than at the bottom or in ditches where, were it to conform to received wisdom, it should properly be growing. In any event, like all the flowers on the farm, it is steadily increasing as the grazing is lessened and controlled, and the bracken gradually reduced.

Lady's smock is a herbaceous perennial, so in theory will reappear year after year, but on this hillside it is only because I can get up there once a year to cut the bracken that they are not smothered and have a chance to flower. And, at the 450m contour line that runs almost precisely along that flattish strip, they are a rare source of nectar for hoverflies, and the larvae of orange-tip butterflies feed on its leaves. It is a member of the brassica family and will seed itself. However, some plants are sterile but the fallen leaves can root and create new plants. Apparently, the young leaves have a peppery, rocket-like flavour but I have yet to try them.

Jackdaws

The jackdaws are nesting in the chimney. I cannot blame them. They got here first. When we bought the farm in 2005, it had been unoccupied for a few years and had become increasingly derelict for decades before that.

Jackdaws like to nest in holes and an unused chimney is ideal. One chimney had not been used for more than 20 years and when I got to it I pulled down enough sticks and chunks of wool to half-fill the room. Ironically, it made excellent kindling.

In March, they ferry backwards and forwards to their nests, always with outsized sticks and twigs in their beaks. Whilst the result is messy and even chaotic, you cannot fault them for endeavour. They particularly like the twigs from our solitary larch and their nests are always thickly lined with wool that they scavenge from the hedges and barbed wire, where sheep have rubbed.

We also have them nesting in one particular barn that I use as a workshop. They return there year after year, always nesting in the gap caused by some missing stones on the gable end and always managing to make a huge mess of droppings, sticks, wool, distinctive black-mottled pale blue eggshells and the occasional dead fledgling. For four to six weeks they take over, then slowly use it less and less. During that period, I cover everything in the workshop with sheets and barely use it. The barn becomes one enormous jackdaw nest.

Across the country, jackdaws have increased greatly over the past 40 years. They are omnipresent on the farm, flying around in 'clatterings' – small, noisy groups that chatter with that hard 'chack' call that has given them their name – staying local and feeding on practically anything they can find. It is this adaptability that has allowed them to be so successful.

It seems that they have none of the more unpleasant habits of the corvid family and whilst I am sure they would not pass up a helpless baby bird, they certainly do not attack the lambs like their crow and raven cousins. Their little beady, white-irised eyes, street intelligence and slim build make them more of an artful dodger than a thug as they duck and dive, alert to everything and always looking for a deal.

And there is something charming, even noble, about the devotion that pairs show each other, bonding for life, living busily together throughout the year.

———

Dawn Chorus

The dawn chorus starts not long after 5 a.m. and has now acquired that magical depth that is so characteristic of this time of year. The bright, clear song of a blackbird in the foreground and behind him, receding across the fields and hedgerows and woods, waves of distant song. The loveliest sound in the world.

———

Irish Yews

The blue and great tits love the Irish yews in the Cottage Garden and the yew cones in the front. They cling to their surface, picking off the insects, and then disappear inside them. Across the eight large Irish yews and the eighteen cones there must be dozens of nests – a whole community of tit families. They enter the densely clipped yew like someone slipping through the books of a library, through a secret, hidden door into another interior world.

———

Herb Robert

When weeding the borders in a shady corner on one of the first warmish days of early spring, there is always a smell that rises up from the handful of weeds – a musty, warm fragrance, touched with hamster cage and very distinctive. This is herb robert (*Geranium robertianum*) that spreads all over the borders as a kind of benign gate-crasher. It also weaves its way along paths and through walls and seems hardly to need any soil to take root. It has particularly ferny leaves for a cranesbill but the flowers, although smaller than most, are familiar in shape and a pretty pink. It was particularly prevalent in our little London garden, 40 years ago, where the soil was so much thinner and drier than our heavy clay here.

It was used as an insect repellent and also, I have just discovered, the leaves were put in dogs' beds to deter fleas. I shall try this and report back.

———

Dusk Chorus

By mid-March the sap is rising and the new surge of energy pulsing through the natural world flows in my veins, too. Every day, more new leaves break bud and the hedges at Longmeadow start to glow with new green like stained glass. The garden takes on a substance, acquires body and fills out from the bony starkness of the winter months. By the end of February, that skeletal outline had become the norm. Winter was now the status quo. So, when the growth appears, filling the voids, rounding the edges and gradually smudging across bare lines against the sky, it always does so with a flare of surprise, a gift that arrives unexpectedly, despite the predictability of the calendar.

With it comes the fragrance of warming soil. In practice, this warmth is hardly anything – just the faintest trace of eau de earth rising, but enough to start opening out all my senses. For the dogs, this must be heady stuff – to them, spring earth must be fine wines and truffles, a leather or cabinet maker's workshop perhaps, all filtered and sifted and sorted, plus a thousand other scents we can only guess at.

Of course, March weather can be vile – heavy snow, ice, biting east winds are all possible and even probable, but no March weather stays long. Everything about the month is predicated on change, even from hour to hour, and this continues as the month progresses, moving from winter into the full tide of spring.

But of all the changes, the one I love most – and which is better in March than at any other time of year – is the dusk chorus. The dawn chorus gets most attention and reaches its peak around the end of May. The dusk chorus of March is much briefer, more limited and, because the light is sinking, much more defiant.

I have often stood as the cold dark creeps in and through, hearing that brave sound wrap around the garden as it dissolves into the dusk. The songs are more individual and clearer than at dawn, when the competition is greater. There is a thrush that always sings from the same spot on an ash tree in the coppice, and three or four blackbirds challenging each other, clattering away indignantly if I get too close. Robins, wrens, tits and sparrows all tune in and pipe up but the effect is more syncopated and less confrontational than at dawn. At the beginning of March, the chorus lasts barely 20 minutes, although by the end, with the clocks going back and dusk easing itself out between half past seven and eightish, there is a full 40 minutes of avian evensong.

I remember one March when I was a student living in the middle of a town – and feeling homesick for the countryside with its space and peace – my father sent me a cassette tape of the dusk chorus from the garden at home. I could hardly bear to listen to it because it was so moving, so redolent of all that was lacking from my life then.

Thus, whilst the dusk chorus is beautiful, it is always touched with melancholy. Rather like the Japanese notion of *wabi-sabi*, this can add to its beauty and transience. But unlike *wabi-sabi*, which is essentially an autumnal emotion, with the fading of the year reflected in everything from the colour of the leaves to the earthenware glaze on a cup, the dusk birdsong on a March evening is wistful rather than sad. March's tomorrow always holds the promise of more light, more day, more sunshine, more growth – even more birdsong.

———

Blackthorn

Clouds of the tiny white flowers of blackthorn (*Prunus spinosa*) dust the uncut hedges along the lanes and fields. The flowers of this 'blackthorn winter' are made on last year's growth, so if a hedge has been smashed into regularity by a flail, it will be blossom-free, but fortunately there are enough left uncut for this flowery snow to reappear year after year.

This, the earliest blossoming of the year, can happen any time between February and April, and although pear, almond and apricot blossom all appear before their leaves, blackthorn is the only blossom that decks bare branches.

Those branches, curiously black and almost fossilised, are equipped with the wickedest spines. They are very long, very sharp and very brittle, so break off just below the skin. If they pierce a joint, it can turn septic and then gangrenous, and lead to amputation in days. Only hedge-layer's pigskin gloves, as thick and unwieldy as a deep-sea diver's boots, will resist the thorns. Sarah gave me a pair of those gloves for my birthday some years ago, and although I have put them on too seldom, I treasure them above much else.

No scrub is denser or more impenetrable than blackthorn – it throws up suckers that quickly make it into a thicket that only rabbits, mice and small birds can get into or, more pertinently, get out of, unharmed. This has made it a common hedgerow plant. As an individual tree, it is just too spiky and troublesome to deliberately nurture. It is almost never found in thick woods as lack of light quickly suppresses, then kills it off. Like hawthorn, it will quickly invade open land and become scrub, where it protects trees from grazing animals. These trees then, in turn, grow and suppress the blackthorn.

Sloes, which are the fruit of the blackthorn, are small, oval-shaped blue plums, mouth-puckeringly astringent when eaten off the bush, at least until a frost has softened them and increased their sugar content. They are best made into gin by pricking the fruit, adding sugar to a jar crammed with them, then topping up with gin and leaving them to infuse for at least three months. Few drinks are more richly warming on a frosty day.

———

Song Thrush

Until the late eighteenth century, the song thrush was probably more common than the blackbird, whereas now most of us see one song thrush for every 50 blackbirds. But they are here in the garden and their song is not hard to winnow out from the dawn, and especially, the dusk choruses.

PREVIOUS PAGE The W.B.C. hive at the far end of the Orchard with apple blossom
for the bees to gorge on.

TOP The hillside above the farm still completely bare in early spring.

ABOVE LEFT The winter floods leave pools in the field at the edge of the garden
that can remain for months.

ABOVE RIGHT The newly planted potato fields create a corduroy, strangely linear landscape.

OPPOSITE Nigel on a lovely May day shortly before he died.
Still handsome to the very end.

OPPOSITE Nosy neighbours! This gate is all that separates the garden
from the water meadows around us.

TOP LEFT The ditches that cut through the water meadows are perfect cover
for otters and, in spring, froth with cow parsley.

TOP RIGHT The writing garden is entirely based upon the lovely lightness
of cow parsley in spring.

ABOVE The orchard meadow in spring. It is perfect for insects and is cut
in August to allow the wild flowers to set seed.

TOP Nellie amongst the cow parsley, hogweed and grasses of the orchard.
ABOVE Bluebells amongst the coppiced hazel on the farm.
OPPOSITE Looking down the valley on the farm, across the wild-flower meadow.
OVERLEAF The winter-flooded fields around the garden are ideal for buttercups.

Although blackbirds and thrushes can superficially sound very similar, blackbirds have a deep, flutey tone, whilst the song thrush has a distinctly clear, silver song, with many short, repeated phrases. I remember being told as a child that the way to distinguish between blackbird and thrush song was that the thrush always repeated its refrain. That is almost true, but a blackbird can confuse the issue by developing and embellishing its melodic theme. Apparently, the song thrush's musical phrases are passed on from bird to bird and generation to generation like musical folklore. Thrushes are also good mimics, not just learning from each other but copying sounds they hear around them including other birds.

Song thrushes have no identifiable difference between the sexes and are noticeably smaller than blackbirds, although their legs are proportionately longer and, of course, they have the speckled breast, the speckles running in rows down an ochre front, and a chestnut upper wing and back feathers. In flight, the underside of the wings is a warm ochre, almost orange, hue.

Like the blackbirds, the thrushes in this garden take up familiar positions each evening – the fig tree in the Walled Garden is a favourite spot, as is the ridge of the main roof of the house and the big wild cherry in the coppice. Their song cuts through the evening air.

Although less eccentric in their choice of nesting sites than blackbirds, I usually find a nest or two each year tucked into a hedge or a climber – they also quite often nest in the yew cones in front of the house – and see the female sitting tight, hunkered down, beak thrusting and eyes wide with alarm, but not moving a muscle or making a sound. Beneath her will be the familiar bright blue eggs sitting in the typical basin of smoothed wood pulp that invariably lines their nests.

Magpies are a major predator, taking both the eggs and the young. When they fledge, the young birds often scuttle around the garden, barely able to fly or feed themselves, desperately vulnerable to cats and, I am ashamed to say, the occasional dog. This stage lasts for a week or so but if they get through it, they can then look after themselves.

If singing were all it did, the song thrush would always be welcome in any garden but it also is a voracious predator of slugs and snails, and the 'tap tap tapping' of a thrush breaking the shell of a snail on a stone or paving slab is one of the ways of knowing they are around. I will often see a thrush hopping in a border or on the grass of the orchard, stopping, head cocked to one side so it can hear better, and then plunging its beak down into the soil and extracting a worm. In fact, worms are its preferred food but to spear them, it needs the soil to be damp – when it is hard and dry, the thrush turns to snails instead. But if there is a really hot, dry summer, snails become hard to find and then the song thrush turns to spiders for sustenance. However, there is evidence that song thrushes have been hit badly by the use of slug pellets and it seems to me to be an act of wanton vandalism to sacrifice these lovely birds for the sake of a (largely ineffectual) reduction in slug or snail numbers. The song thrush is also, like all members of the thrush family, very fond of windfall apples in autumn and early winter.

———

Bees

A few years ago, I set up a couple of hives (with a great deal of help and guidance from my local beekeeping association in Monmouth), not so much to harvest the honey, but to encourage more bees into my garden. The honey is a nice by-product.

Although bees hardly need 'keeping' and look after themselves very well indeed, they do need all the help they can get. Bee populations are in decline and if gardeners can plant to encourage and sustain them, they will be doing bees and themselves a great service. If they can keep a hive or two, so much the better.

If you cannot keep bees yourself, then at least add as many bee-friendly plants to your garden as possible. Honeybees like saucer-shaped flowers that are easier for their relatively short tongues to dip into. Plants like musk mallow (*Malva moschata*), common mallow (*Malva sylvestris*), small scabious (*Scabiosa columbaria*), cornflower (*Centaurea cyanus*) and wild clary (*Salvia verbenaca*) are all ideal.

Bees also love fruit trees – in fact any flowering trees – and all legumes, such as peas, beans, clover and sweet peas, as well as dandelions, blackberries, asters, ivy, and willow. They need pollen and the smaller flowers of unhybridised species are likely to be a much richer source of this than huge show blooms that are the result of elaborate breeding.

It was first noticed that bees were in trouble when the varroa mite arrived from its Asian home to the UK in the late 1980s, and the disastrous impact on bee populations began to make headlines. At the same time, it began to be apparent that the unrestrained use of pesticides, insecticides and fungicides was not just affecting the perceived 'pests' (a blunt, lazy term) but also the pollinators, such as bees.

Bees, it seemed, were being affected by neonicotinoids. These are a class of systemic insecticide used by many farmers on a wide range of grain, vegetable and fruit crops. Thus, bees that foraged on, for example, oilseed rape showed twice the decline as those that did not feed on agricultural crops.

There is some doubt about how – and even if – neonicotinoids are the culprits, but the evidence is weighted heavily against them. One study pointed to the effect on bees' homing systems – they were travelling to gather pollen and failing to return to the hive, eventually dying of starvation. Other studies indicate that the neonicotinoids weaken the bees' immune systems, making them more susceptible to diseases such as varroa. However, nothing is proven beyond reasonable doubt.

On the one hand, no farmer sets out to kill bees, but on the other, the world population of bees is falling to dangerously low levels, which impacts powerfully on humans to the point of being a matter of life and death. It has been estimated that 80 per cent of the western diet is dependent on pollination by bees. The message is stark – no bees equals insufficient pollination equals insufficient food for people and mass starvation.

So, I nurture bees in the garden and on the farm – we have a tree at the top of a very steep field that has had wild bees in it ever since we have been there. In summer, you cannot go near it without being attacked. But in the middle of one winter on a freezing day, when I knew the bees would not be active, I plucked up courage and peered closely into the tree – a field maple – and saw that it was almost completely hollow. From the ground to the top, the trunk was filled with cells rising to 10ft or more. The tree had become little more than the outer wooden casing of a high-rise hive.

Diving Crows

When, out walking the dogs, I disturb a crow perched on a tree, it always flies down, swooping away towards the ground. After about 20 yards, it rises up into the air, although it never flies up and away from the branch. Why is this? Is it because a predator is more likely to get it as it slowly picks up speed? Is it safer on the ground than in the air? The only real predators are goshawks and peregrines, and a peregrine would

never take it from its perch. Would its behaviour evolve so specifically to combat these threats? And if so, why would it regard
dogs and humans as a threat unless it feared being shot – in
which case, a speedy descent makes it less of a target than the
slow rising up of a big, heavy bird. My guess is that crows are
clever enough to suspect that a man with dogs could well have
a gun and mean them no good, and so they have worked out
the best way to evade trouble.

———

Wood Anemones

Wood anemones carpet the ground around the dogs' graves
in the coppice like fallen petals. The flowers, white but
touched with pink and set in ferny, soft green foliage, open in sun,
follow the sun's progress across the sky from east to west, then
close at night or in cloudy shade. It is a plant of woodland and
light shade but flowers best in the flush of light that follows the
regular cutting of coppice.

Anemone nemorosa needs dampish conditions so is not a plant
that grows under large trees, whose roots suck up all moisture. It
likes our little coppice and is slowly spreading to a wide carpet
from the eight original plants that I put in there some 20 years
ago. 'It would', Sarah said the other day, 'be better if it covered the
whole of the coppice floor.' This was part-wishful, part-reproachful,
implying negligence or laziness on my part, but actually it has not
done badly by its own anemone lights because it is notoriously
slow to spread. The seed is rarely fertile so it increases by root
growth, covering barely an inch a year of new ground. So, our
spread – whose positively frisky expanse is nearly double that – is
something we should be grateful for. Once they have finished
flowering, the leaves die back and it is as though it has never been.

Because they are so slow to colonise, a broad expanse of them in a wood is a very good indicator that this is long-established woodland, many hundreds of years old. Wood anemones can also be found on banks and in some meadows, although the latter may be relics of woodland cut down long ago. It is as though its movement is so slow that its retreat from a now-changed habitat takes a correspondingly long time.

Its flowers do not produce any nectar but lots of pollen, and our bees love them for this. Hoverflies love wood anemones, too, but no animal will graze on them because they apparently taste bitter. Since it is poisonous to people, this is not something I choose to verify.

———

Strange Call

As always, the first thing I do is take the dogs outside. Nigel shuffling into the light, Nellie pushing forward like someone trying to get to the front of a queue. It is a clear morning, scudding clouds, the light still banded and growing in the eastern sky.

There is a strange noise overhead – half-quack, half-seagull, half-rook – and two peregrines fly over, quite high, calling.

When they are almost directly above me, one carries on straight, heading west, whilst the other veers off south, almost at right angles. A distinct parting.

Two males? They seem the same size. Was one the male I saw a few weeks ago and if not, how many peregrines are there flying around these skies? I still reel at the wonder of them, and want them to remain a thrilling, rare encounter. I would feel short-changed if that terrible beauty were suddenly as common as ravens or buzzards.

But it was such a strange, harsh sound in the fragile spring dawn.

———

Mountain Ponies

The spring of 2013 was brutal. The snow lay thick on the hill-side to the end of March and took weeks to melt. The fields in the valley remained parched and sere, with the trees without hint of leaf well into April.

It was lambing time and the lambs that did not freeze to death were desperately exposed. The wind was vicious, lowering the temperature into minus double figures for days on end. It remained cold, with the ground hard and frozen, and no grass for the animals. Many ewes died as their udders froze solid and their lambs starved. It was a desperate time.

Sheep were not the only creatures to suffer. As the snow slowly melted, it revealed other casualties. It was not until the end of the month that I was able to walk up to the very top of our boundary, where it borders the open hillside, and found two dead ponies, huddled up against the fencing. Both were white, albeit muddy, and small and thin but – apart from the inevitable desecration of the crows taking their eyes – as yet untouched by the foxes.

Any sheep farmer becomes accustomed to dead animals. But a dead pony is a shocking thing, partly because it is so big. To have two within a few yards of each other was like some appalling crime scene. In fact, in that bitter spring, pony deaths became horribly normal. During the course of the next week, I found two more and one of my neighbours said he had come across nine on the hillside. Presumably there must have been dozens, scores, more.

But these two felt personal because the ponies had clearly come down as far as they could to get shelter from the cold and look for food. Our fence – the one that I continually repaired to stop the sheep and ponies getting in – had stopped them getting into the shelter of the wood and, exhausted, hungry and freezing, they had simply collapsed against it and died.

When ponies have endured a harsh winter, they are at their lowest ebb if a cold spring strikes. But the situation had been made much worse by a chain of bureaucratic events.

Welsh mountain ponies are a distinct breed. There is some evidence that they descended directly from the prehistoric Celtic pony that was around before 1600 BC. So, they have adapted and evolved to cope with very poor grass and scrub, and the worst of winter weather on the hillside. Only the oldest, weakest or youngest were likely to die of exposure and hunger.

But then mountain ponies were used in the valleys as cobs to pull carts and sledges on the steep hillside, and farmers rode them for the 'gather', when the sheep would be rounded up and brought down for shearing or dipping. The farmer across the valley from us apparently had a remarkable ability to train these completely wild ponies and earned enough from doing this and selling them to buy his land. One spring day, about ten years ago, I followed him down the little valley road as he escorted perhaps ten of them for about a mile to a particular field, droving them like cattle but gently, and with man and horse completely at ease and in tune with each other.

Then, as a result of the foot and mouth outbreak in 2001 that devastated the countryside, livestock became much more highly regulated. The fee to register the movement of a pony to take it to market was around £30. When the animals were worth hundreds, this was painful but acceptable. But suddenly, the market slumped. Ponies were fetching less than it cost to register their movement, so even if you could sell them for horse meat, you were paying to do so.

The result was that hundreds of tired old Welsh mountain ponies were dumped on the mountainside like Christmas dogs on a motorway. But these animals had had a lifetime of being fed high-quality hay and lush grazing, and had none of the hardiness that was bred into native mountain ponies. By the time that the terrible onslaught of snow and ice arrived in late winter 2012, they had little chance of surviving.

When I went back to see the bodies a month later, they had been stripped back to the bone, and by high summer they were perfectly bleached skeletons. They, who had died such a slow, miserable death, made beautiful bones.

_____

Wooing Buzzards

The buzzards are busy mating – or rather the males are busy attempting to catch a mate. Yesterday, two flew out of a tree in the coppice, the male calling loudly.

Now, six buzzards over the garden for much of the day. They clearly make three pairs or would-be pairs, with one, the female, noticeably bigger than the male. The males make all the running – mewing, chasing, performing – whilst the females soar nonchalantly. Exactly like my teenage years . . .

_____

APRIL

Wild Garlic

At the beginning of April, I always make a little detour down a track that I only use a few times a year. It is very narrow and the banks are high, so that by mid-spring the hedges and the growth on the banks brush the car and for a glorious week or so in May it is like going through a car wash made of cow parsley.

But now the growth is just beginning, the bracken not yet up and the grass just gaining some colour after a long, cold winter, here on the lower slopes of the Black Mountains. This is the moment that the long, spear-like leaves of the wild garlic (*Allium ursinum*) appear. There is one patch of bank on this lane where I can reach out of the Land Rover's windows and tear handfuls from the bank, filling the cab with their tang. Within 20 minutes I am in the kitchen, separating out the wisps of grass and weeds that inevitably are included in the snatched trawl, then chopping and mixing it with oil and sea salt to make a rich, green, garlicky pesto. It is one of the truly delicious, fresh tastes of the season and over the coming week or two I will return to gather more to eat with pasta, potatoes, bread, egg, and anything I can dip into it or mix it onto. All the Mediterranean flavours are usurped by this northern cousin, gathered months before the garlic bulbs are ready, fresher and tasting of all the thrilling greenness of spring.

The plant goes on to produce a delicate white allium flower ball on a long stem but ramsons should only be planted with caution in a garden because they can spread to the exclusion of all else. I have planted a few bulbs in the garden on the shady side of the Mound, but despite this supply a minute from the back door, that I could carefully harvest with scissors and place in a handmade trug, I still return to my remote mountain lane each spring to lean out and snatch a few handfuls from that one special spot.

Otter

I was taken otter hunting 50 years ago by a much older cousin. I don't think we caught anything but I remember the beautiful Dorset countryside in spring, the lovely hairy otter hounds and my first visit to a pub, trying to look nonchalant as I drank a pint of bitter. Any moral qualms I might have had were far outweighed by the anxiety of trying to make the right impression.

I was eventually to see others – but they were rare glimpses and few and far between. On a trip to the Outer Hebrides in 1981, we watched a sea otter lying on its back in the rocky shallows as it ate a crab and then, another ten years on, not long after we had moved into this house, I was washing up and saw what appeared to be a dolphin in the river. It was in fact, my brain eventually worked out, the back of an otter arcing out of the water. A few years later, driving home down the tiny lanes late one night, an otter popped out in front of the car and ran in front of me for fully 50 yards, back arched like a great thickset cat, before slipping into the ditch by the side of the lane. Sarah once looked out the kitchen window and saw a whole family of otters playing in the field by the house at the river's edge, and we often see their spraints when we take the dogs for a walk.

But a few years ago I had a strange experience of seeing an otter very close indeed. I had set off early to the farm to check the cattle. It was a cold April morning, Easter Sunday, bright but clear. Just before I reached Hay-on-Wye, I noticed a body in a field gateway. The sad truth is that bodies of animals on roads are not that uncommon. But this one was both different and strangely familiar. I stopped, reversed and saw a full-grown otter lying in the frosty grass.

It was unmarked, eyes open and mouth parted in a slight grimace, but rigor mortis had left the head raised and cocked to one side, curiously alert. For a moment I was not sure if it was actually dead. I slowly – I knew otters have a fearful bite – bent down to touch it. It was rock-hard and very dead.

What do you do with a dead otter? Ignore it? Report it? Who to at 7 a.m. on Easter Sunday? So I put it in the back of the Land Rover, intending to report it to a suitable authority later, without having any idea who that might be.

As well as being shocking and mysterious – if hit by a car hard enough to kill it, why was there no visible mark and why was its head raised up still? – it was surprisingly big and well, *ottery*. Death had not in any way reduced its essence. The broad head with its blunt muzzle and little ears, the fur of the lower jaw and the neck paler, flecked with white. The front paws that were curiously hand-like despite the covering of short fur, its nails blunted and squared off by digging, and the back feet turned up to show the fleshy, calloused soles. The tail was long – almost as long as the rest of the body – and covered from its hugely thick base to the tip with dense brown fur. The body was both sleekly elegant and powerful, even in the frozen attitude of death.

I rang the relevant government body the next morning to report the dead otter but it was a bank holiday and was told that no one could deal with it for a few days and that, by then, and I quote, 'it would be stinky'.

In the end, we took the body down to the river by the edge of the garden and slipped it into the water with a blessing before the river gods bore it away.

———

Arrival

5 April. An almost full moon is rising after a long, hot day. I see a tired little bird bobbing and sliding through the sky. The first swallow. A heart-leap of recognition like seeing a lover in a crowd. There is another by the end of the day. I feel an overwhelming sense of the return of an old, much-loved friend, who will share my garden for the next five months. It is a great surge of happiness and a sense that spring can really begin. No going back.

These first comers are the males arriving in dribs and drabs, exhausted and half-starved from their epic journey from South Africa, and have returned to within a few hundred yards of where they were born. They cut arcing shapes in the sky as they reform intimacy with the garden and the familiar details of the house and its sheds.

Frighteningly few survive the 9000-mile journey there and back. At least half of the young never make it to Africa on their first migration, dying of starvation or predation on the way.

If they do complete the first trip, they have a much higher chance of subsequent survival because they are stronger and more experienced, but 25 per cent of all adults die on the annual migration, and very few live more than four years. Thus, not only does the population not become overcrowded but each pair will have two, and sometimes three, broods in a summer, with four or five young per brood.

I have been to South Africa a number of times during our northern winter months and wondered if any of the swallows luxuriating in the sunshine and abundance of insects have made that journey from my garden, and if they will make it through that extraordinary journey back again in spring.

The ones that do make it feed and rest silently. But then, when they are joined about a week later by the females, the males' bubbling, piping, whirring chatter starts before dawn and will continue on and off throughout the day. That sound, along with their busy aerial elegance, is as central to this garden in summer as any plant.

Then they build a nest and at least two batches of young are reared in the cool, dark and cave-like tool shed. This involves their whizzing in and out a hundred times a day through two doors and the intervening potting shed. A film crew does not deter them but merely becomes another obstacle to twist and swerve around as they dart in and out.

I always check their height in the sky for the next day's weather because they follow the insects, which rise and fall according to the air pressure. So when the swallows are soaring high, there is a good chance of fine weather the next day and when they are swooping just inches from the ground to pluck insects with astonishing dexterity, the pressure is low and it is likely that rain will follow.

Dandelions

Walking with the dogs through the sheep-cropped fields at the beginning of a dry week in April I see that hundreds of golden dandelion flowers have opened in the warm spring sunshine. The stems are invisible, the flowers sitting apparently directly on the ground like little starry pools of brilliant yellow.

Dandelions thrive on being chopped back, whether by nibbling sheep or a lawnmower. If one of the definitions of a weed is a plant that has adapted to difficult circumstances better and quicker than most others, then the dandelion's ability to recover and thrive despite regular decapitation makes it a super-weed. The shorter the grass is cut, the more light reaches the dandelion leaves and the stronger it will grow. It will, of course, not produce seed if cut regularly but the deep taproot, the wide rosette of leaves and a lifespan of up to ten years mean that it can bide its time and then, when the conditions are right, quickly flower and only take about ten days between the flower forming and setting ripe seed.

The flowers open in the morning sun, flower for a couple of days, then close. The seeds develop inside the closed flower head, with the stalk growing longer, extending to hold the fluffy seed 'clock' high, all the better for the breeze to catch the seeds and cast them to the wind.

Our last house, 20 miles east of here, was set on a hillside and had a meadow rolling down from the garden in front of the house. In May it shone yellow with thousands and thousands of dandelions. One of the first pictures I have of my eldest son – himself a father now but then just two – is him holding a dandelion with two hands and blowing the seeds. It is incredibly sweet – obviously because this is my lovely little boy – but also because that image of a child blowing the gossamer seeds of a dandelion clock has become a kind of shared folk-memory, a communal experience that has reality even if it did not actually happen.

A Handsome Visitor

10 April. Looked out of the kitchen window and noticed an unusual bird (for us) at the bird table. With its coal-black head, I thought it was a blackcap but the black bib and chestnut back streaked with black made it more like a fancy-dress sparrow with a longer tail. It turned out to be a male reed bunting. I have never knowingly seen one before. Whether the field of rape next door has attracted him – apparently they like nesting in rape fields – or whether the fact that we are in low-lying wetlands means that there are lots about but rarely in the garden, I am not sure. The latter I suspect. But he is a handsome bird.

Cowslips

A couple of miles up the road between garden and farm is a crossroad. Stop, look both ways and there, for a couple of glorious weeks in April, is a bank covered in cowslips. Cowslips (*Primula veris*) are related to primroses but are different in a few critical ways. For a start they are not a flower of coppice woodland but of sunny, open places – hence this south-facing bank. Perhaps they are most acquainted with chalk downland and as that is the countryside I was brought up in, I think of cowslips as the open field yin to primroses' woodland yang.

Cowslips used to be very common and even in my youth they were remarkable for their loveliness rather than their mere presence. They have seen some resurgence but their main problem has been lack of habitat, especially due to the ploughing up of ancient grassland, although herbicide use has also been catastrophic. Herbicides have now been greatly reduced, so cowslips are making a comeback on roadside verges and particularly on motorways and big new road developments, thanks to the often superb yet under-appreciated planting and management. Nevertheless, the obsessive and utterly unnecessary flailing of verges along minor roads means that cowslips, along with many other spring flowers, are cut back before they can set seed, so they are gradually being wiped out.

Although open chalk downland is their archetypal habitat, as long as the soil is not too acidic, they can thrive in wood, meadows, glades and verges. I planted about 50 at the edge of the coppice 25 years ago. Since then, the trees have grown and cast rather too much shade for them but the cowslips still come up. However, many have hybridised with the primroses, which they do very readily, making a 'false oxlip', which looks like a primrose flower on a cowslip stem. It is very handsome.

They are perennials and, given the right circumstances, can live for decades. The seeds drop and seedlings emerge very close to the parent plant, so they evolve and spread in patches and clusters, which, helped by gravity, will invariably be down any slope.

Cowslips are the food plant of the caterpillar of the Duke of Burgundy butterfly – although not, I suspect, the cowslips we have here. I have never seen one in this part of the world and they are more likely to be found further south.

———

Slugs

When you encourage people to create a wildlife-friendly garden, it inevitably results in a hierarchy of what is 'good' wildlife and what are 'pests' (how I hate that label!) and therefore somehow not part of the cosy image of a cheeping, cooing, buzzing garden. If honeybees, hedgehogs and songbirds are top of the list of the acceptable face of nature, then right at the bottom, amongst the undesirables, come slugs. They inspire a visceral, simmering hatred in most gardeners. At best, they are yet another challenge but at worst they exist to spoil our best-laid horticultural plans.

But slugs are superb at recycling waste vegetative matter and are an essential part of a compost heap. The problem is that they do not discriminate between a fallen leaf and a delicious young seedling, both of which they consume with a mouth filled with over 20,000 teeth.

Unlike snails, that live largely above ground in nooks and crannies, slugs – essentially snails that have evolved to leave their shells behind – live largely in the soil and emerge at night to eat tender young growth as well as feeding on roots and tubers underground.

Although there are over 30 species of slug in the UK, there are four main garden ones and the biggest do not necessarily do the most damage. The keeled slug (*Milax budapestensis*) is probably the biggest problem despite its small size. Black, with a thin orange line down its back, it spends most of its life underground, feeding off root crops, but will also eat what it can when it surfaces.

The garden slug (*Arion hortensis*) is shiny black with an orange belly; its party trick is to eat off bean plants at ground level and riddle potatoes with holes. The grey field slug (*Deroceras reticulatum*) will eat anything and produces three generations of up to 200 eggs a year. Slug eggs can lie dormant for years before hatching when conditions are right. The leopard slug (*Limax maximus*) is big, often spotted (although not so much in woodland) and lives mainly off fungi and rotten vegetation – and occasionally other slugs – so does much more good than harm.

Finally, the black slug (*Arion ater*), which, despite its name can come in almost any colour, is a whopper and can reach 8in long, but is the least harmful of all.

It is far better to find ways of living with slugs than wasting time and energy trying to get rid of them – and in any event, that is doomed to failure. What you see is actually a tiny percentage of the population. Densities of over 250,000 slugs per acre are common, which makes a mockery of any attempt at slug control.

Slug pellets are harmful to hedgehogs, birds and dogs, so should never be used. Beer traps can work but only very locally and look ugly. Gritty, scratchy surfaces such as gravel, hair and eggshells have some effect but limit slugs' activity rather than stopping it.

I try and live with mine using three techniques. The first is to have a slug-free growing zone, where I raise tender young plants and check for slugs daily. The second is to grow healthy, unstressed plants that are much less likely to be attacked, and the third is to encourage lots of natural predators such as birds, beetles, frogs and hedgehogs, who, between them, make a much better job of controlling the slug population than I can.

———

Jack-by-the-Hedge

Garlic mustard (*Alliaria petiolata*) is one of those wild flowers that has collected dozens of folk names, including Jack-by-the-Hedge. It can be seen carpeting roadside banks, hedgerows and under trees in woods. It has vaguely nettley leaves – although the serrations are less sharp and completely without sting – held in ordered, stately tiers up the stem, which is topped by clear white flowers standing above the foliage. So far, so decorative, but its main claim to attention, if not fame, is that it is very edible, tasting gently of garlic. It is good eaten raw or cooked and can be made into a sauce or pesto.

It is a biennial member of the brassica family, which accounts for its slightly mustardy tang, and it flowers in its second year. It is the main food source of the orange tip butterfly, which is a close relative of the cabbage white, which likewise feeds off brassicas.

———

Blackcap

10 April. As I walked through the Jewel Garden this morning, a particularly sweet, rich song rang through it, more substantial than a robin's, bigger and richer than a wren's and less fluting but more bubbly than either a blackbird's or a thrush's. I finally located its singer in the branches of one of the purple hazels. It was a male blackcap, head adorned with a jet-black beret and pale grey body no bigger than a sparrow's. It is a big song from such a little bird.

I hear blackcaps in the garden much more than I see them, a little bird lost in the higher branches and foliage of the trees, its voice soaring out like a daytime nightingale. It is a woodland bird and the more trees and shrubs a garden has, the more the blackcap is likely to visit and even nest.

Whilst the male has his smart black toupee, the female's hairpiece is a chestnut-brown and, like almost all female birds, she does not sing.

Blackcaps are members of the warbler family and are summer visitors, although, as our winters have got milder, more birds seem to be going only as far as the southern half of the country, rather than to their usual winter homes in North Africa and southern Europe. In fact, we have increasingly had blackcaps coming to Britain to winter from alpine Germany and Austria.

This winter influx has resulted in an unlikely side-effect. Blackcaps are one of the few birds, along with thrushes, that eat the berries of mistletoe. But unlike thrushes, who excrete the seeds, blackcaps usually wipe them off their bills and in so doing wedge them into crevices in bark. The upshot is that mistletoe has spread hugely.

When the weather is really bad and snow and ice set in for days and weeks – which has not happened for quite a few years – we see male and female blackcaps at the bird table outside the kitchen window, but in a mild winter, never. That seems to be not because they have gone south but because they are finding plenty of food without resorting to our daily buffet. Their diet is normally based on flies, insects, caterpillars and berries; they are not naturally seed or fat eaters although the evidence is that they are adapting and evolving quickly to the enormous increase in bird food put out by householders over the past ten years or so.

The male bird, as well as singing operatically, will build a number of rather half-hearted nests to lure a mate who, if tempted, will complete it and make it into a neat cup of grass lined with moss, feathers and hair. The eggs are incubated for about twelve days and the chicks fledge about two weeks later, although are able to leave the nest a week after hatching if need be. Given such a quick turnaround, they often manage two broods a summer.

A week later, as I sit in my room, locked down and locked out of the garden by electricians laying cabling for TV cameras so *Gardeners' World* can be filmed without a crew present, there is rising birdsong floating through the open window. It is the blackcap, his soaring, sibilant song rising above the strangeness of these days.

————

Morning Murder Amongst the Topiary Yews

13 April. As I drew back the curtains, I saw a puff of feathers and the twisting dart of brown wings. A sparrowhawk had snatched a bird from one of the yew cones, twisted round between another, turned right between two more and dropped out of sight – all in half a second. Whilst my brain was making sense of what I had seen, the feathers were still falling gently to the grass below.

I went outside and gently crept down the path, expecting the bird to still be there, mantling over its kill. Nothing. No sign of it. Not a feather.

But as I relaxed and turned back, there was a clatter of wings from the holly hedge behind me and the sparrowhawk burst out – all-brown, female – within touching distance, wheeled round me as though I was a tree trunk or yew cone and flew off. Down in the bottom of the hedge I could see a half-eaten blackbird.

Such excitement! And all before seven in the morning.

————

Badger Track

There is a gate that opens onto a crossing over a stream and onto the next field. It sticks and every time I go through it, I resolve to mend it. I have been resolving this for the past eight years. It is the Gate That Sticks and will probably remain so until the gatepost rots. But because it sticks, the dogs stand impatiently whilst I lift and jiggle to get it to open and there is time to notice the narrow mazy track beaten into the bright green but still short grass. It starts underneath the gate, curves out into the field, then wriggles down to the hedge where it disappears. Finally, getting the gate to open, I see that there is a groove worn underneath the fence at the edge of the stream and a few bristly hairs caught on the barbed wire.

This grooved, narrow track takes me up the dingle, with its strip of sloping, wooded banks either side of the stream. The trees shimmer a pinky grey with rising sap but have no glimmer of leaf yet and are fully ten days behind the garden, which is daily prickling into green, but the bluebell foliage is dense already, although it will be another month before the flowers appear. No bluebells but lots of violets – little blue stars, not in clusters but dotted all over the ground. We hardly ever come here, partly because it is fenced-off to keep the sheep and cattle out, and partly because it does not go anywhere. It is one of the various places around the farm that have, without any particular plan, been left pretty much to themselves. We could call it rewilding but that would be to aggrandise it. It has just been left.

Which is probably why the badgers use it as a run. At least, I think it is badger. However, I then come to a slight clearing that confirms the badger theory because an area about ten yards square is flattened and pocked with small holes and divots, each one occupied by a good dollop of badger poo. This is a badger lavatory. My first thought is not, how interesting, but that I must stop the dogs rolling in it as there is nothing more fragrantly enticing to the average dog than badger poo.

But, dogs safely restrained, it *is* interesting. The fact that a dedicated latrine exists at all is unique to badgers and this is certainly the largest I have seen. It is also, as far as I can make out, some distance from the nearest sett, which implies that it is a marker, probably right at the edge of these particular badgers' boundary and acting as much as a deterrent to other badgers as a loo.

The track that I had been following then heads back up the hill, crossing the stream, up the other side of the bank, following the field edge there, and then under the fence – more dirty white hairs on the lowest strand of barbed wire, more lifting of dogs up and over, Nigel, distinctly unimpressed, cuts across the corner of another field, under another gate. And then – disappears. Completely. I spend 20 minutes scouring the area for any signs, willing the inner tracker in me to notice the tell-tale crushed grass, smoothed soil or paw print, but there is nothing at all.

We have always had badgers on the farm, as proven by the remnants of three very visible setts, although never more than one is occupied at any time. I had assumed that the badgers' track went downhill towards the lusher grass near the valley floor, but perhaps it is made by badgers coming uphill to visit us, defecate, amble about a bit, feed and then return home to the relative lowlands. The dogs seem uninterested by any scent on the badger trail. Perhaps it is too obvious to them and their noses read it as a heavily sign-posted badger motorway. Perhaps it is less recent than it looks.

Lots of 'perhapses' and 'don't knows'. But there is time. One of the many luxuries of having a patch of land is that you can watch and wait and let the stories unravel at their own pace.

Geese

19 April. Geese are in the middle of the field, the female – presumably – lying down and the male standing guard. He honks agitatedly as the dogs and I come nearer. I wonder how long this pair have been together because I know that they pair for life and geese can live for ten, 20, even 30 years. I steer the dogs well clear but the geese cannot tolerate us at all and take off, honking, disturbed and disturbing. Nobody ever crept up on geese and for all their domesticity, they are wild, proud creatures.

Geese were always kept on local farms by the farmer's wife and sold at Christmas. She and the other females in the family would do the plucking and keep the money from the sales. I remember we kept geese when I was a child and I have a vivid memory of looking out of my bedroom window on a frosty morning and seeing my father walk up the garden with two dead geese, their long necks draped over each arm. They were plucked in the garage with electric heaters on to keep the bodies warm and make the plucking easier and the floor grew deep in goose down.

Dog's Mercury

Dog's mercury emerges from under the hedges lining the lanes in the valley at the same time as leaves start to prickle the bare branches. It also grows in the dingles under the beech and ash trees, and between the overgrown hazel stools that have not been coppiced since at least the last war.

Mercurialis perennis is very common where it grows and can be a thug, spreading by underground rhizomes, particularly in shade, but it is a reliable indicator of old, long-standing woodland. It is poisonous to grazing stock and humans but the stock avoids it and even if you cannot identify it, once handled, its distinctively unpleasant odour should be enough to put you off eating it.

Being poisonous is not, in itself, a moral flaw but is typical of many woodland plants. Bluebells and wood anemones are just as dangerous for grazing animals. For us on the farm, this is not terribly significant because we do all that we can to keep the sheep out of our woods, but in Wales, well into the twentieth century, wood pasture was important and used extensively. Both farmers and animals had to know what was nutritious and what was harmful.

But although humans, cattle and sheep may avoid it, woodcock like to lie low in its cover during the day, and the little green flowers of the female plants (it is dioecious, with separate male and female plants) provide seeds that birds and small mammals eat. A decoction of dog's mercury was also used for curing warts and the leaves and stems produce a very good indigo-blue dye, but with the one major fault being that it is hard to fix, turning red in contact with acids and destroyed by alkalis.

———

House Martins

House martins are the other side of the swallow coin. If swallows are poetry, martins are witty prose. Swallows are all elegance and scything grace, whereas martins are tumblers and high-wire daredevils. Swallows break your heart when they leave and martins put a smile on my face every day they are here.

The two are inevitably yoked together for me, just as they almost always are in the sky above the garden – although not above the farm, which has no martins other than the occasional visiting group. For some reason, they do not nest outside our farmhouse or barns whereas the swallows do so in a number of the sheds and byres.

The first to arrive are always swallows, with the martins reaching here at least two weeks and sometimes a month later. Although superficially similar and using the sky in the same way, once you get your eye in they are very different. Martins are slightly smaller and stubbier, with shorter tails and wings, and dark navy-blue backs and white undersides, whereas swallows have longer tails, lighter blue feathers and a distinct patch of red at their throat.

Their flight patterns are very different. Swallows cut arcs and wheels in the sky, using more space, carving arabesques in the air. Martins work a smaller area, swooping and bobbing, ducking and diving, returning again and again to the same aerial patch until they have exhausted the insects, then move on. As many as 50 at a time can do this towards the end of summer, when there is one or even two sets of young hunting along with the adults, who are feeding the third brood.

But in April, they come in ones and twos, dribs and drabs, returning to last year's nests. These are mostly on the east and north sides of the house although there has always been a nest or two just above our south-facing window, too. They repair the nests and build new ones out of mud, dipping down into puddles to scoop mud without breaking flight. It is a major feat as the average nest takes about a thousand beakfuls of mud, a thousand flights to and from the nest site, to construct. A very dry spring causes real problems, which is why destroying old nests (some people think them 'dirty' or untidy) that will probably be reused is vandalism.

Outside the window of the room where I am writing, overlooking the Herb Garden, there are nests inches above the window frame, which means that from May to mid-September I cannot open the windows for fear of disturbing the birds. It is a small price to pay. In fact, the only time they get opened in summer is to let out a swallow that has flown in through the downstairs door, come up the stairs, along the landing and into my converted hop-kiln work room.

Throughout the summer months swallows fly in and out almost daily but we rarely have martins. This is because swallows instinctively look for a cave to nest or roost in and our permanently opened doors to the garden in summer obviously look cave-like. But martins prefer to remain on the outside of a building, on the surface of the rock face, avoiding the interior and the potential for danger within.

One of the great pleasures of my life is the burbling, chirping busyness of the nesting martins at dawn outside our bedroom window. The rising sun silhouettes their constant swooping arrival up to the nests, where they are greeted by a hubbub of chittering from the young and then plunge down from the nests in a constant pendulum of feeding.

Between the swallows and the martins, the summer sky above the garden is always busy. Unless there is heavy rain or gale-force winds, there are always dozens of them hunting, sometimes almost out of sight because the insects are so high, sometimes just feet above my head. But they are always there and when they go the absence is painful.

The only real predator of martins above the garden are hobbies. I confess I am torn between wanting to see more hobbies and therefore wanting them to hunt – and catch – prey above the garden, and also wanting the pretty little martins to be safe. On balance the exquisite and rare hobby wins the toss every time but nature makes harsh choices.

Martin numbers are falling, partly because modern houses are less suitable for their nests but also because they suffer badly from the use of insecticides. They feed mainly off flying aphids and the more of these that there are, the better the second clutch size will be and the greater the chance of a third brood.

I used to wonder why martins, both during the breeding season and on their travels south, used to focus so clearly on the sky above this garden but now realise why. We are effectively a service station for them – a refuelling stop-off.

Finally, there is one great mystery about house martins. Given the domesticity of these birds and their familiarity, the way that they are literally part of our households, it is astonishing that we do not know where they go in winter other than somewhere in

Africa. That is it. Unlike most migrating birds, which are mapped and tracked, we also do not know how they get to this unknown place. There is speculation that they do much of their winter feeding at high altitude above the rainforest and are therefore rarely seen, but that is pure guesswork.

————

Spurges

The wood spurge (*Euphorbia amygdaloides*) is so much a garden plant that it is easy to overlook the fact that it is a native wild flower. As its name indicates, it grows in broad-leafed woodland and particularly in coppiced woodland, responding to the flood of light that follows each coppice cycle, then becoming less prolific as the canopy grows and closes in. It is a handsome plant with its yallery-green flowers, which, like all euphorbias, have no petals or sepals but are tiny and held in bracts that surround it like a ruff or collar. The flowers – that are pollinated by flies – change from green to electric-yellow and it has rightly become a garden favourite, but looks best when grown as naturally as possible beneath trees or shrubs and accompanied by bluebells, primroses, anemones and other woodland flowers.

The flowers and bracts are the main source of food for the larvae of the drab looper moth, which, having pupated, changes its diet and the moth feeds off thistles. It is rare and I have never seen one. But I see that it occurs in Monmouthshire and, given that the farm is just within that county boundary, it means I might have the chance to do so some day.

The caper spurge (*Euphorbia lathyris*) pops up all over the garden in single stems like a kind of giant asparagus. It can reach 4ft to 5ft tall and is fringed with leaves that grow rather rigidly out at right angles. Eventually, this solitary shoot produces a pair of flower stems and the origami-green flowers hold the caper-like fruits that give it its name.

It has a long-standing reputation for repelling moles and I have solemnly placed cut stems into mole holes, but without any noticeable effect. Even if the moles do not like it, they simply come up somewhere else and make yet another molehill.

Blackbirds in the Tool Shed

There is a blackbird nesting in the tool shed. More precisely, there are two blackbirds nesting on top of a rubber rake hanging up in the tool shed. The nest is interwoven with the rubbery tines backed by the wall behind it.

To get to the nest, first to make it and then to feed the young, the birds have had to fly in through the potting shed and turn at right angles through the doorway to the inner tool shed that has no external access. When we are filming in the potting shed, with lights, cameras, monitors, cables and three or four people crammed behind the camera as well as a couple more in the tool shed, the birds still rush in and out, dodging round and through us, and practically colliding, but more irritated than frightened. It is obvious that people are the least of their worries and the nesting site is chosen for maximum safety from hawks and perhaps, if they are street-wise, cats.

Eventually I took out the Perspex sheet that was covering the slats of the window that is right by the nest, which meant that they could now slip between the bars directly to the nest, whilst still protected from any predator. But it took a while for them to work out that this was a new, easier access and the old route was still preferred for days, despite its complications.

Newts

Newts famously have enormous bureaucratic powers. Motorways, shopping centres, kitchen extensions and housing estates can all be curtailed and postponed by the presence of great crested newts so as not to destroy their habitat. Once, when there were far more dew ponds and ditches throughout the country, they were not uncommon but their spread has dramatically declined – hence the extreme protection afforded to them. In fact, wherever you have any, you almost always have plenty, but because they need water, their spread is limited.

The great crested newt (*Triturus cristatus*) is the largest you will see in Britain and can be up to 6in long. It has warty skin and although, despite the name, the female never has a crest, the male grows two crests in spring, one on its back and another on its tail. Like toads, they excrete a poison from the warts on their skin so they tend not to be predated. They spend winter hibernating on land before moving to water in the breeding season.

We made our pond eight years ago and did not stock it with anything other than a range of plants. Frogs and water beetles quickly took up residence, dragonflies skimmed it, birds bathed in the water and bats zig-zagged down to pick off the insects that gathered in little clouds above it. But there were, as far as I knew, no newts. Then, after a few years, I was skimming off the algae and depositing the wet green vegetation on a stone at the edge of the pond so that any creepy crawlies could return to the water before I tidied up, when something halfway between a lizard and tadpole – a kind of tiny alligator – walked down into the water followed by a couple more. These were newts – the first that I had noticed in the pond. There are now masses of them.

These are the common or smooth newt (*Lissotriton vulgaris*).

It is brown with a wavy crest along its back that it grows in the breeding season to increase its seductiveness. They develop their front legs first and then the back ones (which is the opposite to tadpoles) and are a favoured food of many fish. Once they are fully formed, they leave the water and live in damp places on land. Newts are carnivorous and will eat whatever they can catch – usually tadpoles, worms, shrimps and insects in the water, and worms and slugs when they move to dry land.

Dead-nettle

Growing along the lea of the hedges, white dead-nettles (*Lamium album*) have the brightness and freshness of a really good pudding – albeit a green-and-white one. The fact that they look all nettly but are not related to nettles and do not sting (hence the 'dead' bit of their name) gives them an aura of cheer that their stinging lookalikes can never have.

The flowers make a ruff of white petals touched with green – always a good combination in any flower – rising up the stem in orderly tiers, and they are hooded with a lower lip that acts as a landing stage for bumblebees and other pollinators. The nectar that they are after can be sucked from the base of the flower and I can remember being shown this as a child, and drawing deep of a succession of flowers, confirming that I could taste the lovely honeyed nectar when in truth there was nothing other than a faint flowery taste. But I was loathe to disappoint my elder sister, who showed me the trick.

Like stinging nettles, the leaves and flowers are both edible but unlike stinging nettles, they can be eaten raw in a salad as well as cooked.

There is a red version (*L. purpureum*), although the flowers are pinky-mauve rather than red. It is more likely to grow in the open and as a weed than white dead-nettle, which is a true woodland edge plant.

————

Sedge Warbler

Normally we stop feeding the birds when it is mild enough to put out the pelargoniums. These will take a little frost, so mid or even early April – around Easter – normally fits that bill. This transition is not dictated by timing but space. The pelargoniums stand on the stone table in the back yard that is the bird table in winter. In April, we remove the bird table's logs and weatherbeaten branches and scrub the whole thing down, like shaking a tablecloth of the crumbs of one meal and laying it for the next.

But this year we have delayed the transition. This has meant that all kinds of summer visitors are coming to feed that we normally never see, such as blackcaps, buntings and, today, a sedge warbler.

It was immediately recognisable as different if not identifiable. Superficially another little brown job, it has handsome chestnut-and-black-streaked wings and back – like the reed bunting – a pale head, slim beak and a very obvious pale primrose-yellow stripe above each eye. The underside is pale buff and the tail is long with noticeable white flashes on the edges, like a skylark.

It is like a skylark in another way, too, having a song flight, rising vertically and singing away before spiralling down with outstretched wings. Its song, whether in flight or in the reeds that give it its name, is brilliant, flashy and very varied. Much of this variety comes from its ability to mimic other birds' calls, incorporating and modifying them into its own. This medley is never repeated note for note and every time it opens its mouth, its performance is live and unique, never to be repeated exactly the same again. The song exists only to attract a partner and has no territorial function at all. So, once it has won him a mate – and the more varied and longer the song, the more attractive he becomes as a potential breeding partner – the male ceases singing altogether, save for the few that take up with another mate – which he will do as soon as his female number one has started laying in the nest woven out of grasses, flower stems, hair and spiders' webs, and attached to reeds, low down near the ground.

This tiny bird weighing about a quarter of an ounce, will have come to my garden almost direct from sub-Saharan Africa, flying up to 2000 miles without a break for three and a half to four days.

In fact, it has come not to the garden but to the wet, flooded, lowland beyond the garden fence that pretends to be dry agricultural land for a few months in summer but is really a mere. There are certainly rivers, streams and ditches enough in the vicinity for the sedge warbler to feel at home, even in a dry summer.

———

Alkanet

Green alkanet (*Pentaglottis sempervirens*) has such lovely clear, bright blue starry little flowers, yet it is always a bit-part player, a supporting act somewhere between wild flower and weed. In some places, it crosses that line convincingly and becomes invasive and its deep taproots that resprout even if cut hard to the ground make it difficult to control.

However, it is more than welcome in this garden but it crops up all too sporadically here, leaning against walls and hedges. I wish it would spread itself more enthusiastically but it really prefers a drier, more alkaline soil.

In fact, it is not a native but comes from Spain and was introduced primarily as a dyestuff. With its strong green foliage and intense blue flowers, it comes as something of a surprise to learn that the dye, extracted from the roots, is red. It was often grown in monasteries for this purpose and can sometimes be found in their ruins, like ghosts haunting their cultivated pre-Reformation days. The name alkanet is a relic of the Moorish occupation of Spain, via the Arabic for henna – *al-hannat* – although green alkanet gives a fainter red than dyer's alkanet (*Alkanna tinctoria*).

It looks a bit like comfrey and a bit like pulmonaria, and is a member of the borage family, related to anchusa and sharing the same cobalt-blue flowers. The leaves are one of the food plants for the scarlet tiger moth and the flowers are much loved by pollinators such as solitary bees and hoverflies.

Green Woodpecker

You are more likely to hear the green woodpecker than see it. But whereas with the great spotted what you hear is its drumming, it is the call of the green that is so distinctive and far-carrying. It is a shrill, hyena laugh, a repeated note rising in an alarmed crescendo known as a yaffle. It also has a repeated 'clue clue clue' call, which is a bit like the call of a kestrel, although the woodpecker is more fluting and without the hard consonant at the beginning of each note.

When you do see them, it is either as they fly from open ground to cover, looking as though they are bouncing on an invisible piece of elastic, dipping and bounding in the air, or on the ground as they feed. It is one of the most colourful birds of all, their backs and wings a rich green, heads bright red with a black bandit eye mask (which in the male has a bright red moustachial stripe) and bottoms a vivid flash of yellow. Its beak seems bigger and stouter than that of the great spotted but in fact it is much weaker, which means it is more inclined to make its nest where the wood is damaged or rotten, very often choosing an oak for this. They mate for life but live mainly apart, the established pairs occupying the same neighbouring territories all their lives and then reconnecting each spring with answering calls.

We never see them in the garden, not least because we do not have a lawn as such. However, we do see and hear them regularly on the farm, where they feed on the yellow ants in particular. These colonise uncultivated but regularly grazed pasture, making great mounds (or 'tumps' as they are known in this part of the world) that the woodpecker probes with that powerful bill, its extra-long, sticky tongue scooping up the ants as they are exposed.

I remember the winter of 1963 having a disastrous effect on the population and they disappeared for a few years. The winter of 2010 was also very damaging because snow or frozen ground mean that they cannot get at their food and will starve to death.

Water Mint

When walking in our fields, high up on the hillside, negotiating ditches and boggy pieces of ground, there will suddenly be the pungent aroma of mint as your feet crush the plants growing out of the wet ground and running water. This is the wild water mint (*Mentha aquatica*), with its coarse, almost watercress appearance and purple undersides to the leaves. It grows in really wet spots, so you can pull up great clumps from the wet soil, but like all mints it spreads by rhizomes and will do so from the smallest section.

The flowers are puffs of mauve and ruby held up on burgundy stems; they make a pretty little posy in a jar, filling the kitchen with the minty fragrance of the hillside.

Docks

As one of the last generation of children brought up almost entirely, year round, in shorts until I was about eleven, the top of my calves, knees and bottom of my thighs were easy pickings for stinging nettles – especially the older, taller, more vicious ones. We ran and played outside all day long, which often meant dashing through a patch of nettles, thinking this time, this one time, I will get away with it. We never did. The stings left great weals and pain every single time.

But we had a remedy – broad-leafed dock – the application of which for nettle stings I have talked about in the March chapter.

Rumex obtusifolius is a member of the sorrel family. It has a deep taproot and can become a dominant weed in grass, especially if horses have been grazing because, unlike cattle or sheep, horses will not eat it. However, the leaves are a favourite food for moth caterpillars and Richard Mabey, in his book *Weeds*, recites a litany of the names of all 33 varieties known to feed upon it.

Just cutting or 'topping' them will stop them seeding but they quickly respond by growing more foliage and, given the chance, a flowering stem. I have a 'docking spud', which is like a chisel or very straight, narrow hoe blade on a long handle. Farmers would walk their fields on a Sunday morning before church, carrying a spud with them and using it to jab into the ground to sever the dock's taproot a few inches down, which was what was needed to stop it regrowing.

If allowed to flower, it develops really tough stems which, along with the seeds, turn a deep rust colour, making a late-summer paddock look like it has been jagged with spikes of scrap metal. Docks seeds, like poppies, need disturbance to provoke germination, but can lie dormant for over half a century before cultivation springs them into life.

Wood Sorrel

Around Easter time the banks of the dingles on the farm become carpeted with tiny white flowers set amongst hanging, folded, bright little leaves, like triple butterfly wings, like timid clover, faces averted and held down. This is wood sorrel (*Oxalis acetosella*), which is not related to clover at all. It grows out of moss on logs and stone, and from leaf litter, seemingly not needing soil at all. We don't have any growing in the garden, although there are plenty of garden hybrids, but it is very common in the dips and gullies on the acid hillside all around the farm. The leaves respond to light and weather, and fold up at night and when it rains, opening wide in sunlight – although it grows best in the dappled shade of woodland.

The leaves are edible and faintly lemon-flavoured. They are rich in oxalic acid, which is also found in spinach, chard and rhubarb. Eaten in moderation, they will do you no harm but too much will give you tummy ache.

The spring flowers produce little seed but it often has a second, almost inconspicuous flowering in summer, which does result in seed. Although not definitive in isolation, the presence of wood sorrel in a wood is a good indicator that it is semi-natural ancient woodland. In practice, that means that our dingles have been like this, more or less, since the last Ice Age. The wood has been harvested almost continuously since then, but it has remained constantly woodland, moving and changing and staying exactly itself, just like the stream that runs through it.

Cuckoo

There are triggers that unlock doors through which memory pours. The first cuckoo is as potent a trigger as any. Cuckoo call is like blossom, like snowfall. It is as much a symbol as its actual self. But what may have been a universal experience, as much a measure of spring as mistletoe or robins are of Christmas, is becoming rarer. Cuckoo numbers are down by 65 per cent since the early 1980s and are still falling.

Going back over the past ten years of journals, I see that the first cuckoo is always in the last week of April, with a variance of no more than five days. This is amazingly consistent, given that the poor bird has flown in from the Congo.

That haunting, fluting, two-note call that cuts through the daylight like a trumpet. Summer is icumen in. It is not the same bird, of course – cuckoos live about four years – but always the same effect. But it *is* always the male that arrives first, having made his long and extraordinary journey, almost entirely at night, flying high up at about 15,000ft. The male gets here about a week before the female. She will almost invariably return to the same site year after year, laying eggs that are uncannily camouflaged to look like the hosts' – even though the variety of host parents requires quite a wide range of cuckoo egg markings and colourations.

The female cuckoo does not have the archetypal 'cuck-oo' call but instead has a rising, bubbling cry that mounts to a quick crescendo, like a diver surfacing from water. Once she arrives, her attention is focused on finding a suitable host for her eggs, and with us, it is most likely to be the pipit on the farm and the dunnock in the fields around the garden.

The male has no part in any of this but is solely interested in mating with as many females as possible, whilst deterring all other males. In practice, given the territory size of the cuckoo, many females lay eggs sired by up to four males and males may, given the opportunity, mate with up to four females.

You hear cuckoos much more than see them, but I do see them flying over the garden and across the face of the hillside at the farm – and with his dove-like head and sparrowhawk body, the male is instantly recognisable, circling his breeding range sometimes for 20 minutes or more, during which time he will call hundreds of times. The resemblance to a sparrowhawk, not just in outline and flight pattern but also in colouring, with its barred grey-and-black chest, seems to be an evolutionary work of camouflage, both to protect the cuckoo from attack by hawks and to scare host birds away from the nest as the cuckoo approaches. In fact, cuckoos have no way of defending themselves from attack nor of harming any other bird, yet other birds seem to be taken in by the deception.

Their favourite prey consists of hairy caterpillars – the only British bird that does eat them. The caterpillars are mostly found on trees, especially in woodland and orchards, and cuckoos will travel long distances – up to fifteen miles – to a spot with a rich supply. The hairs that are so irritating to other birds are shed in the cuckoo's stomach and regurgitated as a pellet. I have noticed that we have much more evidence of cuckoo activity on the farm than around the garden, which may have something to do with the greater proportion of woodland to open fields there.

Cuckoos do not call when feeding or going to and from feeding sites. The call is only used around the breeding area (I was going to say 'nesting area' but this is the one bird that never nests), which they mark out by song and which is relatively small, covering around 75 acres or about 40 football pitches. One of the quirks of their call – which is always made in flight – is that the bird turns its head, which has the effect of throwing the sound.

The combination of the moving bird and the thrown sound means that the cuckoo can be quite hard to locate, which adds to the slightly wistful, ethereal effect – although if you happen to hear it as the cuckoo passes overhead, then the call is surprisingly strong and loud.

The calling stops by the end of June and by the middle of July, the cuckoos are gone, heading first to the Mediterranean to feed up and then back to the Congo. They arrive there in November, joining the swifts that also migrate there from Britain.

One sobering thought. I have always thought of cuckoos returning here as coming home, of being part of our summer as much as the leaves on an oak tree. But the truth is that they spend 70 per cent of their lives in Africa. We are the holiday destination, and they are as African as the gorillas that occupy the mountainous rainforests beneath them.

———

Bluebells

It is strange how we feel that certain flowers are ours by right at certain stages of the year, almost as though they provide a public service. Snowdrops in January, daffodils in March, bluebells in April and May.

But on the farm the bluebells have become an astonishing gift, renewed and celebrated each spring.

Sarah and I walked every inch of the farm in the first May we were there and I not only counted the bluebells but plotted out exactly where each one was on my farm map. By the time we had finished, I had a grand total of nine crosses. Just nine solitary little flowers. A few were in the scattered, heavily grazed patches of woodland but more were on isolated pieces of hillside that would soon be dense with a cover of bracken. Bluebells do not normally grow as a meadow flower, so where they occur in an open field, it is an indicator that it has been woodland of some kind in the not-too-distant past. By overlaying the 1880 Ordnance Survey map over my plan with the crosses, I could see that every single cross was in an area marked as wood back then.

Bluebells are woodland flowers but do not grow well in dense shade. Managed coppice suits them best and the hazel coppices with beech, standards of the countryside around my childhood Hampshire home, were perfect for them. Coppiced wood is good because, after the coppice cycle – every eight to twelve years in the case of hazel – the wood floor is flooded with light for a couple of years and bluebells, primroses, anemones and violets, in particular, burgeon, setting more seed and spreading quickly along with plants that grow from seed that has lain dormant during the darker part of the cycle but is triggered into germination by exposure to light.

Sometimes this wait can be very long indeed. Wood spurge seed (*Euphorbia amygdaloides*), for example, can lie dormant for well over 100 years before light bursts it into growth. Meanwhile, there is enough shade from the standard trees and the rapidly growing new shoots of the coppiced stools to suppress the grass and bracken that would otherwise take over.

Then, as the new hazel growth increases and the canopy closes over, the light levels increasingly drop, and by the end of the cycle the plants are clinging on in conditions that are too shady for comfort. Then the hazel is cut and the cycle starts all over again. It can continue in this way for millennia.

Gradually, year by year, our original nine multiplied. It takes about five years for a bluebell seed to develop into a bulb so, however successful the growth and pollination of existing flowers, there is a time lag before they start to spread.

But now, over fifteen years after that first set of nine crosses, bluebells carpet our dingles and woods. The nine have now become at least 9000.

One in a hundred bluebells is pure white, an albino missing the pigment that makes a bluebell blue. Well, bluish. When you see bluebells by the thousand, the effect is broadly blue. But look at an individual flower carefully, and you will see that most native British bluebells, whose flowers typically hang modestly to one side (the Spanish bluebell is much more upright and does not hang to the side) are mauvey/purpley/blue. This is not surprising when you consider that the pigment for making them blue, anthocyanin is, in fact, red. Look at the bluebells again, and you will see how that reddish-pink tinge shines through.

And as the dogs and I walk through the bluebells, following the badger tracks up the hillside through the woods and along the banks of the streams, I am overwhelmed with a sense of good fortune. To have access to all this, on this day, in this light, brings riches beyond measure.

———

MAY

Hawthorn

Hawthorn is a fixed part of my landscape, both in the garden and the countryside around. And not just around here. Travel to any area of British countryside where there are hedges, and hawthorn will be the overwhelmingly dominant hedging plant. When the common land was enclosed on a mass scale in the eighteenth and nineteenth centuries, hawthorn was used above all else to form the boundary hedges – over 200,000 miles of them. Any straight hedge dividing fields is likely to be almost entirely hawthorn, planted to enclose land in that period. A more meandering, curving hedge, with a number of different species, will be much older and often the remnant of a wood thousands of years old. I have used hawthorn hedges in the garden where it moves towards less formality, although keeping them tightly clipped produces a strictly linear fuzz of spiny tangled branches in winter and a soft green blur of leaves from April to October.

On the hillside above the farm, on the tree-scattered *ffridd,* the scrubby, lightly wooded land above the pastures of the lower slopes of the hillside and below the open moorland at the top, individual hawthorns, short, weather-tormented trees, magnificent in their dogged resilience, are remnants of a much more wooded past. In blossom, they form a creamy froth stretching all along the valley as far as the eye can see.

However, one of the most noticeable manifestations of the different flowering times that altitude dictates shows in the 30 miles between the garden and the farm. The expression 'Ne'er cast a clout till may is out' refers not to the end of the month but to the blossoming of the hawthorn, or may, tree. By 1 June, our hawthorn blossom in the garden is over but, on the farm – at 1000ft – it is still going strong, whilst right up on the tree line, at about 1600ft, the white of the blossom speckles the hillside until the second week of June.

That blossom becomes fruit and in a good year – and 2019 was an astonishing year – the trees can be bowed down with small red berries. Birds love them and the thrushes, in particular song and mistle, blackbirds, redwing and fieldfare – all fall on them with huge and greedy enthusiasm. But they tend not to do so at first. The berries are ripe and ready to eat from September but it is not until the first cold snap – usually in November – that they get eaten up fast. It is as though the birds know that they will keep perfectly well on the tree until well after Christmas, so can be left in reserve whilst other food supplies are available.

The tree is armed with vicious thorns – not the worst in the armoury of British trees, that crown is worn by blackthorn – but at any one time I bear the wounds and embedded thorns from my encounters with hawthorn. But its dense tangle of thorny branches is the perfect cover for small birds, both in winter and when nesting in summer.

The common hawthorn, which dominates all those thousands of miles of hedges, is *Crataegus monogyna* and one of the ironies of its use as hedging is that it actually grows naturally as a tree of rather open places rather than in dense stands or as thick undergrowth beneath larger trees. Until my early childhood, hedges were mostly cut by hand and laid – that is, each hawthorn stem would be cut through until held by just a slither of wood and bark, and then inclined over onto its side and bound in, or 'plashed', at 45 degrees. This way an overgrown hedge that had not been cut for ten years or so would be reduced to a dense, stock-proof line just 3ft tall. It would then be largely left uncut until the next time to lay it, in a decade or so. But now the flail hedgecutter reduces all hedges to a four-square, neat, ordered line. Whilst this results in very dense hedges – and that is good cover for small birds – what is best for a wide range of wildlife is a mixture of low and tall hedgerows, with some trees along their length, but the flail smashes everything into uniformity in its remorseless path.

Hawthorn is one of the very few British trees that can seed, grow and establish into a tree whilst being constantly grazed, and is one of the first trees to pioneer abandoned grassland, or indeed, any waste ground. This makes thorny scrub, which in turn protects the less confident colonisers like oak from being eaten by rabbits or deer.

So this modest, ubiquitous hedging tree of the British countryside is a true savannah tree. It has been a feature of the very earliest, more open wooded countryside, where herds of grazing animals roamed through and around woodland, since the last Ice Age.

However, *C. laevigata*, the woodland or midland hawthorn, is much less common – although before the mass planting of hedges, this species would have been at least as common as *C. monogyna*. It is one of the prime indicators of semi-natural woodland, which means that a hedge or patch of scrubby woodland with *C. laevigata* in it is very likely to have been proper woodland continuously throughout human history – older than any cathedral, older than any Roman remain. In the Anglo-Saxon charters, thorn trees – and these would have almost all been *C. laevigata* – often feature as boundary points, in other words, single trees that were noticeable and memorable along a hedge or field line.

The easiest time to differentiate between the two types of hawthorn is when they flower. *C. monogyna* invariably has white blossom, whereas *C. laevigata* can flower various shades of pink and tends to flower rather earlier. It is from this that most of the garden cultivars, such as the famous 'Paul's Scarlet', are bred.

Both types of hawthorn make superb firewood as it is very dense and hard and burns very hot. So if an old, sizeable tree blows down, I cut up every scrap for burning. But I would never cut one just for firewood. I like them too much. One of the only surviving two trees in the garden from when we came here in 1991 is a hawthorn in the coppice, bent and leaning, and having hardly grown any taller in the past 29 years. But sometimes the old trees grow surprisingly straight and true. I have a couple of favourites on the farm with straight trunks and with the bark twisted and fluted like strands of rope; they have real venerability and dignity.

Red Campion

Red campion (*Silene dioica*) is a tremendous weed of this garden. It pops up along the edges of paths and borders and hedges, and across quite a few of the borders, too, if given the opportunity. Its simple pink whirligig flowers start to appear in the middle of April and stay flowering into June. The flowers' simple accessibility means they are much favoured by all kinds of pollinators. We pull up and compost barrowloads of them every year but they are steadily increasing nevertheless.

It will grow in deep shade without flowering, then exposure to light will trigger the flowers, so it is often found in coppiced woodlands. It is one of the indicator plants of ancient woodland, so if you find it growing in a wood, regardless of the apparent age of the trees, it is a sign that there has been woodland there for a long time. It is dioecious – each plant is either male or female – so you need both to produce viable seed.

Bladder campion (*S. vulgaris*) is a plant that does not occur naturally in the garden but a single specimen planted in the Walled Garden 25 years ago has become parent to great rafts of it around the garden. I, innocently, chopped chunks off and put it around the borders, but it has become so entrenched that it is effectively a weed. But it's a particularly lovely weed, with splayed, little white petals fringing a pink balloon or bubble of calyx – the bladder in question. It naturally grows in grassland, where it has to work harder to compete than in the rich soil of a border. I have recently been lifting and dividing the border plants and redistributing them into the rougher areas of long grass. This is not as easy as it might be because, despite the prettiness of the flowers, the roots quickly become incredibly woody, almost like a fused log.

They are pollinated by long-tongued moths attracted by the clove-like scent that is given off at night, and froghoppers, with their protective cover of cuckoo spit, are also drawn to it. The leaves are edible and can be used in a salad, whilst the woody roots contain saponin that was used to make soap.

Magpie Murder

11 May. From my bedroom window I watch as a magpie emerges from the hedgerow with a baby bird in its beak. It swoops off into the Walled Garden. A few minutes later it returns and lands in the same ash tree growing in the hedge, and sidles into the interior. There is a commotion and it comes out again, a little naked body dangling from its bill.

The murdered young might be sparrows, blackbirds, thrushes or anything. There is no hierarchy in this murderous predatory cycle. It is deeply disturbing but happening in every hedge, every row. Nature knows no sentiment.

Cow Parsley

Cow parsley has the power to steal my heart anew every year. I am made dizzy with joy by its soft clouds of white flowers sitting in creamy umbels on tall stems bolstered by feathery foliage, the whole thing multiplied a thousand-thousand times and coursing down the lanes, fields and hedgerows, along miles of British countryside.

There is nothing in this world so beautiful as cow parsley on a May evening beneath uncut hedges of may blossom. Nothing, outside the arms of those you love, that so exactly fulfils the promise of the reasons to be alive.

Anthriscus sylvestris is a humble enough weed. It is fine growing singly but a single plant cannot compete with the massed effect. Whereas some plants are operatic in the richness of their swoop and scale, cow parsley is choral and works for me like a floral version of the Sanctus from Bach's Mass in B minor, soaring and sweeping into ecstasy.

About 30 years ago, one spring, when I was very depressed and fragile, I was driven half-mad by the council cutting the verges, smashing and shredding mile upon mile of cow parsley just when it was in flower. I found it a kind of torture. Even when at my strongest mentally, I consider it terrible – a kind of box-ticking municipal vandalism. Luckily, cuts to local government and a growing awareness of the importance of roadside verges for wild-life have reduced the cutting, as well as leaving it later which gives the seed a chance to ripen. But there is still far too much gratui-tously vandalised.

Cow parsley is a member of the carrot family and is under no threat despite the brutality of council verge-vandalism. It is a survivor. Indeed it is something of a thug and shades out many more fragile plants growing in its lee. It will not grow in very wet places, although it completely invades our Spring Garden, which always floods in winter, the water bringing in fresh cow-parsley seeds each year. They could not be more welcome.

Cow parsley seems to have spread over the past 40 years as a result of both its management and the increasing use of nitrogen on agricultural fields. When the council trashes the verges, it leaves the smashed stems and leaves where they fall and they rot back down into the soil to enrich it. This is detrimental to many flowers but not to cow parsley, which grows best in rich soil. That is why it likes the lovely clay loam of our Spring Garden that I further enrich by mulching every year. Also nitrogen and other chemical fertilisers scattered by farmers as pellets onto fields then run off in the rain to the roadside verges. This has the effect of encouraging thugs like cow parsley (and nettles, goosegrass, hogweed and brambles) but further discourages the delicate and much wider range of possible roadside wild flowers.

There is a price to pay for everything. The few weeks of glorious cow parsley are an exquisite monoculture – but the cost of that beauty is loss of diversity. It is the Sanctus played at full volume drowning out the delicate song of the lone singer.

———

Dipper

I used to see a dipper frequently, its black-and-white bobbing body on a stone in the water, tail cocked like a wren, where the path crosses the stream in the dingle. But the sightings are more fleeting now and, as I write, I have yet to see it this year.

It is such a particular and charming bird, and so unusual in its habits that its presence on the farm was a kind of good magic. Its flight is a spurt of wings and stumpy body low over the water, following the line of the stream to the next rock or low branch to perch on.

The water of the dingle tumbles down over rocks and at times becomes a torrent, crashing and swirling, but the dipper seemed indifferent to this liquid violence. It would stand on a partially submerged stone, dipping up and down as though on springs – hence its name – then plunge into the water like a kittiwake or gannet before emerging with an insect larva or freshwater shrimp caught off the floor of the stream as it walked along under water. Dippers are apparently the only bird in the world that can do this, clinging to the ground with their toes to steady themselves against the current. They also have the almost unique feature that the females sing and regularly do so as part of the dawn chorus. Robins and starlings are the only other species where the female regularly joins in the morning sing-song.

Bryony

There was a girl in the sixth form with extraordinary long, thick hair that hung almost to her waist. In an era when almost every girl had long hair swinging down her back, hers was remarkable for its abundance. Her name was Bryony and, 50 years on, I still think of her when I see the tendrils and broad palmate leaves of bryony sneaking across the face of the yew hedge in the Walled Garden. This is white bryony (*Bryonia dioica*) and it is the only British member of the gourd family. It tends to be found in the south but is common here along the Welsh border country.

We cut them back to preserve the purity of the green yew wall but by midsummer the bryony in the field hedge by the house is a tangled mass. The tendrils are curled and corkscrewed and it has little whitish-green, greenish-white flowers, with the males, which are on separate plants, bigger than the females. These in turn become bright red and very poisonous berries. All the plant is toxic, with the roots the most poisonous of the lot, and occasionally grazing stock are killed as a result of eating them.

Black bryony (*Tamus communis*) is not related, despite the name, but shares the distinction of being a solitary British member of an exotic family – this time the yams. The yam link gives it its name because the 'black' comes from the colour of the underground tubers. It also climbs (always twisting clockwise) but without white bryony's tendrils and with heart-shaped glossy leaves and yellower flowers that become long strings of bright red berries like beads. These are also poisonous – apparently acting as a violent laxative – but the visiting redwings and fieldfares gobble up both types of bryony berries without any apparent ill effect.

Redstart

A little bird flits out of the stable as I walk through the door. She does this every time and we almost greet each other in passing, like two people who get their Sunday papers at the same shop each week. In fact, I suspect she has spotted me before I reach the door, braces herself for disturbance or worse and, at the last moment, beats a hasty retreat. She is a redstart and is nesting in a cavity of the thick stone wall. This was a bird I had not noticed before we came to the farm – robin-sized and splashed with robin red, except the red is on its tail rather than chest and it is a distinctly rusty chestnut rather than the redbreast's orange.

I know it is a female because, other than her distinctive rusty bottom, she is brown above and her chest feathers – if I could see them – are a pale, sandy colour. Her mate, on the other hand, is positively tropical, with a jet-black face and throat beneath a grey head, the black flowing down his back, and with a rusty, orange chest and tail. He has a liquid, sweet, if rather brief song, which I hear much more than I see him. Both birds have a simple 'wheet' call that I often hear when walking in the trees by the dingles.

Having become aware of the redstarts, I realised that they were common locally, their red tails (the name is a corruption of the Saxon *steort* or 'tail') popping out of the hedges every 50 yards or so as I drove along the lanes between fields. But they are a summer visitor and rather localised. They are particularly drawn to Wales by the *ffridd* that runs as a band between about 1300ft to 1500ft. Their close relationship to flycatchers can be seen in the way the males take insects in the air and hover at the tips of foliage to pluck them from the leaves.

Yellow Ants

We have one field we call 'the anthill field'; not a very poetic name I admit but very descriptive. Half the field is hummocked with tumps about 20in apart and the same height and width, each one grassy and shaggy, giving the whole field a lumpy and bumpy texture. These are the anthills of the yellow meadow ant (*Lasius flavus*), who occupy each anthill to the tune of 10,000 per tump.

Some of these anthills can be over a century old and their presence is one of the indicators of grassland that has not been ploughed or cultivated for years. The tumps gradually get bigger over the years and some can be almost 40in tall and the same wide. They provide a habitat for a greater range of plants than would otherwise be present, both as a result of the bumpy surface and the fact that the ants radically improve the drainage.

The yellow ant is the food of choice for the green woodpecker, which will break into the anthills to lap up the exposed ants with its long tongue. As a result, many of the tumps in our anthill field are disturbed and broken as though a dog has half-heartedly been scrabbling at them. But the connection is very specific and very clear – if farmers 'improve' old grassland by levelling the anthills, then the green woodpecker loses an essential supply of food.

The chalk hill blue butterfly also depends to a great extent upon the worker ants burying their caterpillars, which protects them from predators until they hatch and fly away.

————

First Hobby

Watering the pots in the Jewel Garden on a glorious clear May morning, I look up and there, against the pure blue sky, is a hobby, flying straight overhead, low enough for me to see its barred black and grey tail. Long, sharp wings, long tail, pearly grey. Slicing through the sky, streamlined for speed. This is by far the earliest in the year that I have seen one here. The day is made.

————

Sweet Vernal Grass

The first two meadows on the farm have had a curiously chocolate-brown haze over them for the last week, which forms a kind of geological map of the wetter parts of the fields. It comes from the flowering spikes of sweet vernal grass (*Anthoxanthum odoratum*), which is one of the first of the grasses to flower here. Just walking through it, crushing the stems underfoot, fills the air with the scent of newly mown hay in a way that no other grass does fully three, if not four, months before the grass will actually be cut for hay.

The stems of the vernal grass are thin and short, and the leaves sparse so make slim pickings for grazers and haymakers alike, compared to an 'improved' meadow with its lusty, almost rowdy rye and annual meadow grasses. But it is part of the rhythmic patchwork of the field and a sure sign that the meadow, having lain bare, muddy and derelict all winter, is starting to enter its magical couple of months, when it is transformed from just another hillside pasture into a richly flowering mead.

―――――

Cabbage White Butterflies

The only caterpillar that really wreaks havoc in my garden is the cabbage white. There are actually two types, the large and the small white. The large white (*Pieris brassicae*) lays its eggs on the leaves of any brassicas (cabbages, turnips and radishes as well as wallflowers, crambe and nasturtium) and the emerging yellow-and-black caterpillars cover them by the hundred, stripping the young plants to a skeleton. The butterflies are attracted by the mustard in brassicas, which the plant develops as a defence against insects. The butterflies take on the mustard taste in their own tissues, which works effectively against predation by birds.

The males are creamy white with dark grey wing tips, whereas the females have a pair of distinct spots on the upper side of their wings. They have two and sometimes three broods a year, the first laid in May and the second in July. The larvae hatch after a few weeks and eat the outer leaves of their host plant, so are usually fairly easy to see.

The small white (*P. rapae*) lays deeper into the plant and has pure green, very well camouflaged, caterpillars, which do their work less conspicuously but to just as noxious effect. Spraying the plants with saltwater can help, but the best cure is prevention, covering the plants with fine net from the minute they are planted until October.

Otherwise, you must go through each plant every day, picking off the caterpillars by hand and dealing with them as you deem fit.

Most of the large whites that you see in spring have migrated from southern Europe, whereas the small white is hardier and can survive a mild northern winter. They go from egg to adult in about 30 days and the adult will live for around three weeks, feeding on nectar from bluebells, dandelions, clover thistles and a variety of other native plants, pollinating as they go, so do not exist solely to destroy a gardener's cabbages.

———

Hogweed

The giant hogweed that seemed to be relatively common 50 years ago is now banned, proscribed and generally packaged with a health warning. This is because its sap creates a phytophoto-dermatitis reaction when in contact with skin, which then blisters and becomes sore in otherwise mild sunshine. However, when I was a child, we used to make blowpipes from the hollow stems of young plants or from mature sideshoots that carried the umbels of white flowers, and we would swat each other with the stupen-dous 15ft main stem – all without any ill effect. The change is probably down to the change in the ozone layer rather than the chemical content of the plant. It was, is, a magnificent plant – stately, statuesque and, if not applied to bare skin, utterly harmless. Nevertheless, it is now outlawed.

However, its little cousin, *Heracleum sphondylium,* or lesser hogweed, is a flourishing weed in my garden and has increased hugely over the past five years. As weeds go, it is a lovely thing and for a few weeks in May, it fills the orchard with its stately white umbels of flower as gloriously as any cow parsley, albeit with a more compact, tightly formed flower head. But the roots are deep and the seeds fall by the thousand and in a wild-flower meadow it elbows out competition until it becomes an unwelcome intruder. The answer is to individually decapitate it at every opportunity, which will stop it seeding and weaken its growth.

It is worth noting that, although giant hogweed gets the blame for all the phytophotodermatitis, in fact lesser hogweed is just as bad. A common complaint for those that strim it with bare legs is angry red weals where the flayed hogweed has taken its dying revenge by emitting a spray of furocoumarin. Which is one of the many reasons that I never garden in shorts.

––––––

Yellow Corydalis

The fragile, ferny leaves of yellow corydalis, or yellow fumitory, soon followed by hanging flags of bright yellow flowers, grow out of the bricks and stones of the shady house and garden walls, and along the cobbled edging of paving. When we had 64 big clipped box balls planted to the north of a large hop kiln – so, mostly in shade – with cobbles set in mortar between them, the corydalis would grow to the point where it looked as though the clipped green shapes were sitting in a yellow flowery foam.

Very harsh weather turns it to mush but it has always returned vigorously enough. The flowers, which are pollinated by bees, perform here for months at a time between mid-spring and late summer, and longer in a sheltered spot in the south. It does not grow directly out of the bricks and stones but in the mortar between them and, as a lime-loving plant that relishes sharp drainage, is especially associated with old walls. These were invariably made with lime mortar until the twentieth century.

Yellow corydalis is not a native but originates from the southern Alps and was probably introduced by the Romans. Although it likes the walls of old buildings, it does not spread very far on natural rock faces. Nor do we have it at all on the farm, probably because the dry-stone walls are too acidic, too wet and too cold.

Its only, very manageable, drawback is that the foliage forms a soft cushion under which snails live very happily. Every now and then I go hunting for them, rummaging under the billowy strands of corydalis in a manner reminiscent of looking for coins down the back of the sofa.

———

Small-leafed Lime

Up the road half a mile and then across the fields is a route that the dogs and I take to pay homage to one particular tree. It is not much – hardly a tree at all really, just an overgrown piece of hedge at the edge of a field near a bend in the road. But its significance is huge.

It is a small-leafed lime (*Tilia cordata*), with neat, rounded heart-shaped leaves tapering to a point. These are good to eat on a hot summer's day, slightly mucilaginous but refreshing.

I remember reading Oliver Rackham's seminal work, *The History of the Countryside*, where I learned about small-leafed limes for the first time, and then, a few days later, chancing upon this one tree, tucked away in a remote Herefordshire lane. It was like striking gold.

Small-leafed lime, or pry, is a tree of woodland and was once common right across Britain, dominating woods across the south and Midlands across to the Welsh border. In fact, we here, as with so many other plants, politics and animals, are right on the border of its territory. This raggedy tree is probably a remnant of the edge of the native post-glacial wildwood that was cleared to make agricultural land some time between 5000 and 8000 years ago, leaving a ribbon on the outside to serve as a hedge. But, for all that, Herefordshire does have a surprising amount of these limes, albeit unobtrusive and often unnoticed.

Lime is a bad coloniser because it does not grow easily from seed and needs warm summers for fertile seed production. Six thousand years ago it was widespread due to the combination of weather, habitat and the thousands of years it had to establish, but once these wildwoods began to be cleared around 7000 years ago, they did not easily regenerate.

Left to grow to its own devices, it makes a large but neat tree, with strongly fragrant flowers that attract the obsessive attention of bees, who pollinate it and then make especially good lime honey. The flowers also make a tea with calmative properties. The leaves are eaten by many species of moth caterpillar, including the lime hawk moth. Aphids also love them, which in turn attracts ants and birds that prey on them or their honeydew.

Lime coppices and the stools can live for 1000 years or more, throwing up fresh poles from the stump, which grows wider and wider. The poles were used as handles and firewood, and larger pieces were valued for their softness for carving – the most famous examples being the work of Grinling Gibbons, whose extraordinarily detailed Baroque swags and cornucopias were all carved in lime. It also had a rather more obscure usage as cutting blocks for saddlers and glove makers – the softness of the wood meant it did not blunt their tools – and as the blocks upon which milliners shaped their hats.

The bark was also used extensively as a fibre, made into ropes, mats and even clothing, and by gardeners as twine and for binding besoms – and a well-bound besom is a beautiful thing.

————

The Lily Beetle

The lily beetle (*Lilioceris lilii*) has become a pantomime villain for gardeners, appearing as an unusual and unfamiliar creature about a decade ago and now ubiquitous. It – and in particular, the larvae that emerge in spring from clumps of orange eggs laid at the bottom of stems – feeds upon members of the lily and fritillary family, reducing them to shadows and shreds of their glorious selves.

It is not indigenous to the UK but comes from Asia and arrived in Britain from the United States in the late 1930s. It spread slowly in the south but, by 2000, was starting to spread across most of the country and arrived in this garden about ten years ago.

As yet, lily beetles have no predator, although that may evolve as they become more ubiquitous. The only way for gardeners to protect their lilies is to hand-pick them off the plants. Although tedious, this is not difficult, because their backs are a brilliant vermilion that stands out from the green foliage. However, their underside is earth-brown and they react to disturbance by falling to the ground and lying on their backs, thus immediately becoming camouflaged. So you have to nab them on the plant. It has been claimed that the beetles utter a distinctly audible squeak when picked up although I have yet to hear it – but then I am growing deaf. For all I know, their shrieks ring round the garden.

Bird Cherry

Around the middle of May, the valley is dotted with white blossom. It is the season of white blossom of all kinds, but this is different. It comes before the hawthorn blossom and is nothing like so widespread, looking like dabs of white paint on the hillside rather than the liberal splatter of the may blossom. It is also absent from the garden and any of the fields and hedges nearby but we have about four trees of it on the farm, and there are hundreds running down the ten miles of the valley.

These white flowers belong to the bird cherry (*Prunus padus*). It is mostly found in the north but there are populations up the Welsh Marches and this valley obviously contains one of them. It likes damp, acidic places and tends to be accompanied by alder, which shares its growing preferences.

The blossom grows in racemes of simple, individual flowers hanging off a main stem, so it is both voluptuous and generous in its quantity of flowering and sparse and elegant in its manner. It has a slightly acrid, fruity fragrance, which has insects flocking to it. Once pollinated, the flowers become little black fruits which are eaten by the birds – especially the thrush family. The caterpillars of many moths feed off the foliage, which is a good thing, but the small ermine moth (*Yponomeuta padella*) can become over-enthusiastic and almost defoliate it. The leaves, however, are toxic to livestock. Our trees grow in the dingles, overhanging streams, so, unless the sheep get out, which they are wont to do, they do not have access to them.

Cherry names can cause confusion. The bird cherry is *P. padus* but the wild cherry, or gean, which I have growing in the coppice in the garden and is substantially bigger than the bird cherry, with edible fruits – if the birds don't get them first – is called *Prunus avium* – which translates as 'bird cherry'. However, you are extremely unlikely to get the gean growing next to or near the bird cherry and the flowers of the gean are completely different – a generous scatter of small blossom on this great big tree, that then falls like snow to the ground.

Pipits

The pipits start to appear around mid-April, rushing in groups (flocks seems too organised and grand a word for such a hesitant, modest bird), uncertain, hurried and yet seemingly always struggling to master flight. By mid-May they are in every field, every scan of the sky.

There are three types of pipit – meadow, tree and rock. These are meadow pipits, small, individually inconspicuous, dully brown. Yet throughout summer I cannot walk across any of our top fields – all well above 1000ft, with rough grass and inclined to bracken and scrub – without a dozen meadow pipits rising one by one before me, each hidden in the grass and each seemingly flung into the air like confetti, fragile and insubstantial, and only sustaining just enough flight to drop down again, hidden.

Yet these are tough little birds that survive the rigours of harsh upland winters and they are an absolutely essential building block in the ecological edifice of these hills, where their lack of distinctive plumage and their ability to disappear into the grass plays an essential part in their survival.

They are the favoured prey of merlins and hen harriers, and many are taken by buzzards, peregrines, sparrowhawks and owls. They nest on the ground and the chicks are predated by foxes, stoats and weasels. Much more specifically, they are the preferred host for cuckoo eggs, the tiny pipits diligently raising the monstrous strangeling that has murdered their young and thus, unwittingly, playing a key role in the cuckoo's clinging on to its rapidly declining British presence.

Every time I hear the cuckoo calling in May and June as it flies along the hillside behind us, I give a nod to the funny little birds that bob nervously up from the grass, a pair of which probably raised this much more glamorous and feted visitor.

Pretty White Weeds

There are a number of umbellifers – and I do not pretend to always distinguish between them – that are beautiful but either easily become a weed or have been classed as such, and are not deliberately grown either by farmer or gardener.

Cow parsley is the best known and hemlock the most notorious, if you discount giant hogweed, which is much less often seen nowadays – and in any event, no one would ever call it pretty.

But in gardens and fields high in the hills around the farm, the delicacy of tiny white flowers carried in the plate of an umbel can be spectacularly beautiful.

Ground elder is every gardener's nightmare. But in flower it is charming and were it not so intransigently invasive, we would grow it – carefully. We have it here but confined to one corner of the front, where the topiary yew cones are. It is mown every week so that it never spreads but stays sulking, biding its time, in the roots of the holly hedge.

Pignut (*Conopodium majus*) grows in field after field on the acidic hillside around the farm. By the end of May, it creates a lovely, wispy white veil like low-lying mist just above the grass. When I was at boarding school, just seventeen miles from my home but with entirely different, very acidic, sandy soil, we would dig down under the plants for the 'nuts' or tubers. They tasted vaguely nutty and nice, but much more important than their culinary rating was the sense of finding food, bucking the system and challenging the strict regime of a 1960s school unchanged since the First World War.

Wild carrot (*Daucus carota*) is another umbellifer that flowers gloriously. This is the original carrot from which our vegetable garden root has been bred, although the long, tapering roots are minusculy slim compared to the garden carrot, and the orange colour was only bred into it in the seventeenth century – the roots' natural colouring is white or purple. The flowers, carried on stems 2ft or 3ft high, although essentially white, are touched with pink and there is often a single pink flower at the centre. It starts out as a distinctly domed umbel and then, as the flowers fade and turn to seed, slowly inverts so that the seedhead ends up as a dish. This is the true Queen Anne's lace, despite cow parsley also often being called that. The name is said to come from the central pink dot of flower that represents a drop of blood after Queen Anne pricked her finger. It is a plant of waste ground and likes good drainage, preferring alkaline conditions to acid. I grow it from seed and plant it into our borders as it does not like our wet heavy soil around the garden nor the acidic nature of the farm.

I grow sweet cicely (*Myrrhis odorata*) from seed and it is very happy in the shade of a wall as well as growing in the coppice. Although it is an indigenous wild flower, its natural habitat is further north and I have never found it growing in local woods. The foliage is particularly ferny and soft, with the flowers growing in delicate, modest umbels spread widely across each plant. The whole plant smells strongly of liquorice – and tastes deliciously of it, too, with the same calmative effect on a troubled digestion. Once the flowers set seed, you can cut it back hard and it will regrow and flower again.

The dark green leaves of fool's parsley (*Aethusa cynapium*) look quite similar to sweet cicely, but crushing the leaves produces an unpleasant smell, like hemlock, although its stems do not have hemlock's purple splodges. However, fool's parsley is also toxic, although not quite so potently as hemlock, and should be handled with gloves and removed from anywhere where edible plants are grown. Nevertheless, it is a pretty plant and another with an umbel of white midsummer flowers.

———

Toads

To one side of our propagating greenhouse, in the potting-shed yard, is a standing-out bay. This is where we put plants for hardening off, those that are ready to be planted but whose destination is still occupied, as well as the inevitable gaggle of plants that we do not know where to put. Pick up any of these, whether in pots, plugs or even seed trays, and the chances are that there will be a toad puffing itself up in disturbance. On a warm day, they will crawl smartly out of the way but in cooler weather they sit, swelling up, brown and warty and radiating irritation.

Whereas frogs in general get a good press, toads have long been reviled. They crawl rather than hop, have dry, warty skin rather than the lustrous glow of frogs, and were all deemed to be poisonous. In fact, they are – the warts are glands that secrete poison to deter would-be predators, but unless you try and eat it, the common toad is not going to do you any harm.

I am always delighted to see them because they are after the small slugs, snails and worms that would otherwise be eating the plants. For all their ugly sleepiness, toads are voracious hunters and will devour small grass snakes and even mice.

We have toads all over the garden. If I go out at night with a torch there will invariably be one staring at me from the centre of a path. The dogs will hear a shuffle in the undergrowth, leap at it and then turn away in disgust or dismay when they discover it is another toad.

Toads will secrete themselves in a burrow in a border or in the greenhouse, and when disturbed will retreat backwards looking distinctly grumpy. You are unlikely to see them near water except in the mating season.

There are two British toads, the common and the natterjack.

Natterjacks have yellowish eyes, whereas those of the common toad are light brown, almost copper, and when fully grown the common toad is 50 per cent bigger. A toad that scurries is likely to be a natterjack and if you hear a loud, rather coarse call, it will be from a male natterjack, which is much more vocal in the summer mating season than the common toad. Natterjacks hibernate in a burrow, ideally in sand, whereas common toads hide themselves away in logs, a pile of sticks, leaves, an empty burrow and, invariably, a dark corner of the cold frames.

I was astonished to learn that toads can live to be 50, although they would have to be exceptionally lucky to do so save in captivity, but adults often make ten years or more. Many are killed on roads as they move from their winter dry grounds to their wetter breeding places in spring, and they can cover quite long distances in doing so.

Toad spawn is distinguishable from frog spawn because instead of being in clumps, it is deposited in rows of black eggs held in strands of jelly. These can be up to 10ft long and are often wound around vegetation. The toadlets that have not been eaten by newts, water boatmen or diving beetles, emerge from the water in August, tiny and speckled and a tasty mouthful for grass snakes, herons, hedgehogs, stoats, weasels, rats or crows – all of whom seem impervious to the white secretion that deters most other would-be predators.

Goosegrass

I remember Lorna Wootton carefully covering Adrian Gould with goosegrass, front and back, his thin white legs sticking out from goosegrass-covered shorts, his hair a crazy goosegrass cowl. He was the Green Man, the Spirit of the Woods, Pan,

Cernunnos – except Adrian Gould would have been no more than seven, Lorna a year older and I, the youngest of all.

That was 60 years ago, when the world was easy and green and distilled of care. We played many of our games on a road that saw perhaps three cars a day and we knew the driver of each. But goosegrass sticks and hooks itself still onto clothing, other plants, anything to hand, so that by mid-May it becomes a clinging layer fuzzing the outlines of hedges, shrubs and even up into the branches of trees.

Goosegrass – or cleavers amongst its many other local names – is *Galium aparine* and is related to woodruff and lady's bedstraw. It is a prodigiously vigorous annual weed, growing up to 10ft in a season with the whole thing covered in hooked bristles that cling to any surface. Apparently, as a result of centuries of weeding, the goosegrass found in arable fields has evolved to have larger seeds, germinate at a different time and to creep rather than climb. It is an aspect of plant behaviour, adapting and responding to the way that humans treat them, that is fascinating.

It is called goosegrass because geese and chickens greedily eat it, as occasionally do people, although perhaps not with the same enthusiasm. The bristles, rather like stinging nettles, soften on cooking. I am not sure I feel an urgent need to try this out. But I do know that it makes excellent compost.

Doves

I have lived through an age when doves have gone from being an icon of peace, the epitome of soft, loving gentleness, to almost a garden pest. Familiarity has bred a degree of contempt.

This is hardly the fault of any dove. The turtle dove – which throughout history has embodied constancy, fidelity and true love

– has become one of the most endangered species in Britain. Numbers have fallen by over 90 per cent since 1970 and are continuing to do so, and there is a real expectation that it will become extinct in the UK.

The turtle dove is a migrant, spending most of the year in sub-Saharan Africa and arriving here in spring to breed. I say 'here' but I have never seen one here and hold out no hopes of doing so. I should recognise it only from pictures, with its undove-like brown wings and slim, almost dainty outline, and know that it is practically half the size of a wood pigeon.

For the record, doves and pigeons are essentially the same – all members of the same Columbidae family and we have divided them up arbitrarily. Even within the family, we give roles to what are essentially identical birds simply through colour or context. The white dove, symbolising peace and rising in a flutter of pure wings from the roof of a dovecote in spring sunshine, is the same bird that hops amongst the fallen chips and litter outside a fast-food outlet.

The decline of turtle doves has been due partly to persecution en route from and back to their African wintering grounds, with the Maltese alone responsible for shooting hundreds of thousands at a time; partly to the lack of suitable weed seed that it depends upon, which has resulted in half the number of chicks being reared; partly to desertification caused by climate change; and partly to the disease of trichomonosis that affects many birds but seems to have affected turtle doves particularly badly.

But can you balance species out? Sixty years ago, there were ten times as many turtle doves in the British countryside but far fewer collared doves. Now collared doves are ubiquitous. The first pair known to have bred in the UK was in the year of my birth, 1955. By 1964, there were around 18,000 breeding pairs and now, in 2020, there are reckoned to be about a million.

The collared dove originated from the plains of northern India, where it more or less stayed until the mid-seventeenth century. No one knows why it suddenly – and in evolutionary terms very recently – started to colonise the world, which it is still doing. Amongst the many oddities of this expansion is that individual birds are remarkably sedentary, never moving far from where they were raised and that they are not, unlike turtle doves that migrate thousands of miles each year, very good at flying long distances.

Collared doves are pretty birds and were they rare, we would treasure them dearly. Small, albeit larger than a turtle dove, they are a lovely greyish pink with a slim black collar and a soft cooing call. Apparently, that coo is a powerful sexual signal and a male that can coo three times in a row, as opposed to a mere twice, is much more attractive as a mate.

What it is extremely efficient at is breeding. It can have over half a dozen clutches a year, although two or three are the norm, usually between March and October but sometimes in every month of the year. Sometimes it can have more than one clutch on the go at a time, with one or two young in each clutch, born and reared in a very rough, twiggy nest.

This means a lot of energy goes into rearing the young and most couples produce about three surviving healthy offspring a year. As they live for around three years, each pair will produce about ten young – which explains the population growth.

They feed on grain and seeds and my pea shoots, picking them off when they first appear out of the ground. It is hard to be too cross because they are very beautiful and their gentle cooing outside the bedroom window makes up for a lot of lost peas.

———

Ash

A sh trees are such a feature of the landscape, both around the garden and in the valley where the farm is, that they blend into a uniform woody backdrop. But the arrival of chalara, or ash die-back, with its threat of wiping out all ash trees in the country, just as Dutch elm disease did to practically all elms in the mid-1970s, makes one realise with panicky focus how important ash trees are to landscape, society and culture. Losing ash trees would be like losing roses or cats.

As if ash die-back were not threat enough, the emerald ash borer beetle (*Agrilus planipennis*) looks to be coming to this country and its effect will almost certainly be as disastrous as that of the Dutch elm beetle. The future of British ash trees looks grim.

Ash trees have grace and often elegance, yet the wood is, in many ways, the toughest and most durable there is. Its branches, although growing almost laterally on some of the old, gnarled trees on the farm, invariably curl up at the tips in a final gesture of refinement.

The wood is straight-grained and flexible as well as very strong, making it ideal for handles of any kind, from spades to hockey sticks, and for anything that needs to absorb jolts and bumps, such as the chassis of carts, wagons, buses and cars – for instance, the chassis of Morgan cars and the half-timbering of Morris Minor Travellers, and it was also used for the bodies of Mosquito aircraft in the Second World War. Its name derives from the Saxon for a spear – *aesc* – because it was the best wood for spears, arrows and pike shafts, able to take heavy blows without splintering or breaking. It was used for ladders, oars, cricket stumps, walking sticks, the shafts and felloes (the outer rims) of wheels, as well as tables, chairs and dressers. As well as this utilitarian use, ash is acknowledged as the best firewood of all, splitting easily and burning well, even when freshly cut and green.

In other words, ash has been, throughout history, prized for the range of its uses, even above oak. Know this, and the shape of the large ash trees growing in the hedgerows and on the hillside starts to make sense. Almost all the older trees sprout numerous branches from a central straight trunk. These are pollards. They have had their branches cut right back to the trunk at a height above the reach of grazing cattle, who would otherwise eat the new shoots as they emerged. Pollard ash and oak, nearly always growing as part of a hedgerow, were intensely valuable on every farm. Whereas oak was cut once every generation, about 30 years, ash would be pollarded about every fifteen to 20 years, so most farmers would get a couple of harvests from them. Stagger that pollarding across a number of trees and you have a continuous supply of high-quality timber for every conceivable purpose on the farm and in the household.

This has all but ended now. The pollards are growing out and most have not been cut for 50 years or more. Some are almost completely hollow, the trunk little more than a rigid sheath from which grow impossibly large branches – a testament to the trees' age and incredible tensile strength. On the farm, we have dozens of outgrown pollards, many on very steep slopes and awkward positions, which must have been incredibly difficult to get at. Up on the thin acidic soil of the hillside at 1200ft, the wood is poor and the grain never very straight. I pollarded one as an experiment and it was difficult and dangerous, and dragging the timber down the hillside to the farm was arduous work. And after all that, the resulting wood was twisted and knotty and not good for much other than firewood.

Yet clearly, the timber, despite its poor quality, was considered so important that people were prepared to cut it and bring the wood down bit by bit with horses and sledges. Even if it was not good enough for making into anything, ash produced excellent charcoal until the middle of the nineteenth century, when coal took over from what had been the very extensive manufacture of charcoal on these wooded hillsides.

I am torn between leaving the rest of my pollards well alone and enjoying their presence as magnificent and beautiful trees, or somehow pollarding them and using the wood – although we would probably have to bring in horses to do that. If I pollard them, it will acknowledge a relationship between trees and humans that is practical and sustainable, as opposed to buying in wooden or manufactured materials, often from overseas.

Another very good reason for pollarding them is that ashes only live to about 250 years as uncut trees. But if you pollard or coppice them you can double their life expectancy – and there are coppiced ash stools that are over 1000 years old. If I leave them, the shoots grow too big and top-heavy for the trunk and roots to support (even ash roots, which are notably extensive) and there is a real risk that heavy snow or wind will split the tree or even uproot it entirely. This has already happened to a number of ours when a layer of heavy snow froze hard.

Ash coppices are very beautiful places. The shade they cast is always relatively light and airy, and so ideal for flowers like bluebells, snowdrops, wood anemones and primroses. The growth of ash coppice is much more substantial than hazel, with the poles 3in to 6in in diameter when cut, and in this part of the world in the nineteenth century they were used by the tens of thousands for hop poles. But the hop yards have largely disappeared, and the ash coppices have grown out or been bulldozed and replaced by fir plantations.

I planted a number of ash trees in the garden, some of which have grown very large in just 30 years and others that I have coppiced and which are growing back strongly. On the farm, I planted 1000 in 2008, intending them to be coppiced to use as fuel for the house, which is heated entirely by wood. But ash die-back struck and nearly all have been affected. The interesting thing is that they seem to react in different ways from tree to tree. A small handful have already died. Some are hit hard but struggle back into growth, and others show little sign of being seriously affected. The latest research indicates that trees that are solitary, such as those in fields or hedgerow, or in mixed woodland, are more likely to survive, whereas a plantation composed mostly of ash trees – such as my ash coppices – is invariably hit hard. The fungus cannot survive temperatures above 35°C, so hot summers are good for them. But all the evidence is that young trees, in particular, are unlikely to survive repeated infection.

The other problem they have had to contend with is that almost all of them, spread as they are in four different plantations, have been eaten at some stage by sheep, who find minerals and trace elements in the bark that they cannot get in winter from grass. It only takes a thin ring of chewed bark around the trunk to kill a tree, although ash will often resprout from below the damage. In snow or hard weather, mountain sheep will find a way through, over or under most fencing, despite constantly repairing it and putting up as good a barrier as possible.

Fencing costs more and takes more work than buying and planting the trees – although I planted the vast majority by cutting four squares of turf, laying the roots of the tree flat on the exposed soil and then inverting the turfs back over the top of the roots, treading them firmly down and staking the tree to hold it in place. None died as a result of this very unhorticulturally pure method and, despite the ravages of ash die-back, most have grown strongly despite never having been watered or weeded, let alone fed. It is a far cry from *Gardeners' World*.

Grey Wagtail

I often see the grey wagtail at the farm but never at Longmeadow, just 30 miles to the east. With its bright yellow breast like a mustard waistcoat under a grey morning coat, and its extra-long grey-and-white tail that flips and juts and rhythmically flicks, it looks like the familiar pied wagtail in a brand-new set of clothes. It likes our dingle, which can change from a steady, quiet flow to a racing, roaring torrent after rain. It does not seem to mind any amount of water-rage but stands mid-stream on the wet stones and flicks and bounces its tail, and shines bright yellow against the dark, rushing water.

———

Comfrey

Sometimes it is hard to know where a garden plant ends and a weed begins. Comfrey (*Symphytum officinale*) fringes the river at the bottom of the garden in great banks of leaf topped by cream bells of flower.

It also grows in the garden as an orderly, planted row, in official horticultural variation with pink and purple flowers as well as very unofficial crosses – it is promiscuous and interbreeds freely – as well as unplanted, unasked for and entirely unwanted all over the place. Easy come, easy go.

There is almost nothing to dislike about comfrey other than its habit of collapsing and smothering its neighbours. But then all you have to do is cut the juicy, mucilaginous leaves right back, and all is openness and light – before it grows back with enthusiasm and vigour unimpaired.

All in all, comfrey is something of a wonder plant. It likes dampness and heavy soil, and its great fleshy roots, fanged like enormous teeth, grow deep down. Its roots are spectacularly efficient at sucking up available nutrients and storing them in its leaves. These break down very fast and return to the soil exceptionally quickly. No plant has more protein in its leaves and few plants are as good at taking in and garnering trace minerals. This makes it exceptionally good as a liquid plant feed which I use all the time. It smells appalling as the proteins break down, but after a few weeks is approachable and incredibly useful, encouraging flowers and fruiting rather than a flush of soft green growth. It is also wonderful in a compost heap – not normally a desirable attribute in a plant but gardeners learn to treasure such things.

Magpie in the Kitchen

30 May. When I go downstairs at 6 a.m., there is a magpie in the kitchen. He doesn't seem unduly bothered but hops from dresser to chair back, and shelf to window with an air as much of curiosity as panic, like someone in a junk shop looking for anything that might catch their fancy. The window had been left open overnight and he had obviously invited himself in but then forgotten how to get out. I opened the other windows and left him to it for ten minutes. When I returned, he had gone. Magpies are such curious birds – magnificent, murderous and fiercely intelligent. For all their brutality, I admire them enormously.

Summer

May is all spring and June is all summer, yet there is but a heartbeat between the two. You pass into June like entering through a door into a grand summery saloon. In fact there are two halves to summer, the end of May until the middle of July that is a burgeoning, full of hope and arrival, and then a second summer season, running well into September, richer, deeper and touched with a closing melancholy.

In June the British countryside is at its peak. Everything has reached a maturity without losing any of its spring freshness. Nothing is jaded. Many of the smaller birds are laying a second clutch of eggs, the wild flowers in the meadows are at their very best and there is a palpable sense of the natural world drawing deep, reproducing, growing, fulfilling the sole focus of its existence, which is to reproduce and keep its niche of life alive.

By late July this changes; most meadow flowers are seeded, the harvest is coming in and all that early June freshness is fingered and worn. The swifts and cuckoos have gone and there is a chill to the night air. But this is also the season of school holidays and is forever associated in my mind with spending hours roaming the countryside as a boy, with my dogs running ahead, immersed in the world of field and hedgerow, woods and lanes. The days are drawing in, adding an extra sense of urgency to the need to relish every moment, every manifestation of life.

JUNE

Buttercups

At the beginning of June – having got back from eight intensive twelve-hour days at Chelsea Flower Show and feeling over-stuffed with fine gardening in the same way a restaurant critic must feel after fine dining twice a day, every day – I long for a simple field of buttercups. Luckily, I have the extreme good fortune to have just such a thing.

Our now-established wild-flower meadow is a complex tapestry of flowers, grasses, herbs and human management, but begins its floral display with a burst of buttercups at the start of June, which makes the whole field shimmer buttery yellow. This is the meadow buttercup (*Ranunculus acris*).

I love the thought that these buttercups, along with quite a few other flowers of modern meadows, were flowering here over half a million years ago and could easily have been munched by grazing hippopotami. However, it seems that they only began to be called 'buttercups' in the eighteenth century. The use of the word that universally defines and conjures them is, in terms of their history, a mere blink in time.

Creeping buttercup (*R. repens*) has roots that seem to claw into the soil and when it is damp – and this buttercup is only really happy in damp soil – it is really difficult to extract, leaving bits of runners and root behind that go on to make new plants. It is low and mat-forming, and gets in amongst hedges and shrubs, which makes it doubly difficult to extricate from the garden. It also likes damp, compacted lawns and those gardeners who care about such things – not me – loathe the way it spoils their precious sward.

But, like all buttercups, its golden flowers are a late-spring and early-summer joy, flooding the surface of damp fields, road verges and ditches, and damp woodland. It is pollinated by bees who, with their short tongues, can easily get at the nectar and pollen in the open, flat flowers.

––––––

Open Door

In summer, I open all the doors when I get up and they stay open until darkness falls on all but the wettest, windiest days. This means that swallows swoop in, do a round of the rooms and then flow effortlessly back out again, robins and wrens pop up in the kitchen and sitting room, and Nigel lies on the threshold, head outside, tail indoors, watching the world go by.

––––––

Elder

The elder is coming into flower with great dish-sized white florets. We collect these by the basketful to make elderflower cordial, drinking that fragrant, slightly musty taste of early summer days. If it were rare and this its summer display, then gardeners would treasure and nurture it, but for much of the time elder is regarded as little more than a woody weed, barely a notch above dandelion or thistle. Elder is here, part of our lives and yet treated half the time as undergrowth – a botanical underclass. But I like it. It is common and scruffy and only deemed fit for most gardens if refined by breeding, but it is more than welcome in any garden of mine.

Elder follows humans like nettles, growing in middens, drains and where humans and animals have been, tangling round crumbling buildings and pushing its gawky branches into gutters and between the remaining roof tiles. It is the sprawling memory of humanity.

Cottagers and country people used elder for a whole range of comforts and cures. Its bark is a purgative and the leaves were used to prepare an ointment for bruises and sprains. It was said to charm away warts and, rather more practically, a switch of it keeps the flies away. The old lady that we bought this house from used to come back and collect the flowers from a particular scruffy elder round the back of a barn to make a face lotion and shampoo. She had done this every year since she was a little girl. The flowers are also used to make elderflower champagne, cordial and fritters.

The wood is exceptionally hard and when stained was used – probably with not entirely honourable intentions – as a substitute for ivory and ebony. The young stems are filled with soft pith which, when removed, leaves them hollow, making excellent pea shooters. The pith was also used for cleaning the delicate workings of watches.

Elder inevitably finds itself in hedgerows although never counts as part of them. In Saxon charters elders are much more common in open areas, such as downland, than in woodland. The implication is that it is little more than scrub. Perhaps some of this is down to the fact that the leaves are poisonous and not eaten by cattle or rabbits, so continue growing where all around them is grazed down.

_____

Larks

I suspect that for every person who thinks they have heard a skylark, or have heard it celebrated on the radio, fewer than one in ten has stood in an empty field and listened to the actual song as the bird flies vertically higher and higher, the song remaining long after it has disappeared to the naked eye as it reaches over 1000ft, and then it slowly floats down before repeating the performance all over again.

Skylarks are small birds with grey, nondescript feathers and a flashing of white on their tail in flight, unremarkable in everything except song. But when you have a song to sing like they have, you do not need fine feathers.

They nest on the ground and, like most ground-nesting birds, the chicks mature quickly. Whereas most small songbirds need five to seven weeks from nest building to the independence of the young, skylarks can lay a clutch of eggs and the young will hatch and mature sufficiently to leave the nest and become independent within four weeks. Thus the parents can raise as many as four broods a year.

Until the second half of the twentieth century, their song filled every part of British open countryside. Where there were fields, especially meadows, there were skylarks. They were eaten with enthusiasm and hundreds of thousands were sold annually as caged songbirds. They were ubiquitous in the fields of my childhood and are luckily still common enough in the countryside around the garden, but the chances of hearing them are getting slimmer.

Despite their potential for each pair to produce up to 20 chicks a year, larks have declined dramatically, the numbers falling by over 50 per cent in the final quarter of the twentieth century. Although, like all insect-eating birds of farmland, they have suffered from the increased use of pesticides and insecticides, their decline is mainly due to loss of habitat. The change from sowing crops in spring – which left stubble all winter and provided food – to autumn has reduced their chances of winter survival. But the biggest change is the transition from haymaking to silage, which dramatically increased after the 1980s. However, as well as being cut several times, the fields are often fertilised with nitrogen or manure between cuts, and perhaps rolled as well. The chances of a ground-nesting bird surviving this are practically nil. A Swiss study showed that when skylarks nested in silage fields, only 0.14 chicks were produced – which means that the birds have to lay an astonishing seven clutches of four to five eggs to result in one live chick.

So the song of the lark, which is inextricably bound up with the beauty of the British countryside and a symbol of arcadian innocence and purity, has been blotted out by agricultural greed and eco-vandalism. We, who seek out ever-cheaper and more convenient food whilst nostalgically celebrating the recorded song of a skylark, are directly complicit in its decline. We get the countryside we deserve.

———

Foxgloves

Foxgloves have two very distinct settings in my life. In the garden they pop up all over the place, especially under hedges and along paths. They grow happily in the dappled shade of the orchard beds and in the coppice, and self-seed in amongst the box hedges (ravaged by box blight) of the cottage garden. They are one of the cottage-garden plants par excellence, their spires of flower with mottled tubes of petals hanging off to one side where they grow against a hedge or clustered around the stem out in the open.

But on the farm they grow very differently. For a start they are later. In the garden they are at their best in the first few weeks of June, although different varieties will last into July, whereas on the farm, 1000ft higher, they do not really get going until July and can last into August. Also the farm foxgloves are noticeably darker than their lowland cousins. Whereas foxgloves in the garden – and we grow a lot of garden hybrids in the borders as well as the naturalised common foxglove (*Digitalis purpurea*) – have a slightly louche, tall, elegant and easy charm, giving the impression of wanting something to lean on, the farm versions stand dead upright, growing out in the open, their leaves hidden by the bracken that swirls beneath and around them, and just the purple and pink flares of flower standing out.

They are most definitely not a flower of meadows, so if you see them growing out in a field it is a clue that it was, relatively recently, woodland. The bracken acts as shade and thus replicates the woodland that the foxgloves originated from, and still mark where woodland used to be. One hillside where they grow best was oak coppice until 150 years ago. Now just one or two rotting stumps of the trees remain under the bracken but the foxgloves are still growing as though the hillside was covered in oak trees.

After the Second World War, many areas that were formerly coppice woodland were planted up with conifers both by the Forestry Commission and by private owners cashing in on the demand for softwood and pulp. Those plantations, which create a shade so dense that practically nothing grows beneath, are increasingly being felled as the market has changed. This is one of the unexpected side-effects of the collapse of the South Wales mining industry in the 1980s and 1990s, for which an enormous amount of softwood was grown for use as mine-shaft props. Now, that wood costs more to cut down and clear than it is worth.

Foxgloves are biennial, which means that the tiny seeds germinate and develop into small plants with just foliage in their first year, then produce a tall flower spike in the second. Then, in theory at least, they die, having scattered their seed. The second year following felling there is often a thicket of foxgloves growing in the new sunlight. Each flower produces tens of thousands of tiny seeds that lie dormant for decades, waiting for the coppice cycle – which in hazel would be about ten years and as long as 30 years in oak coppice – and now the plantations are cut, they explode out into the light.

They are pollinated by bees that have to crawl right inside the flower tubes, dusting themselves with pollen in the process. On a sunny day, almost every flower is busily occupied with pollen-coated bees harvesting the foxglove nectar.

They prefer ericaceous conditions, so the light acidic soil of the farm is ideal but they seem very happy in the neutral pH of the clay soil in the garden. Foxgloves produce digitalis, which is an important heart medication but poisonous if consumed to excess. Best not to eat any part of the plant.

Cuckoo Call

5 June. Sat outside at 9 p.m. with a glass of whiskey listening to the cuckoo. It flew round the farm and up on the hillside, calling without break for fully 40 minutes, as long and loud as I have ever heard. It grew dark at ten and the bats took their turn in the half-lit night sky.

Yellow Rattle

Yellow rattle has a mixed reputation. For most of human history, farmers have loathed it because it is semi-parasitic on grasses and thus reduces the yield of hay meadows and grazing pastures. It gets its name because when the seeds set and ripen, they rattle in the brown seedpod before it dries and splits and they fall to the ground. But recently, it has begun to be appreciated as the 'meadow maker', the plant that enables other less robust flowers to grow, become established and set seed amongst the competition of grass. Therefore, if you want to make or nurture a wild-flower meadow, you certainly want to encourage *Rhinanthus minor*, or yellow rattle.

When we took over the farm, it had been grazed hard for years and effectively ranched. This meant that sheep had been allowed to eat anything and everything in woods, dingles, meadows and pasture, so there was not a lot of apparent diversity other than coarse grasses. But in our second year, at the beginning of June, we noticed one yellow rattle plant growing in a field. This had little yellow hooded flowers on a straight stalk, with small, nettle-like foliage.

The next year it was gone but three others popped up in the next-door field. We then began to manage that particular field under a strict hay-making regime, which meant not cutting or grazing it between the beginning of May and mid-August to allow the plants to grow and the seeds to ripen. By making hay, we took goodness off the land and quite quickly, as the rattle spread, the grass became less dense and the yield dropped. The first year made 100 large bales of hay but within three years this had dropped to just over 30. The ideal is to have many more non-grass plants (forbs) than grasses, in the ratio of about 80:20, but it takes a while to achieve that and even then, it will vary from year to year.

Now that meadow has swathes of thousands of yellow rattle flowers and, as you walk through it from late July onwards, it does truly rattle like a busy band of maracas. However, it is not uniform nor stationary. Some areas in this one three-acre field have no yellow rattle and have never done so. Others are almost all rattle and others vary from year to year.

However, just making hay is not enough because yellow rattle seed is quite particular in its demands and a field can lose the plant as quickly as it gains it. It is an annual, so if the flowers are eaten by grazing stock or the hay cut before the seed has a chance to ripen, there will be no plants next year. On top of that, the seed has no dormancy period and needs to be sown immediately, which happens naturally as it falls, is knocked or cut to the ground. It also needs direct contact with soil in order to germinate, but even though it must be sown in late summer, onto bare soil, it will not germinate until the following spring. And, if all this were not enough, it must have sufficient rain in spring to trigger germination. A dry late winter and early spring can be disastrous.

A farming regime means that the grass is cut short for hay, exposing some bare soil, and then, as soon as it starts to regrow – the 'aftermath' – stock are put into the field to graze it through the autumn and, weather permitting, in the winter. In the process, the animals churn up the grass, exposing the soil and pressing the seeds into the ground. Very badly 'poached' fields – where hooves have made a muddy quagmire of what was a lovely hayfield – is never a disaster for wild flowers though. A harrow in spring will level the worst of it and the flowers relish all that exposure to the earth. Then, when those nettle-like leaves start to appear and the first tentative yellow flower, you know the cycle can start again.

Haymaking takes at least three consecutive days of dry weather, which can be rare on a Welsh hillside in a wet summer. One year, we could not cut the hay until late October because it was so wet. We made a terrible mess but next year's yellow rattle flowers were just as good. For two years it was too wet to cut the hay at all, so we strip-grazed it with cattle, moving an electric fence as the cattle ate the grass down to its roots. Again, the rattle and all the other wild flowers reappeared the following year. But ideally, the field should be closed off to stock by 1 May up there on the hillside (and by 1 April on lower ground) after having been grazed as hard as possible over winter, then it can be mown for hay at some stage in August.

We have now spread green hay from that wild-flower meadow over the neighbouring field so that the yellow rattle seeds have spread in there too and as I write, there are hundreds of young plants showing, ready to become the key that will unlock the door to a magical mixture of wild flowers.

———

Bracken

The weed that consumes by far the most time, attention and expense in my life – to a power of about 100 – is *Pteridium aquilinum*, better known as bracken.

We have no bracken in the garden or anywhere near it. I had no bracken in my domestic life at all until we took on the farm but bracken dominates it just as it dominates the whole valley. In fact, bracken covers up to three per cent of the total surface area of the landscape of Britain – over 3500 square miles – with another 35,000 square miles of rhizome and root underground because only ten per cent of the plant is visible above ground.

These rhizomes, which are black and curiously mucilaginous, spread remorselessly, throwing up fronds as they go. Most other plant growth is shaded out and only those plants that can grow, flower and set seed before the fronds make their cover – and with us that is mid-June – can survive. The upside of this is that some plants, like bluebells, violets and wood anemones, that were growing when the area was woodland, persist because the bracken provides them with the summer shade that they need. But by and large, where you have dense bracken you have very little else.

But it is not all dense and when we came to the farm, some of the fields were infested with it rather than completely overtaken. So I cut them three times a year, at the end of June, in August and again in late September or early October. This knocked the bracken back and gave the grass a chance to grow better. I used every weapon in my armoury, starting with an alpine tractor with a flail that could cope with the steep hills, then working through a 'bracken basher' roller that I pulled behind the quad. I used strimmers, I used a weed slasher and I used my scythe. Recently I have been hiring a robot, remote-controlled tractor and flail to attack areas that are exceptionally steep and hitherto beyond the reach of even me and my scythe. Bracken may be remorseless, but so am I.

After a couple of years of this regime, I reduced the cut to twice a year, in early July and then again in September, with the second cut as much cosmetic as effective. The grass grew and now these fields, which fifteen years ago had areas where the bracken was over 6ft tall, have very little bracken and what there is, is sparse and grows to a foot or so. But if I leave it or it is too wet to get at, then it slowly returns and I know that within five years it will be as bad as it ever was. It will never be beaten, just contained.

There is evidence that bracken has spread greatly in the past 200 years. Between the middle of the sixteenth and nineteenth centuries, there was a mini Ice Age and the consistently cold winters would have made it much harder for the rhizomes to survive. On top of that, cattle were more common as mountain grazers than sheep, which were kept in much smaller flocks for their wool and milk rather than for meat, and the heavier tread of cattle would have exposed the rhizomes to the cold. But the gradually changing climate and farming practices have allowed bracken to spread hugely and man-made climate change is likely to increase that spread even more.

Traditionally, bracken was cut for harvesting and rolled to suppress or reduce it. When you cut bracken, the damaged plant slowly bleeds, drawing resources from the rhizome, which is weakened. Crushing the fronds with a roller, either with a square section or with a series of thick 'blades' that roll at right angles to the bracken, hence bruising as well as flattening it, does not give the same satisfaction as clearing it away but is actually just as effective. That is why whacking the fronds with a stick works. Even just driving the quad through it will leave much weaker growth next year in the tyre tracks. Running cattle through it, especially in winter, is also effective as the cattle disturb the roots and if exposed to frost they will die. But bracken is poisonous to stock if eaten in spring and we had some heifers die from bracken poisoning, so you have to be careful not to expose them to it too early in the year. The spores are also carcinogenic to humans, so when cutting, I wear a surgical mask.

One of the unexpected effects of cutting back the bracken, especially in the areas outside the fields, where there had been woods, was to reveal green lanes, stone walls, terracing and even a building that had been completely hidden in the bracken.

It will not grow everywhere. It needs acidic soil that is reasonably well drained and fertile, and it does not grow above 1500ft. This means that there are patches where it abruptly stops and there is a clear bracken line on the hillside, above which the moor grass and heather take over.

Historically, bracken was an important harvest and cutting was banned in high summer so as to preserve a supply. It was used for winter bedding for animals, for thatch and as kindling – bracken has a greater amount of lignin than wood and burns hotter and more fiercely. It is also high in potash, so the ashes were used as the base for soap. I use it to make an ericaceous compost and it is one of the viable substitutes for peat when growing plants like rhododendrons, camellias or blueberries in containers.

It is also important for wildlife. High brown and pearl-bordered fritillary butterflies live almost exclusively in bracken, where they find the violets they need for food that would have otherwise died through lack of cover. Bracken also provides cover for ground-nesting birds like merlins, skylarks, lapwings, nightjars, pipits, ring ouzels, whinchats and others. Foxes, badgers and smaller mammals will use the cover of bracken and adders use it, too, coming out to bask in the sun. It is also, in itself, beautiful. There is just much too much of it.

Horse Flies

I forget – and then the little bastards get me by surprise. Throughout the sunny days of May and early June, sleeves rolled, and just very occasionally wearing shorts, I forget how effectively horse flies can ruin your day. The first bite of the year is almost always around mid-June, when I am either driving the tractor up a particularly tricky, steep slope and unable to take a hand off the wheel, or when I am mowing, happily cutting paths through the long grass and bracken.

The first thing you feel is the sharp bite as they gnaw into you and start sucking your blood. If you do see them and if your hands are not encumbered, they can be swatted but you have to be quick because they are one of the fastest flying insects of all and have been clocked at 90 mph.

Horse flies are only just behind a bee or wasp sting for unpleasantness and, having evolved to puncture the hide of a horse or cow to get at its blood, human flesh is, in every sense of the word, easy meat. The least you can expect is for it to go on hurting for an hour or so and then become really itchy and swell, sometimes very impressively.

The only answer is to button up sleeves and necks, wear a hat, tuck trousers into socks and be watchful, because they particularly like places like knuckles and fingers and the back of your neck that are hard to protect. They are also attracted to dark clothes and sweat. As I tend to wear dark blue and am always working outside in the sun – and therefore inevitably sweating – I am fair game.

There are 30 species of horse fly in the UK, all with exceptionally colourful eyes that I am told are beautiful, although my relationship with them is based upon them trying to eat me and me trying to kill them rather than gazing into each other's eyes. There was one filming day in the garden last summer when we were all being bitten by deer flies, smaller than the long brown horse fly (*Haematopota pluvialis*) or cleg, that we have on the farm, and with black-and-white markings on its wings. But the bite hurt just as much and some people had a truly unpleasant allergic reaction.

Only the females bite and suck blood as they need the protein to make eggs. Males have weak mouths that cannot cut into flesh, so they feed on nectar and are good pollinators. It is the cutting that hurts – they have none of the stiletto precision of a mosquito but crudely saw away at your skin until they reach a blood vessel, inject it with an anti-coagulant and then set to work drinking their fill like miniature vampires.

They like water and damp places but are also likely to be found wherever there are horses, cattle or sheep, especially in midsummer and especially if it is warm. They have normally gone by August although invariably, after a few days without seeing or being bitten by one, I let down my guard, roll up my sleeves and then promptly am attacked again.

The larvae will hatch and find moist soil, where they live for a year feeding on slugs, snails and worms. The adult only survives for a matter of days before the female lays her eggs and then, mercifully, dies.

Wild Roses

The dog rose (*Rosa canina*) grows in the hedgerows and on the hillside with equal ease, scattering its delicate pale pink flowers in amongst and over the arching briars. Around the garden, it is a plant of the hedgerows and lines the lanes, flowering where the flail cannot reach but otherwise curtailed brutally like all modern hedges. But on the hillside on the farm, it grows as a romping, sprawling, untidy, unruly, lovely bush – the antithesis of all that is horticulturally organised and pruned. There is a horticultural connection because dog rose was used as the rootstock for most cultivated roses adding hardiness, health and intensity of colour until replaced by *R. laxa*. However, dog rose also has a propensity to throw up suckers and I have a wonderful specimen in the corner of the garden, established from suckers that long ago swallowed up the grafted named variety.

As with everything else, we have two showings, the first in early June in the garden and then a few weeks later, around midsummer and into July, up on the hillside. But both produce the red hips that birds and mammals love. These rosehips are rich in vitamin C and during the Second World War vast quantities were collected to make rosehip syrup as part of the war effort to keep people healthy.

Less healthily but much more fun, we children would collect the hips, then carefully break them open and remove the little hairs that lay between the flesh and the seed. These made brilliant itching powder and when stuffed down the neck of friends or brothers and sisters caused merriment all round.

The field rose (*R. arvensis*) grows very like the dog rose but flowers a few weeks later and tends to be pure white. Things can be confusing because sometimes dog rose flowers are white as

PREVIOUS PAGE The grass borders in June.
TOP Our lovely Welsh Black cattle knew that the rattle of a bucket meant food!
ABOVE LEFT I made this gate that divides the soft fruit from the orchard
from one coppiced chestnut post.
ABOVE RIGHT A drift of wild thyme growing on an ant hill high on our Welsh hillside.
OPPOSITE All the apple trees in the orchard have rambling roses trailing through their
branches.

OPPOSITE The wild-flower meadow on the farm that we have carefully
nurtured for the past ten years.
TOP Nellie trying to camouflage herself as a wild flower.
ABOVE LEFT Common Spotted Orchid.
ABOVE RIGHT The orchids have occurred naturally and are steadily spreading.
The meadow now has three kinds that flower between May and the end of July.

TOP LEFT The water on the farm constantly rushes down the dingles from the hillside with a series of dramatic waterfalls.

TOP RIGHT The water in the garden is all introduced and varies from the highly controlled bubble in the Paradise Garden...

ABOVE ...to the little pond in the Wildlife Garden.

OPPOSITE Madonna lilies in flower. They are pollinated by moths but also host the dreaded Lily beetle.

OVERLEAF We let foxgloves grow wherever they seed themselves – and the bumble bees love them as much as we do.

well. It is also more a rose of woodland and woodland edge than of fields and it is more likely to make itself at home in the light shade of the dingles than out in the open.

R. arvensis is more of a climber or creeper than a shrub and the wood tends to be dark crimson, and whereas the thorns of the dog rose are straight, *R. arvensis* thorns are curved and especially good at snagging at clothes and flesh as you push past. But its form and demeanour are so light and charming that you can forgive the occasional blood sacrifice.

———

Voles

Meg, my son's sheepdog, rootled around in the tussocky long grass and then suddenly pounced, lifting her head with a little creature dangling from her jaws. Then, without any hesitation, she swallowed it whole, licked her lips and went on hunting for more.

I have often watched our dogs, whatever the breed, snuffling around in rough grass and every now and then one will triumphantly catch a vole and consume it. I do feel a bit squeamish about this – after all, our dogs live primarily off dried dog food kept in a dustbin in the back kitchen, plus a few scraps. This was a bit of a leap to the rawly primeval. But the cat purring on your lap will happily bite the heads off beautiful songbirds and crows take the eyes out of lambs as they are being born. Nature knows no propriety so there is no reason why dogs should not hunt and eat voles any more than they do rabbits. And voles – especially the short-tailed field vole (*Microtus agrestis*) – are clearly delicious. The vole population is the key nutritional building block for owls, kestrels, weasels and buzzards. Without them, these animals almost immediately go into decline.

There are apparently 75 million voles in the UK and they thrive in rough grassland. And when they thrive, they really thrive, with the population rising to explosion point after about three years, when it suddenly plummets – presumably because they eat themselves out of house and home. However, these population surges can sometimes result in vole 'plagues' and they go from eating the roots and seeds of pasture, to eating crops and, occasionally, the roots of much-loved garden plants.

Given that the average life of a vole is just one year and in that time they can reach maturity and then produce up to half a dozen litters, each of six or seven young, it is easy to see how the population can grow fantastically fast. Predators – especially barn owls – thrive in almost direct correlation to the vole population, so produce more and healthier young when it is rising, then struggle for a year or two whilst it rebuilds.

Voles love rough grassland – a field left uncut for a year or two is ideal – but any unintensively managed grassland or moor is good for them, as well as strips of unploughed headland along the edge of arable fields or a wild-flower meadow in a larger garden. Keep the voles happy, and you have food for much rarer predators – as well as the odd snack for your dog.

Hawkbit

It is easy to gloss over the variations of yellow daisy-like flowers that appear in succession amongst meadows, banks and uncut grassland. There are dandelions that everyone knows and buttercups, which tend to dominate at the end of May in wet ground – and then there are more. Quite a few more, all sorts of similar ones, very nice and much enjoyed, if mostly anonymous.

But rough hawkbit (*Leontodon hispidus*) is worth closer acquaintance. It dapples the meadow with yellow star-like flowers in June, each elegantly spaced from the next so as not to jostle or crowd and yet they are there by the thousand, casting a wide blanket of golden yellow across the field. This yellow contrasts with the purple and pink of the orchids, and the burgundy of the red clover, flowering at the same time amongst grasses that are still very green and, in the case of our main meadow, now very short and thin. A modern commercial farmer would regard it with disdain.

Although it looks like a simple flower, with petals splaying out around a central boss, in fact these 'petals' are individual florets, each making its own seedhead. It likes our acidic soil but in truth grows just about everywhere, so I have no special claims to it. It is as common as sparrows in the hedgerow – and just as life-enhancing.

————

Jays

Of all the crow family, jays are the most elusive here. They appear in the garden as though they had been hiding, spending days slipping behind hedges and trees, keeping out of sight. They seemed to be much more common when I was a child, particularly in the oak and pine woods of my boarding school and their distinctive screech could be heard daily as they moved from cover to cover. They are very good mimics and whilst in captivity they will master the expected repertoire of telephone and doorbells, in the wild they can imitate other birds and do so often, especially when they feel threatened.

Unlike rooks and crows, jays are woodland birds and are rarely seen out in the open but if you do see one you know it at once, because it is pink-bodied with brilliant, banded blue wing feathers and a white backside that is very visible as it flies with its idio-syncratic dipping, woodpeckerish flight.

Like all corvids, they have a very wide diet that will include other birds – particularly nestlings of songbirds like blackbird and thrush – small mammals and eggs. But the bulk of the diet that they feed to their own nestlings are beetles and caterpillars of oak-feeding moth species, and their connection with oak trees extends into autumn as acorns are their favourite food. They will take them directly off the tree as well as fallen ones from the ground, and make substantial caches of up to 5000 acorns per bird. On the farm, we find acorns popping up in fields a long way from our only two oak trees, where they have been deposited in damp soil or under leaves (acorns dry out very quickly and will only germinate if they remain moist) and jays are reckoned to be one of the major distributors of oak trees. Perhaps, as the two oak trees I planted 25 years ago in the garden become more mature, the visiting jays may be bolder and busier, gathering acorns and redistributing them around the garden.

Orchids

I remember visiting the Singapore Botanic Gardens that are famed for their extraordinary collection of orchids. This was part of my *Around the World in 80 Gardens* series, so I had a camera crew in tow. The director – who was an orchid expert and obsessive – decided that the best approach was simply to follow me and record my reaction to this orchid treasure trove. But I was distinctly underwhelmed. They were clearly exotic and extraordinary, but laid out one after the other by the hundred as specimens in pots – each a gaudy variation of the orchid theme – was like eating a meal made up of three courses of candyfloss.

Another time, I visited a nursery that amounted to an orchid factory in Hampshire that was producing thousands of orchids a week for sale in supermarkets. They might as well have been made of plastic for all the mystery and allure that they had.

So, my relationship with orchids has always been mixed, at best. But then I found one growing in one of our fields – and it was love at first sight. This little pink flower, alone, in a large field, almost hidden in the grass, was both beautiful in itself and a symbol of unsullied nature. Modern agriculture may produce large quantities of food but in the process has gone a long way to ruining the natural world of the British countryside. A wild orchid is the equivalent of a lone figure standing in front of tanks in Tiananmen Square.

Wild orchids are not actually that rare but they are very particular and easily eliminated. We now, fifteen years on from that first sighting, have three types on the farm and one day I hope they will grow in the orchard and Cricket Pitch in the garden.

That original one I saw was a common spotted orchid (*Dactylorhiza fuchsii*) and every year we have more and more, slowly spreading in the wild-flower meadow. They vary in colour from very pale pink to a quite rich mauvey-purple but all have a spire of flowers and leaves blotched with dark spots. On the whole, it grows best in alkaline soils but, as with all floral generalisations, these rules are proved as much by their exceptions as adherents.

The heath spotted orchid (*D. maculata*) looks very similar to *D. fuchsii* but prefers acidic conditions. I have spent hours pondering over minute differences between the two, trying to establish exactly which is which and not helped by the orchids' extremely promiscuous habits that result in every kind of hybrid.

In May, the first orchids to flower in the meadow are the southern marsh orchid (*D. praetermissa*), which is shorter, a much richer purple and has leaves without blotches. We only have – at time of writing – about 30 of these but they are very slowly spreading. The seed is dust-tiny and is blown by the wind, so new plants can appear quite a way from the parent. Rain washes these minute seeds under the surface of the soil or, in woodland orchids, they become covered with a layer of leaves. They then depend upon fungi in the soil to germinate and grow. Once they have established leaves they can then photosynthesise and feed themselves. Some orchids develop tubers that enable them to store food and live for a number of years, whilst others produce rhizomatous roots that mean they can spread underground and produce large colonies.

Finally, we have just – in 2020 – discovered a colony of early purple orchids (*Orchis mascula*) at the edge of a green lane which was once solid wood and which we are now planting again as a wood for my grandson. These inflorescences are less densely packed than their meadow cousins.

As a result of the coronavirus lockdown, I have not been able to see the early orchids this year although my son, working on the farm, sends me pictures. I miss them dreadfully and that excitement of discovering them in the meadow, always in different spots, always a few more and, every now and then, a new type. Had I felt half as excited on that day in Singapore, I would have fulfilled all and more of the director's expectations.

———

Damselflies

Before any dragonflies appear, the damselflies do a good imitation, zipping round the pond on stained-glass wings. Whereas dragonflies can be strong flyers and appear all over the garden, hovering and turning at right angles in the air like an amphetamine-fuelled helicopter, the smaller damselflies stick closer to the water and do not fly nearly so well. The four damselfly wings are equal in size and always fold back against the long, needle-thin thorax when it is perched. Should you be in a position to observe such a thing, a damselfly's eyes are always separate, whereas a dragonfly's will touch. Both have extremely good eyesight.

Like the dragonfly, 95 per cent of a damselfly's life cycle is spent in or under the water, with the eggs laid underwater and the emerging larvae and, subsequently, the nymphs, spending all their time in water, too. The larvae will moult a number of times in the water until ready to emerge, then the nymphs crawl out of our pond under cover of night and split apart so the damselfly can emerge and be ready for its wings to harden in the sun.

They then have only a couple of weeks to live, during which time they will mate and the female lay her eggs.

During their very brief life out of the water, they consume about 20 per cent of their body weight daily, feeding off mosquitoes, midges and flies, but often starving – especially if the weather is bad – or becoming a meal for birds like pied or grey wagtails, spiders, frogs or even larger dragonflies. However, they have been following this compressed but exotic life pattern for hundreds of millions of years with no variation or interruption. It works for them.

———

Clover

Our wild-flower meadow's days of glory are in the month of June. But it is not one performance that begins, rises to a crescendo, then subsides over the course of a week or two, but rather a series of waves of flower, overlapping and merging, evolving and growing until the flower heads of the grasses hide all, save the taller knapweeds, beneath a shifting layer of tawny ripples. It is a cavalcade that runs through the field, from the chocolate heads of the sweet vernal grass at the beginning of May, when the trees are still finding their leaves, to the first swathe of freshly cut hay in August or even September.

But June is the best bit. June up here at 1000ft on the wet Welsh hillside still has the freshness of spring and yet the high colour of summer. June is the month of the orchids and buttercups, yellow rattle in flower, oxeye daisies and, last but not least, clover. Clover is humble fare, so common that it is not really fit to be mentioned in the same breath as orchids, but nonetheless, for all its ubiquity, red clover is beautiful, dotted all through the field with its fluffy purple, burgundy and pink tufts of flower.

Red clover (*Trifolium pratense*) is superior grazing for cattle and is undersown in pastures to add high living to the grass. But that is usually a hybridised, bred version designed for maximum benefit to cattle. The native red clover is smaller and although cattle love it, it is especially good for bees of all kinds. A field of clover guarantees good honey as well as fat cattle.

It likes soil that is not too dry and fares better in meadows than pasture, where it is usually eaten before it can set seed. It is a perennial but not a good coloniser, which is why it is deliberately sown as part of grass 'leys' (short-term grazing, often sown as part of an arable rotation), but if allowed to set seed, it will return vigorously year on year.

White clover (*T. repens*) is smaller and more likely to be found in the average lawn and less likely in a hay meadow. It is shorter and fares better where the grass is kept short and does well on poor, compacted but sunny soil.

Clover of any hue is a legume and therefore nitrogen-fixing, extracting nitrogen from the air and leaving a residue in the soil via its root nodes. It also swamps and inhibits other weeds, so makes good groundcover, but in a meadow the long grass and other herbs around it stop it becoming too dominant.

It will withstand any amount of treading and trampling, whether by human or animal feet, and its seed will last a long time in the soil, so will regenerate anywhere that has a history of grassland. The reason that it can take a lot of mowing, grazing and treading is because it creeps along the ground on stems up to 18in long, and roots at the nodes where leaves and flowers rise up from the trailing stem. This means that lawns or grass paths that take a lot of wear and tear stay green longer than if just grass is sown. However, you will often see and read of clover being a 'problem' in a lawn, along with various ways of killing it. Why a lawn should look better as a monoculture I cannot begin to imagine. I regard clover as welcome not just in a wild-flower meadow but as a valued part of any lawn.

In the *Mabinogion*, the earliest prose stories in English, Olwen, beautiful daughter of the giant, Ysbaddaden Benkawr, left a track of pure white clover wherever she walked – which would have annoyed the lawn-fanatic brigade no end.

Merlin

I was fixing a fence in one of our fields, the post having rotted at the base and the wire sagging. This work is constant and as much to keep out mountain sheep greedy for our grass as to keep our sheep in. Bending double to hammer in the bottom strand, I saw, in my upside-down vision, a chocolate-brown bird streak down the tree line on the other side of the narrow field. It was only visible for a second or two but clearly had the electric energy and lethal purpose of a raptor.

Even upside down, with a mouth full of staples, the automatic process of bird identification/elimination kicked in. Dark brown, smallish – too small and fast for a buzzard, too brown for a male sparrowhawk, wings too sharp and tail too short for a female, and definitely too small for a peregrine. Too compact and dark for a kestrel and anyway, not the way they hunt. That only left a merlin. Could it be? I had never seen one before so could not be sure but it ticked all the boxes and the thought it might be certainly enlivened the drudgery of fence mending.

The next day I was with my son doing the same job in another field and we both saw – this time not upside down – the same bird cross the field and head across the valley to the high ground opposite. It was undoubtedly a female merlin. Since then, I have seen another (the same?) female when walking high up on Hatteral Hill and a male zoom across the corner of a field, slate-blue, very small, and very fast. But although I now have half an eye scanning whenever I am up on the hillside, that is all – so far.

In the etiquette of falconry, merlins were considered a lady's hawk, too small for catching game. Merlins live mainly on small birds weighing less than four ounces, which they chase with astonishing speed, following their every twist and turn. Instead, merlins were used for sport rather than the table, with larks the preferred prey. Given the skylark has one of the most haunting and beautiful songs of all, this seems astonishingly cruel and wanton to modern thinking, but medieval sensibilities did not incline that way. In any event, the lark apparently often got away after a spectacular chase. Perhaps it indicates how common – and thus disposable – larks were compared to today.

Like so many birds of prey, the merlin is a success story in my lifetime, coming back from severe depredation due to egg collectors (they have beautiful red eggs), gamekeepers and, more devastatingly, pesticides. It is still by no means common and, given its preference for upland moorland in summer and coasts in winter, less likely to be seen than a peregrine or a hobby. But the numbers are recovering. And when fixing fences or clearing ditches on the hillside, I am always watching for my next sighting.

Honeysuckle

Honeysuckle (*Lonicera periclymenum*) or woodbine is a woodland plant, using trees for support as it rises to the light. But around the lanes of the garden it is a plant I associate with summer hedgerows – assuming they have not been flailed to a frayed but neat stubble by over-zealous contractors. Driving between farm and garden in June and July, great pools of fruity honeysuckle fragrance flood through the open windows of the car. Shakespeare, in *A Midsummer Night's Dream*, calls it 'luscious' and there is an opulence and hint of exotic indulgence about it that marries well with the velvet warmth of a midsummer's night.

It has evolved to release its fragrance at night, triggered by warmth, to attract the moths that are its main pollinators. The scent is powerful, slipping into the car and travelling down the road with us, but moths such as the gloriously pink-and-gold elephant hawk moth particularly love the trumpet-shaped, splayed flowers, and can pick up the fragrance up to a quarter of a mile away.

The larvae of the white admiral butterfly, with its dark chocolate-brown wings banded with a streak of white flashes, rely entirely on honeysuckle leaves for their food, especially those growing along the edge of woodland rides or along shady, untrimmed lanes. We are right on the edge of its territory, which is largely south and east of us, but we do see them. The eggs are laid on the leaves and the larvae hatch and eat the tips of the honeysuckle leaves until the end of summer, when they construct silk shelters for winter. In spring, when there is fresh leaf growth, they emerge to continue feeding then pupate, with the adults finally appearing in mid-June.

The coiled tangle of the bines provides good cover for birds and we have a honeysuckle outside one of the garden doors that invariably hosts a family of robins, blackbirds or occasionally thrushes – even though we go in and out all the time. As well as cover for nesting birds, the flowers provide a mass of berries that are amongst the first to be eaten in autumn, when the weather turns cold.

Owl in the Bathroom

A tawny owl sat on the back of the chair in our bedroom. He looked very cross. It seems that he had come down the chimney in the bathroom. Perhaps he had landed on the edge, misjudged things and fallen in, or maybe he thought the chimney pot was a good hole to explore. Either way, he had emerged into the grate in the bathroom and was not very happy about it. I had no idea if it was male or female but there was something masculine about its sense of affronted dignity.

There was a smashed vase and quite a few droppings on the windowsill, so obviously it had tried to get out to the light. I opened the windows but it flew into the bathroom and took up position on top of the cistern, sitting sulkily under the low ceiling.

As always, when you get up close to a tawny owl, its beauty and size are a surprise. Although I suspect his feathers were very fluffed up in an attempt to look big and scary – not unsuccessfully – he was almost buzzard-sized and a lovely mix of purple, brown and tawny feathers.

We left him alone and went back in when it was properly dark – after 11 p.m. – and he had gone.

Midges

I love Scotland. My half-Scottish blood rises to the fore and I feel entirely at home there, but there is something in my blood, perhaps the English bit, that is irresistible to midges and that can make Scotland in high summer a living hell. I don't use the phrase lightly. We have twice taken holidays with friends on Loch Hourn, just inland from the sea above Knoydart. It is, like all the West Coast, indescribably beautiful. But Hourn is the Gaelic for 'hell' and the reason that it is known as Loch Hell is because the clouds of midges there make life all but intolerable, reducing you to scrabbling at your face – especially ears and eyelids – in a desperate and invariably vain attempt to relieve the burning itch of the midges' bites.

It is a tribute to our friends that we had nice holidays despite this. But any venture outside, even for a few minutes, meant sleeves buttoned down, shirts buttoned up, collars raised, hats on and trousers tucked into socks. It is the only time in the past 30-odd years that I have also smoked a pipe at every opportunity – because the smoke kept the midges at bay. The saving grace was that midges do not venture far from shore, so we took to small boats on the loch for much of the day and had a lovely time.

Although I glibly refer to midges hungering after my blood, in fact they are drawn by odour and in particular, by the carbon dioxide we give off. If midges like you, be comforted – it is because you smell especially nice to them.

Midges are tiny but can be present in vast numbers. A small pool on a peat moor can hold a quarter of a million midges per square yard. They are indiscriminate about their prey – humans, cattle or deer are all equally attractive and it is reckoned that midges are the reason that deer move to higher ground in summer.

Midges also account for one-fifth of all days lost to work for Scottish forestry workers.

Midges are mercifully scant in the garden, although there are always a few small clouds of gnats dancing in the sunlight. These are non-biting midges, although there are some evenings when my scalp itches so much that I am driven indoors earlier than I would wish. If it is not midges, then some other tiny midge-like insect is nibbling away at me.

But by and large, although there are many different kinds of midge and gnat, it is the Highland midge that has earned the fearsome reputation. But they do some good. The larvae, although minute, are present in such great numbers that their burrowing makes them a significant agent of decomposition. And they do keep great tracts of the Highlands of Scotland more or less free from human habitation and, therefore, wild.

———

Sessile Oak

We have just two large oaks on the farm, plus half a dozen saplings. But once the whole hillside was covered with them. One of our two oaks is very large indeed, a vast galleon of a tree, with limbs horizontal and canted at a gentle angle, unsupported out across space for 30ft, 40ft, 50ft, and each with a girth as big as a large tree trunk.

This is *Quercus petraea*, the sessile oak, that grows better on the thinner, acidic soil of these hillsides than its lowland cousin *Q. robur*. It is called sessile because the acorns have no stalks. These acorns get taken by magpies, jackdaws and jays, and then buried or dropped in open fields, where they sometimes, especially if the ground is wet, germinate and grow into seedlings. But the seedlings rarely survive long as young oaks are the favourite food of all ruminants, from rabbits to sheep and deer – which is why you hardly ever see a young oak growing in an open field unless it has been protected from the outset.

The sessile oak tends to grow slightly less tall than its cousin and is less likely to make the huge, straight beams needed for the largest buildings, but it is broader and more branched, and in maturity – which in oak terms is something between 300 and 600 years old – makes a magnificent specimen, like the one that we look out on. When we bought the farm the previous owners told us they had considered cutting it down because it blocked the view. But it *is* the view.

The reason that our two oaks have survived at all is because they both grow zanily out of the near-vertical banks of the dingle, with the stream rushing 30ft below. This meant that it was too awkward to get to for the harvest that so many of the original oaks would have provided.

All the original oaks – and many stumps remain under the bracken – would have been coppiced on a 20- to 30-year rotation, depending on the soil and situation. Modern life does not slip easily into this kind of timescale but coppicing, with its eight- to twelve-year cycle for hazels, fifteen to 20 years for ash, 20 to 30 for chestnut, and 30 to 40 for oak, was a rhythm that pulsed easily through country people's lives.

Hedgerow oaks in the fields around Longmeadow were regularly pollarded. This meant that the tree had all its branches removed every 30-odd years but the trunk, standing tall enough so that the largest cattle could not reach up and eat the young leaves or shoots, was left. In time these trunks become exceptionally thick and gnarled although the mass of branches that sprout from the top never become more than a foot or so in diameter. It was said, well into the twentieth century, that the oak from the pollards was the most valuable asset of a farm and every generation was set up by this inheritance, providing a supply of wood for anything from fencing to building repairs.

Pollarding also extends the life of a tree, although if not done regularly the weight of the extra branches can split the trunk and many old pollards, whilst looking superb, should be cut back to preserve them.

Coppicing is more drastic and involves cutting all existing growth down to a stump, which then will sprout a rash of new shoots that are left to grow, for oak, for another 20 to 30 years. Treated like this, a coppice stump or 'stool' can last hundreds, even thousands, of years.

The oak coppice on the hillsides above the farm had three harvests. The first and most important was for charcoal. This, before the arrival of railways and cheap coal in the nineteenth century, was produced all across the country on a huge scale to provide the best fuel for smelting and for domestic heating and cooking. It is very light, so cheap and easy to transport, can be stored almost indefinitely and burns much hotter than wood, however well-seasoned.

But an important by-product from the coppicing was bark, which was used for tanning and was sent in huge bundles by river down to the tanners, who then ground it and soaked it in urine in pits in which they steeped the leather. Bark could only be taken from cut trees or wood, since ringing a tree of even a thin strip of bark will kill a living tree. Hence, supply was erratic, demand constant and prices always good, especially for coppice oak bark that was of the highest quality. It is reckoned that in 1830, tanners used over 60,000 tons of home-produced bark and imported half as much again.

Whole families would work on the hillside in late spring, when the sap was at its highest and when, for a few short weeks, the bark was easiest to remove. They would slide a special barking tool, or 'spud', under the bark and slide and lever it off in large pieces, which were then stacked and dried in the wind and sun. The tannin stained hands black for weeks but the money was good and the stripped wood could then be made into charcoal, which provided another cash crop.

Timing was vital. I have tried removing bark when there was not sufficient sap; it clings to the wood beneath and comes off in strings and scraps, taking ages and resulting in a messy pile.

So this hillside would have been regularly coppiced, each farm clearing about half an acre a year. But in the mid-1840s, tanners started to use chemical alternatives to the urine and bark mixtures, and the demand for bark abruptly dropped. Railways and deep-cast mining meant that coal became cheap and readily available, so the demand for charcoal almost disappeared. By the 1860s, the oak coppicing was dying out and by the 1960s, most of the ancient coppices had either been grazed out of existence or bulldozed.

But a few remain and the best example near me is near Abergavenny, on the approach to the Sugar Loaf mountain. You walk through a wood of short but multi-stemmed sessile oaks, last coppiced about the time of the First World War, each tree sculptural, balletic and slightly sinister. Here and there, small platforms can be made out on the hillside, perhaps 80in wide and 12ft to 13ft long, which is where the bark would have been stacked and dried and then, once this had been taken away, the charcoal burnt.

This wood is beautiful but in the way that an abandoned building is beautiful. It is a remnant. Working coppice has an energy and a biodiversity that is rich and life-enhancing, from the newly cut coups, where the sun pours in to stimulate a flush of flowers, to the canopied and deeply shaded areas that are next in line for harvesting.

This winter we shall plant a sessile oak coppice for my grandson, George. The site was once a wood that was bulldozed 50 years ago to make a small, steeply sloping field that is poor grazing. I shall not see the harvest in my lifetime but perhaps one day George's hands may be blackened from the tannin of the bark, nightingales will nest in the branches of the uncut trees and, on warm summer nights, sing across the stillness of the valley.

———

JULY

Bird's Foot Trefoil

Around the beginning of July – much later up at 1500ft than in the warmer lowlands – a bright yellow understorey starts to appear in patches beneath the grasses that are now beginning to set seed and fade into a bleached-out, tawny wave.

This is *Lotus corniculatus*, bird's foot trefoil, also known as eggs and bacon, hen and chickens, granny's toenails and dozens of other local vernacular names. The abundance of nicknames is an indication of how common it is and yet it always is a delight, both bright and jolly and precious. It likes grass that is grazed short but also appears in the meadow in seemingly arbitrary patches and swathes, although it prefers drier ground and where the soil is not too acidic. One of the advantages of farming on a steep slope is that the drainage is good and although we have very high rainfall, ground that is farcically boggy one week – too wet to even walk on without slipping over – can be dry enough to drive on the next, so the range of plants remains wide.

The flowers are egg-yolk yellow, with pinky red buds, and are carried just an inch or so above the ground. They develop thin seedpods like a bird's claw – hence the name – containing seeds that shoot out when ripe. They have masses of nectar and so are good for butterflies and bees, and the larvae of butterflies like the common blue and dingy skipper feed on it.

———

Swifts

Swifts do not live here any more. They pay cursory visits but do not belong to these skies. Yet no other creature owns the sky more than the swift and they used to grace us with their supersonic, sleek version of the still ubiquitous swallows and martins. But over the past 20 years, their appearances have become increasingly infrequent, increasingly brief and their numbers increasingly sparse. They used to scream over in groups of a dozen or more, wheeling up into the sky with an astonishing elasticity, or else we would see them high above us on a clear evening, little black crescents making great curves and arcs in the sky as the insects they hunted were carried up into the troposphere.

They nested in the steeple of the village church less than half a mile across the fields, but that stopped at least ten years ago. Nowadays you are more likely to see swifts in the centre of a town or even city than in the countryside. British swifts declined by over half in the 20 years between 1995 and 2015, and the rate of decline is accelerating. Most is due to the reduction in their prey – flying insects and, somewhat surprisingly, spiders floating on gossamer in mid-air – and the effect of pesticides and habitat loss. No surprises there, just the sickening inevitability and sadness.

The reason why birds like swifts, swallows, blackcaps, cuckoos and redstarts migrate here to breed in the summer is because of the range and quantity of insects. Their return journey in winter, when our insect population drops, is for the same reason. The investment in energy and danger – let alone the almost unthinkable scope and bravery of migration – is huge. If insect numbers drop below a critical level, that investment in the journey will not be worth it. The birds just will not come. For humans to bludgeon the insect and invertebrate population with insecticides and pesticides to increase farm production and profits – and for all the sanctimonious, high-minded justifications, it is commercial profit that drives this more than anything else – is no different than locusts or a fungus destroying a crop. It is destructive, lop-sided and fundamentally lacking in wisdom or any understanding of the bigger picture.

But there are still swifts to be seen and celebrated – especially in towns. Their story is one of the most remarkable of all birds. Other than making a nest and laying their two to three eggs, their whole life is spent on the wing. They need a flat surface to nest on and typically, this was under eaves or in a hole in a wall. Although loss of insects is the critical part of the equation in their decline, loss of suitable nesting sites has also had a role. Barns are being converted, old houses repaired and new ones built without eaves, and certainly without the odd missing brick to provide a suitable nesting hole.

The nesting material is all collected on the wing and consists of feathers, grass, wisps of straw and other floating flotsam, all bound together by saliva. They will then return to the same nest year after year, repairing it as needed. The young are in the nest a long time – up to two months – and if the British summer is bad, there can be a high mortality rate. It will also mean that the parents have to travel great distances to get enough food – up to 500 miles a day – but fledgling swifts have the ability to go into a state of torpor if there is insufficient food, which slows down the use of their reserves. Even the embryo in the egg can slow its development down if the parent is unable to return to incubate it and keep it sufficiently warm.

Once the young do finally leave the nest, they spend just a day or two learning to fly and feed before making the long journey south with all the family leaving our part of the world by mid-August. In fact, they are one of the very few migratory birds that has not extended its summer visit to the UK as a result of climate change.

They fly across Spain to North Africa and then down across the western Sahara before heading east to winter in central Africa. But much of their life remains a mystery. Although surviving birds will return to where they nested or were raised, the young will not mature to mate or rear young for four years, although they can live to be eight or even ten. However, they do pair in their first summer and may even build a nest despite not producing any young. It is a kind of playing house. They remain paired for life, returning each year to the same nesting site. But many of the younger birds that do not build a rehearsal nest may spend the first three years of their lives entirely on the wing. It is an astonishing thought.

Musk Mallow

Towards the end of July, a little clump of flowers always appears on a steep bank behind the farmhouse – not far from where the wild thyme grows. The pink, papery petals are on long stems and, because the foliage blends into the grasses growing around them, they appear at first to be without leaves. Unopened buds are apple-green and in a round cluster, giving no hint of the fragility of the flowers about to break free. It is a musk mallow (*Malva moschata*).

What is strange is that there is just this one little patch that has not spread in the fifteen years since we have been here, and there are no others growing within hundreds of yards. The musk mallow likes open, well-drained positions – hence its proximity to the thyme – but is relatively common, albeit not on the farm, where it is a case of a common plant becoming precious because of its scarcity. I suspect that would be true of many of our common wild flowers, where familiarity quickly breeds, if not contempt, then a certain blasé quality.

I know that many consider musk mallow a weed, popping up unbidden in allotments and verges, but our one patch is a treasure, both on that bank and when we take a few stems indoors and the musky fragrance fills the room.

Small Heath Butterflies

The meadow is covered in hundreds of small heath butterflies. They ignore all the flowers but sit on flowering stems of the grasses – fescues mainly – with their wings folded, showing a black dot in a flare of rusty orange. The only time they seem to open them is when they quickly flit to the next grass. The perfectly camouflaged green caterpillars feed exclusively on fine grasses like fescues and bents, which are absent from the rich managed leas of modern agriculture.

––––––

Hemlock

My father once kept gerbils as part of his equipment as a science teacher at my prep school. There were dozens of them and he would let them out in the sitting room to exercise. Of course – inevitably – one day they made a break for it and never came back, some living inside the furniture, others roaming beneath the floorboards. That is another long and strange story but for the moment just breathe deep of the aroma of uncleaned-out gerbil cage. If you have ever kept mice, pet rats, guinea pigs or hamsters, then you will be familiar with that olfactory sensation.

The first year that I cut the grass here – mid-spring 1992 – I noticed that precise and unmistakable odour as I reached the far corner of what is now the orchard. Musty, fusty, mousy and rank. It could only belong to a burrowing, cocooned mammal – except that the culprit proved to be a tall umbellifer, like a giant cow parsley or hogweed, with distinctive purple splodges on its thick stems. This is hemlock, stately, statuesque and stinky.

And – most excitingly – deadly poisonous. *Conium maculatum* contains a neurotoxin that paralyses the respiratory nerves and can cause death by suffocation. The more sunshine it absorbs, the more the poison intensifies. The whole plant contains these toxins but the seeds have the highest concentration.

The leaves are very ferny and the flowers lovely white umbels like cow parsley. It is impossible to mistake it for anything else because not only does it reek, but it is also enormous – over 6ft tall – and has those purple splodges.

We still have hemlock in that corner and I, who hardly ever wear gloves to garden, always put them on to cut it back or pull it up. It is biennial, so in the first growing season, it just makes a rosette of finely cut leaves and then, after a winter, will develop its hollow, noticeably smooth flower stem.

It is quite common around here, liking the wet, heavy soil, and although I am instinctively cavalier about these things, it surprises me that so little fuss is made about it because it really can kill people – as well as most animals that eat it, although the smell is enough to deter almost everything.

———

Bats

Everybody has a wildlife blind spot. Some cannot abide spiders, others snakes. There are those who are just not cat people and there are misguided people who do not love dogs. There are even people who fail to see the charms of a pig.

By and large, I love all animals, am not spooked by snakes, can see the virtue of rats and don't get fazed by wasps, hornets or moths banging into me as I read in bed on a warm September night. But I am a chiroptophobic. I hate bats.

Well, not exactly hate. I have no objection at all to them as long as they stay well away from me. But I do hate the way they bomb me at dusk when I am working or walking in the garden, hate the way they swoop and skim around outside the house, and really, really hate it when occasionally they fly into the house.

I used to hate birds fluttering around indoors but seem to have pretty much grown out of that – mainly through handling chickens and because it is so lovely having swallows flying in and out of the house all summer long. So, I suspect that my panicked reaction has to do with the bats' zany flight and fluttering, rather than the fact they are ugly mice borne on repulsive leathery wings.

But I know that bats are fascinating and should be encouraged. I approve of them wholeheartedly – but would happily never see another bat in my life. However, we have lots in both garden and farm, so I am sure to see them daily between April and October for the rest of my life.

They are preyed upon – hobbies and tawny owls can and do catch them, and anyone who has had a cat knows that sooner or later it will turn up with a bat. But the only real threat to them comes from loss of habitat and insect prey rather than any predation. Only the great crested newt is as championed and protected as bats.

The one fact that everyone knows about them is that they eat a huge quantity of insects. Some bats catch insects as small as midges, whilst others eat moths, beetles, craneflies and even flying ants. The pipistrelle – the smallest and commonest of our native bats – is reputed to eat up to 3000 midges every night.

Many catch their prey in the air but some, like the lesser horseshoe bat or the natter's bat, will pick prey off leaves and branches as they pass. Some, like the noctule, fly high and others, like horseshoe bats, fly low to the ground and even hunt from perches.

I know of these things but I cannot say that I go out of my way to observe them for myself – other than one slightly surreal night when the late David Bellamy and I went bat spotting in the grounds of Buckingham Palace. But I do like watching the noctules flying on a summer's evening like swifts, high in the sky and surprisingly straight and fast. And pipistrelles are so common with us that their flight paths, like the tracery of a sparkler in a child's hand waved randomly in the dark, are part of the pattern of dusk. Having watched pipistrelles in the garden here for more than 25 years, despite instinctively avoiding them, I cannot help but notice that they have set hunting grounds that are very local and specific, and that one or sometimes two bats will work them for 20 minutes at a time. Around the hop kiln is one, the Mound another, the path up to the Paradise Garden a third. Obviously, this is due to the prevalence of insects at those places but it is interesting that those hunting grounds are so particular.

There are eighteen species of British bat. I have seen pipistrelles and noctules in the garden and pipistrelles and a barbastelle on the farm. The latter are very rare; we disturbed one that was roosting under a flap of bark on an old tree. Barbastelles like woodland near water and are only found in South Wales, Sussex and Devon. I have a friend who has horseshoe bats in his cellar and another who had to accommodate – with a specially built dormer bat entrance – horseshoe bats in his attic.

I was leaning out of the bedroom window one lovely September morning as dawn rose, when two bats swooped in about an inch from my face and disappeared into the gap between the window and the frame. Given my feelings about bats, you may imagine I was not entirely happy about this. But I accept that we share our home and outbuildings with them, and probably the woods, too. Having them in the garden is entirely a good thing and the surest way of encouraging them is to make life good for your insect population. Also, bats will be drawn to water, partly because of the way it attracts insects but also because they need to drink, so a pond will always encourage them to any garden.

I remember, when filming *Around the World in 80 Gardens*, going down a side-tributary of the Amazon in a motorised canoe as dusk fell. Suddenly, out of the trees that flanked either side of this river – tiny by Amazonian standards but about the width of the Thames as it goes through Westminster – thousands of bats streamed out over the water, criss-crossing back and forth as they hunted. They had large, sharply pointed wings – bigger than any British bat – and for about 40 minutes, they flew around and amongst us. On the one hand, this was my worst nightmare, but on the other, it was fascinating and I had no choice but to give in to the experience and try to relish it.

If you are not sure if droppings come from mice or bats – and they look almost identical – then there is a sure test. Crush one and if it is at all sticky or malleable, then it is mouse. If it crumbles, it is bat because bat droppings are made up entirely of the wings and bones of their prey and have almost no liquid content at all.

———

Wild Clary

Salvias in the garden, other than sage (*Salvia officinalis*), tend to be rather exotic and tricky to keep happy in our heavy, wet soil. But on the farm, there is a salvia that grows easily and freely on the hot, sunny banks of thin soil over sandstone. This is *S. verbenaca*, the wild clary.

I have it now in front of me in a little white milk jug on the kitchen table. It is not dramatic, not a star, but has a simplicity and distinct style that is lovely. The stems are typically square, with side-shoots going off symmetrically at 45 degrees at equal but widely spaced intervals, and the purple flowers are also evenly spaced, like ruffs up the stems.

It feels as though it should be a summer visitor up here on the

Welsh hillside, like the swallows or cuckoos coming north for a few months to breed before heading south for the winter. But it has made a home here, come snow, icy winds or endless winter rain. As have I.

———

Kestrel

I saw a kestrel cross the garden this morning, her brown body (I think it was a female – no hint of grey) as neat and sharp as a perfectly cut suit. When I was growing up in Hampshire, kestrels were the one bird of prey that was common. I used to see them almost daily and until the 1990s, you could not drive on a motorway for ten minutes without seeing at least one hovering above the verge, hunting for voles. Their rattling call – 'kee kee kee kee' – was as common over that rolling, chalky farmland as the buzzard's mewing cry is here. I used to think back then that we took them for granted – the token, rather unexciting birds of prey in lieu of the real stars like peregrines and hobbies – but that if kestrels were rare we would think them the most beautiful of birds, as stream-lined and finessed for purpose as any living creature.

And now they are rare.

I do see a hunting kestrel about once a month up on the hilltop above the farm, hovering easily above the exposed, tufty grass, the binoculars showing it twisting and shifting and adjusting almost by the second, giving the appearance of holding stock still above the horizon. But this female was the first I have seen above the garden for a year. In truth, gardens are not really kestrel territory. They like verges, hedge banks and grassy fields; gardens are too much like woodland.

The kestrel is the only British bird of prey that truly hovers. Buzzards, kites and harriers will hold steady into the wind but need the right airflow and updraught to do so. A kestrel can hover as and when it chooses, which it does a great deal, descending by degrees until it will drop onto the mouse or vole it has spotted. Gerard Manley Hopkins' poem 'The Windhover' – the best poem about a bird in the English language – has it exactly:

> I caught this morning morning's minion, king-
> dom of daylight's dauphin, dapple-dawn-drawn Falcon, in
>   his riding
>   Of the rolling level underneath him steady air, and striding
>   High there, how he rung upon the rein of a wimpling wing
>   In his ecstasy! then off, off forth on swing,
>   As a skate's heel sweeps smooth on a bow-bend: the hurl
>   and gliding
>   Rebuffed the big wind.

My father-in-law had a pair of kestrels nesting in a barn, the birds raising their young on a wide beam within the floored-off roof space and flying in and out through a large air hole in the gable end. We could watch them from an upstairs window, busily going to and fro feeding their young, until three appeared at the entrance, fledged, getting braver, until they were ready to go. It was a sobering thought that two of the three were statistically unlikely to survive to their first birthday and only 20 per cent of young reach the breeding age of two. Nevertheless, despite this high mortality rate, numbers maintained and even grew.

But that was nearly 30 years ago and the latest report by the Department for Environment and Rural Affairs, published in 2019, shows that numbers have almost halved since 1970. Kestrels have become as rare here as peregrines were back then. Who would ever have thought it?

A number of reasons have been offered for their decline. It is undoubtedly influenced by modern farming, which favours autumn-sown wheat versus the spring-sown barley that was ubiquitous in the Hampshire of my childhood. The difference might seem arcane but it means that stubble is now rarely left for more than a few days, whereas it used to stay in the fields until as late as April, providing cover for the mammals the kestrel feeds on in winter. As well as the preferred voles and mice, this almost exclusively ground prey will include shrews – which is rare as most raptors find shrews disgusting and avoid them. But they will take anything from worms and beetles to a young rabbit or rat and, on occasion, lizards and slowworms.

They can and do catch birds in flight but to a far lesser degree. This seems odd, given what an elegant and streamlined flyer the kestrel is, but it seems that it is bad at catching birds. There are records of them catching bats, swifts, pigeons, lapwings and petrels off oil rigs – but that is because these are effectively their lowest hanging fruit.

Around us, most fields are ploughed to an inch of the hedge line, leaving no room for a 'headland'. This is a strip of rough grass anything from two to ten yards deep that was originally left unploughed to allow horses, and then tractors, to turn when ploughing. Now tractors are hugely more powerful and drag four-furrow reversible ploughs three times as fast and can turn on a sixpence. The upshot is that there is less cover for voles and therefore less food for kestrels.

Perhaps also, the significant increase in goshawks, peregrines and buzzards locally has been at the cost of kestrels, since these larger raptors, especially the goshawks, will attack and eat kestrels. At the very least, it would be enough to scare them away.

Whatever the reason, I miss the familiarity I once had with this neatest and most elegant of birds.

———

Ladybirds

One of the oddities of modern life – or perhaps just my modern life – is that I see as many ladybirds in winter in my bedroom as I do outside in the garden in summer. They spend their winter months in the house which, being mostly a Tudor timber-framed building, has countless nooks and crannies where they can secrete themselves. Then, when the heating is on, they come out to have a fly around, which often includes landing on the bed as I am reading and then very slowly, very gently, crawling over me.

Every gardener knows that ladybirds are a Good Thing because they eat aphids (up to 60 a day each) which are officially a Bad Thing. That is probably about the extent of people's knowledge, other than that we view ladybirds with a kind of affectionate domesticity that we afford to few other beetles.

There are quite a few ladybirds to feel affectionate about. The most common is the seven-spot but you may also see two-spot, four-spot, ten-spot, sixteen-spot, 22-spot or 24-spot versions, although for some reason, the four-spot is excluded from Ireland. In total, there are 42 species of British ladybird but to all intents and purposes – and I realise this is going to offend all coleopterists – they merge into one shiny red beetle splodged with varying black dots.

But, however many spots they wear, ladybirds have real charm. It is partly to do with the intensity of their red backs and black spots, and partly to do with their rounded, almost semi-spherical shape that gives them the air of a brightly arrayed rural vicar bumbling along in a Morris Minor. Then they open their carapace and reveal wings that transform them, with a James Bond sleight of hand, into a helicoptering, zooming insect like all the others.

It is not just the adults that eat aphids but the larvae do, too, but they, by default, are much less conspicuous affairs. They hatch from the eggs after about a week and immediately start eating. They pupate a month later inside a hard, dark casing that looks like dark bird droppings, then emerge a fortnight later into full ladybird colours. The adult will live for about a year, with the female laying two or three sets of eggs between early spring and midsummer.

As well as aphids, they also eat pollen, particularly on angelica, cosmos, marigolds, thyme and lavender.

You can get ladybird population explosions and then they become too much of a good thing. However, although these have been recorded every 20 years or so, the last time it happened in Britain was in 1976. I remember it well. It was reckoned (by the British Entomological and Natural History Society) that there were 23.65 billion of them in the southern counties of England by late July and people complained of being attacked by them, although it seems more likely that the thirsty ladybirds were trying to drink people's sweat rather than bite their skin.

It seems that the population explosion was created by a huge increase in aphids during the warm spring followed by the drying up of plants in summer, which meant the aphids had little soft growth to feed on and their numbers collapsed. In its turn, the ladybird explosion that ran parallel to the aphid increase suddenly went hungry – so swarmed in search of alternative sources of food.

Thistles

Unlike so many plants that prefer one of the two very different soils, climates and terrains that we have in the garden and on the farm, thistles do not discriminate. They are a bane that has spread right across my landscape. Yet they can be beautiful – after all, I grow and carefully nurture lots of ornamental thistles like *Cirsium rivulare*, onopordum, echinops, eryngiums and glorious cardoons. And like everything else – literally everything – they are a thread in the infinitely complex web of life.

Thistle seeds make up to a third of goldfinches' entire diet and are eaten by many other birds including greenfinches, linnets and siskins. Peacock and meadow brown butterflies feed on thistle nectar and painted lady butterfly larvae feed on the leaves, especially of creeping thistle. Overwintering insects often use the hollow stems of various thistles as a safe haven.

In the garden, they are prickly and the classic 'wrong plant in the wrong place' but on the farm they cause real problems to sheep as the prickles puncture their lips as they graze the grass around them and the resulting wounds can get infected with a soil-born viral disease called orf that manifests itself with scabby lesions around the sheep's lips and mouth. These lesions then cause feeding problems, especially in lambs, and as a result they do not thrive. And as anyone who has kept sheep knows only too well, a lamb that is not thriving is very likely to quickly become a dead lamb.

So we try and manage the thistles by topping them. ('Topping' is when you cut off the seedheads of weeds like thistles and docks, and the tops of grasses, reducing the height of growth of the whole field to about 4in.) I have spent hours with a scythe doing this in the pastures where the anthills of the yellow ants mean that the tractor and cutter cannot go without damaging both anthills and machine, but by and large we use a topper. This is not difficult and part of the round of agricultural jobs. However, timing is critical. The old rhyme says, 'Cut thistles in May, they'll grow in a day; Cut them in June, 'tis too soon; Cut them in July, then they will surely die.' Leave them till August and the fluffy white down of the seeds floats like river mist, hundreds of which seed in this garden and across the fields of the farm.

But one of the oddities of thistles is that just when you think they are a major problem and seem to be getting thicker and thicker, they can dramatically reduce. Some of this is climatic – although thistles do well on rich soil they do not like damp grassland and we have noticed that the better-drained fields always have more thistles. So a really wet year will not be good for them.

There are at least fourteen native British thistles but the one that we have most of in our fields is the spear thistle (*C. vulgare*), which makes a large, very prickly plant with mauve flower heads. Worst of all is the creeping thistle (*C. arvense*). This one can grow like a prickly thicket and as well as spreading by seed, has creeping roots that will make new plants if broken. It has pale lavender flower heads and although the stem is smooth, the leaves are horribly prickly. As well as spreading with astonishing efficiency, it also exudes pheromones that inhibit the growth of most grain crops.

In the garden, we also get a lot of sow-thistles (*Sonchus asper* and *S. oleraceus*), which, in well-cultivated soil, are sappy and easy to pull up and then compost.

The other intrusive thistle into this particular garden is the burdock. It grows to at least 6ft on our rich soil and the burrs snag appallingly on a jersey and the dogs' coats all winter long. The answer is to cut it at ground level as soon as you see it, and to go on doing so until it weakens and dies. Along with a few other plants, the giant leaves were used to wrap butter in and the roots made dandelion and burdock beer, which was sold in every newsagent and village shop alongside ginger beer and cola 50 years ago.

———

Green Hazelnuts

The hazels are already covered in pale green cobnuts sitting like boiled eggs in their fringed husks. It is a mast year and the trees are laden with nuts – as are the beech and oaks. But it is deeply frustrating that the cobnuts fall so early when still green, and the squirrels plunder them before they can ripen for harvesting.

————

Nightshade

Nightshade tangles and roams the hedgerows just outside our kitchen window and sprouts from a Walled Garden wall but it is beautiful in its own sprawling way and not all nightshade is deadly. Ours is woody, both in name and habit.

Woody nightshade (*Solanum dulcamara*), also known as bitter-sweet, has a purple Turk's cap flower, with the petals bent-backed revealing a cone of bright orange stamens. These develop into green and red berries and are eaten by songbirds like thrushes, blackbirds and robins in late summer as much for the liquid they contain as for their food value.

Woody nightshade may not be deadly but it is poisonous and best left untasted. It grows rather like a late-flowering clematis, twining through the hedgerows, but its nearest garden cousins are not clematis but potatoes and tomatoes. It likes damp places and will even grow in shallow water but our heavy soil keeps it happy at any time of year. Deadly nightshade (*Atropa belladonna*), on the other hand, prefers chalky or limestone soils although will grow elsewhere.

————

Adder

I have never seen an adder in the garden but then I would not expect to. Too wet, too low, too agricultural. But I have seen them twice on the farm and once, when filming on the North York Moors, I practically stepped on one. Luckily it slithered away rather than defend itself.

Adders are Britain's only venomous snake and, although you are unlikely to die from an adder bite if you are reasonably healthy, quite a few dogs are killed by adders as they poke their noses at them. They hunt by biting their prey – usually a vole, mouse or ground-nesting bird – which will then attempt to shoot off but movement accelerates their absorption of the poison so the snake can take its time, following and then consuming it. The poison also breaks down tissue, making it easier for the adder to digest.

When I was at school, we would tell each other stories of the horrific effects of an adder bite – we were convinced that the sandy coniferous woods we played in were full of them although no one had actually seen one – and that the affected limb would turn black as coal and that a hideous death would surely follow. The only remedy was to take a knife and cut two deep slashes across the bite (I never worked out why two were necessary but did not want to appear unknowing), then suck the poison out before spitting it manfully away. It was always hard to know which was worse – the prospect of being bitten or of having to suck the poison out of someone. Fortunately, I was never called upon to exercise either option. For the record, apparently this would have been the worst thing to do. If you do get bitten by an adder, stay calm, reduce your activity to slow the spread of the venom, and go directly to A&E.

Adders are smaller than grass snakes, rarely reaching more than 2ft (a mature female grass snake can be twice as long as that).

They have a very distinctive black zig-zag pattern down an olive-green back for a female, and a grey back in the male. They hibernate in winter, choosing a rabbit hole or under a rock or roots. Unlike grass snakes, who lay eggs, they give birth to as many as 20 live young in late summer.

The young are venomous and semi-independent from birth but tend to stay together as a family group, finally dispersing after hibernation. Adders can live for ten years but many of their young are predated by birds of prey, crows and even pheasants in the first few weeks of life.

Adders like heath, moorland and wild grassy hillsides, where you will see them basking in the sun. They do this to raise their body temperature sufficiently to become active, although on warm summer days, the air temperature is high enough for them to hunt all day. The two occasions I have seen them at the farm were both in late spring as they sunned themselves on the south-facing slope.

———

Snails

There was a time, if you walked out of our front door after dark on a warm, damp evening, your feet would scrunch over 1000 snails. Torchlight showed them carpeting the ground. They were everywhere. These were all garden snails, long-bodied and with pebble-like shells looking like a distillation of a tortoise. By day, they lived in the hidden dryness of the yew cones and hedges, and because they did not eat the yew or the lawn, there was no other evidence of their presence. But it was spooky.

Snails used to be a big problem here, inflicting all the usual snail damage on the garden. We used to collect them up and put them in a bucket of saltwater, killing them by the hundred. But it was completely ineffectual because snails have a sophisticated way of controlling their growth rate in response to population density. The more slime they come across, the slower they grow. So by removing easy-to-see, catchable adults – that make the most slime – you are merely increasing the rate of growth of the hitherto smaller, slower-growing snails. Or to put it another way, the more I killed, the more the reinforcements came through to fill the gaps.

However you do it – and there is no moral high ground here – the more snails you kill, the more snails you will get. So killing snails – or slugs – is to completely misunderstand their role and place in a garden and in the ecosystem at large. For a start, it achieves nothing. No plant is saved as a result, no good is done. It also perpetuates the misplaced idea of mankind as the controller of nature.

Snails, like slugs, eat decaying plant tissue. However, garden snails and a few slugs have discovered that young seedlings and some garden plants resemble decaying tissue and so are exceptionally good to eat.

In the natural order of things, they would come across these plants infrequently or, in the case of introduced plants like hostas, never. That we provide a vast banquet of the rare delicacies is hardly the snails' fault. To put it another way, if you found that song thrushes had a particular penchant for tulips and ate the buds as they appeared, would you systematically kill every thrush you saw?

As it is, thrushes eat snails – and are the only bird that has evolved a technique for smashing their shells. Ducks will eat snails, too (especially Indian runners and khaki campbells), as will frogs, toads, hedgehogs, carob beetles, centipedes and slowworms. In fact snails are pretty much at the bottom of the food chain, which means that if you use slug pellets, you are damaging a wide range of wildlife.

Cold is the garden snail's greatest enemy and snails used to be surprisingly absent in the colder north, but that is something that climate change is reversing. I marvelled at the quantity of uneaten hostas when I was visiting gardens in Philadelphia but realised that their winters are invariably too harsh for the garden snail.

You could, of course, eat them. Escargots are simply garden snails. They need 'cleansing' first, so catch them and put them in a contained, damp environment for seven to ten days, feeding them grated carrot and water. Then put them on a fast for two days before cooking and eating them. I have not tried this nor do I intend to.

———

Crayfish

I found a large crayfish in the grass – a good 100 yards from the river.

I was amazed at how like a mini-lobster it is. I had imagined it to be shrimp-like but it is five or six inches long, silvery grey with reddish claws and tries to nip Nellie's nose when she investigates.

It is a signal crayfish, an American introduction that has, since it arrived in the mid-1970s, been reaping havoc in waterways like the river and brook that run near us. This is because it eats everything from the native crayfish to frogs, fish and tadpoles, as well as spreading disease. The best analogy with our own crayfish – which are much smaller – is that of the grey squirrel and the red. They are predated upon by otters and mink so presumably the success of the crayfish is helping the rise of otter numbers.

It is illegal to release crayfish back into the waterways so I took it home, put it into a jar of water and went indoors to have a cup of tea and think about how to deal with it. When I came out it had gone. So it either trekked back through the garden and across the field to the river or has set up home in the pond, ready to terrorise the frogs.

———

Tansy

Tansy (*Tanacetum vulgare*) has become the dominant weed in our Dry Garden. In late summer, the stems can be pulled up with a satisfying rip of root from the soil but if left into winter they become like iron and blunt my secateurs when I try to cut them. But despite their robustness and the way that, however many I pull up, just as many return the following year, they hardly spread at all. They are confined to the two borders of the Dry Garden and a few growing by the gate where we park, and I have never found one anywhere else in the garden in over a quarter of a century.

It is not unattractive and I only remove it because it is a thug and muscles out other things that need space around them to be fully appreciated. The flowers are a bright egg-yolk yellow carried in a series of little buttons making a loose plate. The leaves are ferny with a characteristic bitter smell. These leaves are said to kill intestinal worms but I cannot personally vouch for that and, if they taste as they smell, then I will be happy to leave them untried.

It grows in the Dry Garden and in the parking space partly because they are at home where the soil is poor and compacted and the deep, nourished loam in the rest of the garden would be too rich fare for them.

But the Dry Garden backs onto the Walled Garden, which is where the house's vegetable and herb garden was for at least 400 years and I suspect the tansy was grown in there as part of the medicinal armoury that every farmhouse had at its disposal. It was widely used as a catch-all disinfectant to cleanse and purify the body. A tansy cake was traditionally baked at Easter, made from the young leaves mixed with eggs and was thought to purify the blood after the Lenten fast. Tansy juice was rubbed over meat to act as a fly-deterrent and bundles of tansy flowers and leaves were laid on windowsills to stop insects coming in and out of kitchens. The Elizabethans mixed tansy in with the straw of their bedding, presumably to keep the bedbugs away.

So these weeds, bullying their way into our finely tuned borders, are probably fascinating relics of the Tudor apothecary plants that grew in this garden 500 years ago.

Hares

Two hares are in the road in front of me, black tips to their long ears, bodies surprisingly elongated and leggy compared to rabbits. One slipped into the field as I slowed down but the other ran ahead for a few hundred yards before ducking under a gate into a field of uncut wheat.

This is noteworthy because I rarely see hares in the fields around the garden when I take the dogs for a walk. It is not hare country although I do see them on the mountain road, solitary and part of that much bleaker, harsher landscape.

But 50 years ago, walking dogs in the chalk barley fields of north Hampshire, I would expect to see at least one, and often more, every time I went out. Their zig-zagged dash evading anything that my dogs could hope to emulate. I had one particular dog, a labrador called Gretel, who was exceptionally well trained and biddable – unless a hare was involved. I took her with me 40 years ago when I worked as a beater on some

North York grouse moors and for a week she showed up all the expensively trained dogs that the 'guns' had with them. But on the final drive a hare popped up in front of her and she took off after it, yelping in an embarrassing fashion, and was not seen for four hours.

Where rabbits can only aspire to cuteness, hares have always been creatures of mystery and magic, and laden with symbolism in many cultures. Like rabbits, they are not indigenous to Britain but were brought here from Asia some time during the Iron Age. But unlike rabbits, they do not burrow or live communally, their 'forms' are a bare scrape on the ground and they spend much of the day lying low, ears pressed back against their body, camouflaged against the bare soil. The more open the space, the better they can exploit their legendary speed, twisting and doubling back on themselves so that only the fastest and most agile predators have any chance of catching them. They then feed mostly at night, eating exclusively grass and the young green growth of cereal crops.

The young – leverets – are born with eyes open and are fed once a day by their mother for the first month but are otherwise left to fend for themselves. They are heavily predated by foxes and birds of prey but the doe can have three or even four litters between February and September, each of two to four young.

Although hares are largely solitary, in spring and the mating season you can come across groups and gangs of them in a field, 'boxing' on hind legs (usually a female objecting to the overpersistent attentions of a male) and behaving in a skittish manner.

Their numbers have declined substantially in the past 100 years, mainly due to changing agricultural habits and practices such as sowing cereal crops in autumn rather than spring, the use of herbicides and the increase in monocultures. But they are not protected and it is reckoned that about 400,000 are shot every year – partly as sport but also by farmers culling them to limit their consumption of young crops. I would happily shoot rabbits to eat and enjoyed jugged hare many years ago, but to kill one now would seem wrong and inviting bad magic.

———

Grasses

The wild-flower meadow sounds floral – as though a border has escaped the constraints of the garden and broken free to flow like spilled wine across a grassy field – but it is a crop. It is grown for making hay that will be used as fodder for sheep and cattle in winter and early spring when the grass in the fields is not growing. Farmers – and especially dairy farmers – obsess about the exact nutritional value of grass and study it in a detail that the layperson can scarcely imagine. Put very simply, grass contains most nutrition when it is growing fastest, which tends to be from mid-spring to early summer.

Grass is over 80 per cent water and most of the goodness for grazing animals is in the leaf rather than the stem. This has meant that over the last hundred years, farmers have focused on growing perennial ryegrass over other, more stemmy kinds. Ryegrass produces most of its leaves in spring, so to get the maximum nutrition, modern farmers cut it for silage or haylage in spring, let it regrow and repeat the process once or even twice more before autumn when it becomes much more stemmy and therefore has less food value. Then, as the weather cools and drops below 5°C, it does not grow at all. In fact, the temperature range at which grass grows best is remarkably narrow – the ideal temperature is only 10°C. Higher than that, and the rate of growth slows.

To keep growing, grass needs a good deal of sunshine and a constant supply of moisture. This obviously becomes a relationship between how much moisture can be stored in the soil and how often it is replenished by rain. Put all that into the grass-growing equation and you can see why Ireland and Wales are much better for growing grass than East Anglia or the counties of the much drier south-east.

But hayfields do not work like that. They are inimical to modern intensive dairy or meat production. Good hay (as opposed to silage or haylage) is made from a mixture of grasses, all of them rather stemmy, plus, ideally, many other plants or 'herbs' (what the Americans call 'forbs'), some flowering and others foliar. The virtue of this mixture is the potential depth and richness of nutrition but that depends upon skilful haymaking. However, at the very least, hay provides winter roughage which is essential for any ruminant. In a long snowy or frosty period, any farmer other than perhaps a dairy farmer, is more concerned with keeping his animals alive and healthy than with them putting on weight.

Modern ryegrass is the antithesis of a good wild-flower meadow. It is strong-growing, produces leaves that swamp out everything else and tends to be a monoculture. That is very good if you want maximum protein for your herd or flock, but disastrous for wild flowers. In effect, ryegrass is a very successful weed. As well as being the main grass crop for farmers, it is also the main component of sports fields and any tough, hard-wearing lawn as it takes a lot of trampling and mowing and recovers quickly.

So to have a good diverse mix of wild flowers and forbs, you must first reduce the amount and vigour of the grasses – and in particular ryegrass. The best way to do this is to introduce yellow rattle. This, once established, will take nutrients from the ryegrass, which will then quickly start to decline. That allows other grasses and forbs to get established. Then, if the grass is mown and the cut material removed – as bales of hay – the grass loses even more nutrition. A farmer would normally fertilise the field either with artificial nitrogen or manure and would re-seed every five to ten years to re-energise it. But if that is omitted, the ryegrass quickly ceases to be a thug and the conditions for a thriving wild-flower meadow are created.

Whereas the garden was nearly all ryegrass when we came here in 1991 – and the grass paths are still dominated by it – we inherited very little ryegrass on the farm. The fields were too poor and neglected for that. But it gave us a good opportunity to start a wild-flower meadow. Our plan was to get one right and then, when we had really mastered the best way to deal with it given our specific conditions, extend the plan to other fields. But by default, as well as our one sublime flower meadow, most of our fields are now flower-filled without us doing anything at all save harrow, graze and top them.

Our main field grasses are crested dog's-tail, cocksfoot, red fescue, sheep's fescue, bent, sweet vernal grass and Yorkshire fog grass. I like the roll and sway of names from a field of grass that is so easy just to see as one uniform sward. The truth is that if you become closely acquainted with any piece of ground, you soon realise that it varies greatly, even within each field. Our wild-flower meadow has a strip running down one side that is much wetter and has quite distinct flora, and the top half of the slope is different from the lower half because water and nutrients drain down the hill.

The red fescue has soft, shimmering seedheads tinged pink and are almost all stem, with the leaves fine and slim. Sheep's fescue is more tufty and is the most common grass on most hill farms – certainly on ours. Sheep will graze it very short but left for a season, it creates a flowing, wispy sea of delicate plumes.

We have bracken growing at the top of the field for a width of about 20 yards. This tends to spread more readily into fescue grasses but not into the more acid-loving agrostis or molinia grasses that grow higher up the hillside and in patches within individual fields.

Crested dog's tail is extremely good as a component of a wild-flower meadow as it has an upright flower head like a soft ear of corn, and leaves that all come off one side of the stem. It is better at withstanding drought than many grasses but never grows lush and verdant.

Yorkshire fog is so called because the flower heads create a foggy miasma shimmering as a pink haze above the long stems. When dry it is velvety soft but brushing through it when it is wet quickly reduces your trousers to a sodden sponge. A field full of Yorkshire fog is a sure sign of agricultural neglect as it makes poor fodder – but it is an excellent component of a wild-flower meadow.

Cocksfoot has a similarly soft flower head, although the flowers emerge from sideshoots elegantly spaced as though carefully pruned for ikebana. The sweet vernal grass is the first of the grasses to flower, with its chocolate heads turning the field dark brown in May and smelling sweetly of new-mown hay when it is still standing and very un-mown.

Rough meadow grass has sheaths around its leaves and grows well on very heavy or damp land. It is often part of lawn mixes.

Common bent has wide branches topped with rather beautiful, delicate panicles of flower. I remember my father's exasperation as the cylinder mower that left the other grasses in our lawn neatly striped refused to cut the bents, so he would cut it again with a rotary mower to extinguish every stubborn trace of it. But it would always quickly regrow.

Every wild-flower meadow will have its own mixture of grasses adapted to the terrain and as much part of the floral balance as any of the much more feted flowers. But to make it work on anything other than a back-garden scale, it has to be cut and made into hay, then grazed hard over autumn and early spring so that it is inextricably woven into the pulse of the agricultural rhythm.

————

Tawny Owl

The other day I was turning into the lane that leads to our house when I spotted an unusual bird sitting on a fencing post. It was large but fluffy – a ball of white feathers with a few awkwardly sprouting splashes of brown like a cartoon. It had great round eyes that looked at me with curiosity. It then revolved its head a full 180 degrees and flew off with silent wings. It was a young tawny owl, still alarmingly vulnerable but clearly fully-fledged and free from the nest.

Although we do not see them that often because they spend most of the daylight hours camouflaged against the tree trunks, there are a lot of owls around us. The garden rings to the calls of tawnies all year but especially from late summer into autumn, when the young are leaving to find their own territories. But for the rest of summer the young will remain close to the nest, learning to hunt and mastering their incredibly silent, dexterous flight.

Some nights a silhouetted figure will perch on a wigwam of bean sticks in the garden and screech with shocking loudness before slipping anonymously away. For such a big bird, tawny owls fly with the muffled softness of a falling snowflake. Their night sight is good but their hearing is better and they will unerringly locate the slightest rustle and the scurrying mouse will be clutched in their powerful talons before the victim has heard a thing.

Some 30 years ago, at our last house, I found a pair of young owls at the base of a large walnut tree we had. They had clearly fallen from the nest so I took them in and started to feed them every few hours with mince. But I was quickly advised to return them to the spot where I discovered them as the parents would find and feed them on the ground and in any event, the fledglings might well half-scramble, half-fly back up the tree. They certainly survived – and screeched and hooted loudly outside our bedroom window for hour upon hour that long, hot summer. I would find them in the day, pressed up against the stems of the apple trees in the orchard, their plumage a rage of brown, ochre and cream, and their eyes a deep, dark, staring purple.

When I was at boarding school in the early 1960s, the matron adopted a similar young owl and it would sit on her head as she walked round the dormitories, nibbling on her grey hair and pulling it gently in its beak. One night it swooped in through the open window of my dormitory and sat on the end of my bed, shifting its feet and looking round with its swivel head. Then, as suddenly and quietly as it came, it flitted, moth-like, back out into the dark of the night.

You never forget such things.

——

Heath Bedstraw

In just one field on the farm there is a patch, perhaps 30ft or so long and roughly 12ft deep, of tiny white flowers that form a mat on the steep slope. This was dense bracken when we came and I remember the acute anxiety of cutting through it for the first time with the tractor. The angle of the slope and the height of the bracken were such that all I could see above was sky – with no sense of how steep the slope was, what the terrain was like or where I was going other than onwards until I reached the top.

Gradually, the bracken has diminished and although it is still there, the grass dominates and the animals graze it well. As a result, these small white flowers of heath bedstraw (*Galium saxatile*) now have a home they like. Added to which, the steepness of the slope means that the goodness is washed out by the constant rain on this distinctly thin, acidic soil, sitting just inches over the rock, so you have heath bedstraw's ideal growing conditions – all at its preferred upland altitude of about 1300ft.

My lack of familiarity with the tiny flower is all to do with the soil. My formative years were spent on chalk, which literally shaped my world-view. Everything I looked at, everything I smelled, even the sound that plants made, were dictated by the pH of the chalky soil of north Hampshire. The fields flowed silkily with barley rather than rustled stolidly with wheat. Beeches and yews were the yard-sticks to measure big trees by and hazel, field maples, spindle and ashes were everywhere. If I saw an oak tree it was invariably *Quercus robur* rather than *Q. petraea*, the sessile oak, which is only really happy on acidic soil. Every field was lapidary with the glassy black of plough-broken flint, and chalk lay as a solid seam a foot or so under the surface.

All kinds of wild flowers loved this – harebells, wild marjoram, poppies, cornflowers, cowslips – the list is long. But some, such as heath woodruff, heathers, devil's bit scabious, ragged robin, foxgloves and sheep's sorrel are happier with some acidity. So the world begins to be framed around flowers, trees, crops and grasses that seem innumerable and common but which are actually very specific to the particular ground beneath your feet.

That is a roundabout way of explaining why I was not familiar with heath bedstraw but the far-reaching effects of geology on my whole outlook on life always stagger me.

———

Vole Holes

The long grass on the bank of the Mound was cut for the first time since last October, the foliage of the daffodils all completely died back and the wild flowers seeded. Once it was all cleared away and taken to the compost heap it revealed just the bleached roots of the grass tufted amongst a lot of exposed soil. To the uninitiated, it is a scene of devastation but this is exactly what was expected and wanted because the seeds of the flowers will only germinate if they have direct contact with the earth.

On closer inspection you could see that the banks were covered in small, round holes, each about an inch in diameter. Standing there with the film crew between takes for *Gardeners' World*, I noticed a single little eye looking out from one of these holes. A minute later, there were two eyes and then a nose. Then a little face appeared, ears tucked against the sides of the hole before, eventually, the full head of a vole peeked out into this newly exposed world. It took one look at us, we took another look at it, and then it suddenly darted out and up into the border above it.

When the grass is long – from late March until August – it provides the perfect cover and environment for voles. Their burrows are completely hidden and they can come and go unseen, the grass a thicket in which they can rummage, relatively protected from their many predators.

By the end of the week, the grass had started to grow again and the vole holes merged into the green.

———

AUGUST

Wild Thyme

'I know a bank where the wild thyme blows'.

On a steep, south-facing bank above the farmhouse is a clump of wild thyme. The rosy, lavender flowers are buzzing with bees and in the hot sunshine this little patch of Welsh hillside is filled with the rich fragrance of the Mediterranean.

This is *Thymus polytrichus*, which is big on scent but low on flavour. Unlike the wild mint that grows just a few yards away in a constantly wet ditch, wild thyme is no culinary substitute for *T. vulgaris*. It is a very localised oddity on this hillside because it does not like acidic soil and only really thrives in two spots. One is here, on this steep bank. Thin strands of grass grow in amongst the thyme but the soil barely covers the slabbed strata of red sandstone and only the thyme is really at home. The stone gets very warm in midsummer and lizards bask there in the sun, heads raised like retirees working on their tan on Miami Beach.

The other spot where we get thyme is in one particular field that we call, unimaginatively, 'the anthill field'. This is because it is dimpled with hundreds of hummocks made by yellow ants. Each hummock is about 2ft across and about the same in height, and the ants have converted the soil to a fine powder. On top of this, as well as grass, grows thyme, sitting on the hillocks as if on raised beds, free-draining, sunny and relishing the position it finds itself in.

———

Kingfisher

For eighteen years we had two identical twin cat brothers. They were Burmese–farm cat crosses, jet black with the sleek slinkiness of a Burmese and the murderous efficiency of a farm cat. The only way of telling them apart was to hold them upside down. It was a high-risk tactic because although one brother, Blue, loved it and would relax completely, the other, Stimpy, hated it and would try and bite you as hard as he could. They fought daily but always slept in each other's arms. Blue died first and Stimpy, the fierce warrior, was lost without him and died a month or so later. Both are buried in the coppice.

Both were expert killers. Blue specialised in mammals and Stimpy in birds. I have watched Stimpy leap to pluck a swallow, arriving exhausted from South Africa, from the sky, maim it and then walk away, bored. One day he arrived in the kitchen with a kingfisher in his mouth. How he had caught it is inconceivable but there it was, very alive still but clearly not appreciating being clamped in Stimpy's jaws.

Sarah extricated it from the cat and held it in her hands. It was an astonishing thing – the shimmering turquoise and flame blue of its head and back, the black beak – half woodpecker, half gannet – the orange triangle behind the eye, and, just glimpsed within the protective basket of Sarah's fingers, the astonishing orange of its breast. No other British bird burns so bright and yet it is so rare to see a kingfisher at all – let alone held in hand in the kitchen. We do see them occasionally down by the river, more often a quick flash of dark bird darting across the water or disappearing into the depths of a tree than a display in full colour.

Both male and female kingfishers are equally brightly, not to say gaudily, coloured. Apart from the astonishing electric blue of their backs and wings, they have more orange than any other British bird. The combination makes them unlike anything else and instantly recognisable – which seems to be the point. The only evolutionary reason for their brilliant colour seems to be so they can recognise themselves.

They start to pair at the end of February but before they commit to the relationship, there is the nest to build – or rather excavate – within the territory that the male has established and defended over winter. These nests, well above the waterline but a foot or two down the bank, are tunnels leading to a nesting chamber and involve both birds, although the male does most of the digging, using his beak woodpecker-style and, as he gets deeper into the soil, wriggling backwards to push the excavations out with his tail. Once they have dug horizontally for 2ft to 3ft, they make a chamber to lay the eggs in, big enough for them to turn round and leave beak first for the first time in a week's digging. The kingfishers' nests that I have seen on a sheer bank of the river at the edge of our garden must have flooded many times, although as long as it remains dry for any two consecutive months between April and August they can raise a brood.

All this work is a big investment for the male because the female will only consent to mate when the nest is complete – and then not always. But if the relationship prospers the first egg is laid by mid-April and will hatch before the end of the month. The chicks are completely blind and helpless initially but the parents bring them vast quantities of fish until they leave the nest, which they will do around the end of May.

Kingfishers hunt from a perch, diving down onto fish like gannets, plucking them from the water with their beaks rather than spearing them. They then stun the fish with a whack on a branch or stone, turn them so they are head-first and ready to present to a chick's beak for swallowing and return to the nest.

It has been calculated that each chick gets a fish about every 50 minutes during the day and there are usually five or six chicks per brood. That amounts to a busy time for the parents, with a total of over a hundred fish to catch and take back every day – as well as what they need to eat themselves. Once the chicks have fledged and are ready to shuffle down the tunnel from the nest to the river bank, they do so all together and never return. That is the end of their parental nurturing. Their introduction to the outside world is short and harsh. Other than a few days being taught how to dive and fish, the parents actively drive them away so they have to fend for themselves within days of leaving the nest. This is because the parents will start the next brood almost immediately and often have three clutches in a summer, sometimes reusing the same nest – which becomes a disgusting slurry of fish bones and faeces – or making a new one. Either way, it is intense, hard work for the parent birds.

Although this means that briefly, for a month or two in late summer, there are an unusual amount of kingfishers about, the mortality rate is very high. The young have to go and find a new territory, establish it and survive the winter, then find a mate and breed themselves. If you see a kingfisher in your garden in late summer it will almost certainly be a young one looking for its territory.

All birds are directly connected to habitat and place, and kingfishers are birds of tree-flanked rivers and streams. The preservation and care of that very specific habitat is essential for kingfishers to remain in the British countryside. The other main environmental threat is agricultural fertiliser run-off that devastates the fish population and thus impacts disastrously on kingfishers. Disturbance, by humans, dogs, wild animals or farm machinery is also a problem. The parents are triggered to fish by the young cheeping from within the tunnel. If the parents are disturbed, they will avoid the nest, the chicks will get too weak to cheep so the parents stay away even longer, and the young can starve.

But even in the ideal environment, kingfisher life can be nasty, brutish and very short indeed. It is reckoned that only half of the fledglings survive their first two weeks and less than a quarter make it through to breed the next year as they are prey not just to cats but to rats, mink, pike, otters, stoats, weasels and sparrow-hawks, as well as to hunger. The average life expectancy is just two years, which explains the birds' need to breed with such frantic intensity.

However, the story of the kingfisher brought into our kitchen had a happy ending. We took it down to the river bank, released it at the water's edge and it darted off strongly, chirping thinly. I like to think that having escaped Stimpy's jaws, it survived to breed the next year and that its descendants are still hunting along the river now.

———

Feverfew

The acrid tang of feverfew clings to the beds around the house. It has hardly spread into the wider garden but remains firmly anchored to the Dry Garden, the Walled Garden and the Herb Garden at the back. I think of it as another of the Tudor ghosts that continue to haunt the place, originally part of the medicine cabinet of plants that every farmhouse would have had growing, and now as much part of the household as the timbers and the stones.

Feverfew has little white daisy flowers with yellow centres, carried on spindly stems with pale yellowy green leaves that are strongly aromatic. I am not sure if I like the smell but it is instantly recognisable. Once smelled, never forgotten.

Feverfew was universally used for migraines, headaches and for reducing fevers – hence its name – and is not a native plant but was introduced in the Middle Ages from the Balkans. The woman we bought the house from 30 years ago – who had lived here for the previous 70 years – used to eat it in sandwiches when she had a headache. I find it very bitter but am assured that it is good for digestion.

It is unfussy where it grows, popping up through cobbles and along the margins of walls, flowering from midsummer into autumn, the leaves ready to provide relief should a migraine strike, just as they have provided relief for occupants of this house for the past 700-odd years.

———

Wasps

It is hard to find many good words to say about wasps at this time of year. They seem to infiltrate the garden in a stripy infestation, appearing at the hint of any outdoor meal, or a single wasp terrorising entire households by buzzing menacingly around the room.

Bees only sting as a last resort, mostly if they feel the hive is threatened, and as an act of ultimate self-sacrifice because they kill themselves in the process. Wasps, however, will attack, seemingly unprovoked, and can sting repeatedly. Bees are noble and endangered and are supported by numerous charities (of one of which, Bees for Development, I am a proud patron) but wasps are just scary.

Bees provide honey and pollination, and without bees, the human race would quickly starve. But what are wasps *for*? Ignoring the absurdity of this human-centric question, they are actually *for* quite a lot. For most of their lives wasps are dedicated carnivores, eating so-called garden pests such as caterpillars and aphids. That alone justifies their existence as part of a balanced, organic garden. It is only in late summer that they develop their sweet tooth and that coincides with both the ripening of fruits in our gardens and a glut of worker wasps that have finished their nest-building duties and are thus free to hunt for sugar in any form. It is a perfect waspy storm. This was never illustrated more graphically to me than when a couple of years ago, the grapes in my greenhouse hosted thousands of wasps – with ten or more on each grape until every last one was devoured.

And as well as predating on garden pests, wasps are part of the food chain, providing a tasty treat for badgers, buzzards and especially spiders which are, perhaps surprisingly, their biggest and most deadly enemy.

Britain has eight kinds of social wasps including the hornet. They all build exquisitely beautiful nests, made from chewed wood pulp, that are astonishingly light but strong enough to house thousands of wasps and their eggs. Each one of these delicate, complex constructions is a little wasp township and a miracle of ingenuity.

But another 230 species of non-social kinds live almost solitary lives. They have many guises and lifestyles but most are digger wasps that have hammer heads and very narrow waists. They excavate holes in dry banks which they provision with live prey – usually caterpillars and aphids but also flies and beetles and even bees.

Only the female stings – male wasps exist only to breed – and her sting is smooth so can be retracted, allowing her to sting repeatedly – and if trapped, she will do so. Wasp stings contain a protein known as antigen 5, which some people can react to violently, going into anaphylactic shock which needs immediate treatment. But they are the unlucky few and for most of us, a wasp sting can be eased with vinegar or an ice cube. It hurts like hell but does no damage. Only one or two people die each year in the UK from the combination of both wasp and bee stings – which is about the same number that are killed by lightning.

———

Meadowsweet

The first few years of owning the farm was a process of perpetual discovery. Every season, every week, bringing new threads to the story of the place and I devoured them insatiably, walking and rewalking every inch, trying to take in as much as I possibly could.

I spent hours every evening researching the history of every aspect of the place, from the type of carts used in the seventeenth century to the vocal variations of birdsong. I went through the inventories of every occupant since records began, sifting through the bedding and copper pots, the good chairs and the three little ricks of hay, the oxen and the sundry tools, like an archaeologist. It was detective work, slowly accumulating evidence and also an obsessive love affair. I stalked my own territory, looking for the slightest clues that tied our bond tighter. This love affair has never waned and, if anything, has grown with every year of greater familiarity.

That first August I found one small patch of meadowsweet growing in a damp hollow in what we call the Top Wood. The feather-duster plumes of ivory flowers were held on long, carmine stems and the leaves, distinctive for their deeply veined, elm-like form and thin, elegant stems, have poise neither drooping nor dominating. This was the most far-flung, wildest bit of the farm and seemingly the least grazed.

I have no memory of meadowsweet (*Filipendula ulmaria*) in the chalk-and-flint countryside of my youth and I have never really clocked it as a wild flower, although in the garden, I have long grown *F. rubra* 'Venusta' – the American prairie plant that is like our wild flower but 6ft tall and less dependent on moisture to flourish. Finding this little patch felt like a real discovery – akin to coming across one or two orchids in the corner of a field.

In fact, meadowsweet grows profusely and easily when allowed to and now we have it growing widely in all the dampest ungrazed parts of the farm. It was used medicinally for thousands of years as a decoction to ease pain, and at the end of the nineteenth century, it was discovered that salicylic acid – hitherto only available from willow bark – could be extracted from the plant and made into a powder. Meadowsweet was then classed as a spiraea, so this new compound was given a name made up of the 'a' of acetylic acid and the 'spi' of spiraea to form 'aspirin'.

The name meadowsweet – so evocative and resonant of flower-filled hay meadows – probably refers to the flavour – slightly almondy – it added when infused in mead and you are as likely to find it growing in woodland or ditches as in a meadow, unless the latter has a particularly damp patch. It has long been used to add fragrance to rooms, either by strewing on the floor or as a bunch of the flowers in a vase, but I find its honeyed, marzipan smell rather sickly and not entirely pleasant – but then, I dislike marzipan.

———

August Night

The owls are busy outside in the warm dark. A few males and some females. How do I know that? Could it be just one of each, moving around and calling to each other? But there seem to be different tones to the males' 'whoos' and variances in the females' 'kee-wicks'. And in amongst them there is the insistent – actually rather irritating – demanding screech of the fledged young. A family perhaps.

———

Grass Snakes

By mid-August, turning the compost heaps will usually reveal a grass snake within the warmest depths. They show their annoyance by beating as hasty a retreat as they can, slipping between or under the boards that make up the insides of the heap. This is alarming or exciting according to your take on snakes. I accept that many people are frightened and alarmed just at the sight of one but I am delighted that we have grass snakes in the garden. In a recent survey of wildlife in back gardens, the two least frequently observed creatures were weasels and grass snakes. I was not surprised by the lack of weasels – they are small, like cover and not very common in gardens – but it seemed both surprising and sad that grass snakes featured so little.

We also find their eggs in the compost heap from midsummer – the female is there not for herself but to lay eggs. In fact, grass snakes are the only British snakes that do lay eggs – the two other native species, adders and smooth snakes, give birth to live young. Grass snake eggs look like an aggregation of puffballs, a mass of white leathery eggs stuck together in a bulbous sack. Later in the year we find these eggs empty and shrivelled and, if we are lucky, the young still there. The snakes also use the compost heaps as a hibernation place, retreating into one in October and only emerging when the weather warms up in April.

When they hatch they are pencil-sized, but females – bigger than males – will grow to reach 5ft long with the thickness of a slim wrist and are Britain's largest snake. A fully grown grass snake has beautiful markings – a distinctive yellow chevron behind its head with a black band, and olive-green skin flecked with black. They live a long time – 20 to 25 years is not uncommon.

They can bite but are not venomous and if they cannot get away from you are likely to play dead and give off a repulsive smell rather than attack you. However, you are much more likely to glimpse one gliding sinuously away from you into cover. In a good year, we can see them almost daily in the garden, often gliding across a path when disturbed by the vibration of our approaching footsteps.

The reason that we have grass snakes in the garden is as much due to our proximity to the river and the two ponds in the garden as anything else. They like water and I have seen them slipping in and out of the pond. One of the reasons for their decline – numbers have dropped hugely in the past 50 years – is the demise of the farm pond, which used to be present not just in every farmyard but in many fields for animals to drink from. Now piped water and drinking troughs mean that most have long been filled in.

They eat frogs, toads, newts, birds, eggs, mice and voles, and swallow their prey whole and often alive, letting digestion do the rest. They also have quite a few predators – buzzards, herons, crows and owls, especially when the snakes are young and small enough to fly away with.

———

Swifts Leaving

14 August. About ten swifts raced across the garden sky this morning, like an aerial display team, heading south. They were not, like the busy, crowded martins and swallows, playing the barometer and hunting the insects where the pressure took them, but flying straight and with real purpose. They were going home.

This is the first shutter closing on summer. The cuckoo has gone already, unseen and increasingly unheard. But the swift's departure feels like the first – and premature – sign of summer ending. They have never been anything like as present here as swallows or martins, and have become increasingly rare visitors above the garden, seen only every few weeks, whereas 25 years ago they were a daily presence between May and the end of July.

Unlike swallows and martins in summer or fieldfares and redwings in winter, which leave such a gap when they go, swifts always come into our sky from somewhere else, so there is no sense that they belong here, no intimacy. We borrow them for a few short months and today they have taken themselves back.

———

Buzzards

The baby buzzards are soaring unsteadily above the garden like a plane coming in to land in a heavy wind, wings tilting and seesawing. They are full-size, big hawks and yet still babies with a distinctive high-pitched whistling, plaintive call. Whereas the adult bird has an instantly recognisable haunting, mewing call, a cry as old and wise as the wind, the young have an incongruous half-whistle, half-mew that always has a note of alarm, like a child learning to ride a bike.

We always have a nest on the farm in one of the taller ashes or alders, but never in the same tree in subsequent years. From mid-July the young, fully fledged and chicken-big, step out of the nest onto the branches and call for the parents to come and feed them. I watched as one made its first flight, the parent repeatedly approaching the nesting tree without landing until finally, the young buzzard launched into the air and then was away and up into the sky with surprising ease and elegance until it tried to manoeuvre and almost became tangled in its own wings, called with its baby cry and needed consolation from the parent. But it was away and could take to the valley skies.

They continue flying very locally until October, learning to hunt although still fed by the parents to top up their own often inadequate returns and then leave the nesting area to find their own territory.

An adult buzzard, with big, broad wings held in a shallow 'V', rides the air with lazy mastery. Crows chase and harry them away but the buzzard avoids them with an easy flick or twist and does not seem to pay them any mind. I have often observed that crows chase buzzards and sparrowhawks as far as an almost determined line in the air, but once across this invisible boundary the threat disappears and they turn back, all necessary defending done.

In the middle of the day buzzards will find the thermals and slowly circle higher and higher until they disappear to the naked eye. It seems that alone amongst raptors, buzzards are very territorial and the soaring that so typifies their flight is often a territorial display. Studies show that the defended area averages about 400 acres per pair but there is also a buffer zone or no-man's-land between territories that can be half as big again and is undefended and to some extent communal. In September I have often seen five or six birds soaring together, which must be parents and fully grown offspring as one family unit.

In my Hampshire youth, I would occasionally see the odd buzzard, always very high in the sky, and treat it as a red-letter day. But they have spread westwards over the past 50 years and are now one of the most common birds of prey, visible in almost all rural areas. This is partly due to the lack of persecution but also to the demise of myxomatosis – that had deprived them of their rabbit prey between the 1950s and late 1980s. In fact, buzzards will eat almost anything on land, and will catch birds, although, despite being big and powerful, they are slow fliers and unlikely to catch anything in an aerial chase.

I have seen four or five waddling around the fields after the flooding has just gone down, picking up frogs and worms left high and dry. They will also hover, not in the high-winged manner of a kestrel but gently, quite low, wings held bent against the wind, hardly seeming to make any movement at all, before dropping onto their prey. I often watch buzzards on the crest of the hill above us, catching the updraught, facing the wind, holding still in the air for a few moments before pouncing and, as often as not, rising almost immediately to repeat the whole operation again and again.

They are hunting for voles in the long, windswept, hilltop grasses and may make a dozen unsuccessful attempts for each kill. They eat as many as 20 voles in a day, so will make hundreds of these hovering mini-dives. But they mostly hunt from a perch, either a branch of a tree at the edge of a field or often from a telegraph pole. In winter, when the hedges are cut and bare of leaves, it is not unusual to see buzzards perched on the flat top of a dense hedge, ready to pounce.

For some reason, Nellie regards buzzards as something between a rabbit and a thrown stick. If they rise up from a field or are even flying low overhead, she will charge off in pursuit. Despite their taking to the air, she will follow them like a child running after a rising kite, until even she can see that they are too high, too far, and the whole enterprise become too absurd. But she will do exactly the same next time, probably to the same bird, who shows remarkable tolerance and lack of concern at the whole pantomime.

———

Ragwort

If you have been brought up with grazing animals – and I realise that excludes almost all the population – then you have learned from the cradle that ragwort is an enemy to be eradicated at every opportunity. It is to farmers what hemlock is to gardeners, only much more common. The reason for this opprobrium is that it contains alkaloids that can cause irreversible and often fatal liver damage to cattle and horses. Yet it is a handsome plant with a spray of yellow daisy flowers held on a tall stem from midsummer to autumn, and is really important for pollinating insects and butterflies. Over 200 species of pollinating insects use it, with 30 depending upon it exclusively, and it is visited by more butterflies than any other UK plant.

Ragwort is a biennial and a member of the senecio family, (although now classified as *Jacobaea vulgaris*), and has a preference for heavily grazed pasture and wasteland, so is often eaten because there are few tempting alternatives. Also the toxic effect is cumulative, so there is no way of judging how damaging it is until it is too late. But where there is adequate grass horses and cattle will rarely touch it because it is bitter.

Curiously, even though horses were once essential for day-to-day life, both agriculturally and for all forms of transport, there is no record of ragwort being regarded as a dangerous poison until the twentieth century. In general it seems that more heat than light has been generated about its danger to livestock.

But as a boy, I remember being dragooned into walking through fields and pulling ragwort out of the ground by the roots and stuffing the ravaged plants into a fertiliser sack tied across my shoulders with a piece of old baler twine. In fact, there is evidence that pulling the flowering plants merely stimulates the remaining sections of root in the ground to produce more plants. Also there are at least as many cases of poisoning from dried plants, usually cut with hay, as live ones, since it is just as toxic dead as alive.

Climate change and warmer winters will reduce ragwort because it depends upon a period of cold in winter to trigger flowering. It also dies after flowering and setting seed, and needs bare soil to germinate – although seed can remain viable for over fifteen years if buried, then be triggered into germination by cultivation.

———

Shrews

Sooner or later everyone has an encounter with a mouse, but unless you have a cat you are much less likely to see a shrew, even though there are an estimated 43 million common shrews in the British Isles and another ten million pigmy shrews. Cats catch them regularly and deposit the little bodies disdainfully on the doormat because they soon find that they are unpleasant to eat – but that does not stop them catching more. Although cats will not eat shrews, they are widely predated by barn and tawny owls, kestrels, weasels, stoats and foxes.

Unlike mice or voles, shrews have pointed snouts and tiny pinprick eyes, and seem to be as much mole as mouse. What I did not know until writing this is that they have red teeth. Unlike mice and voles they are entirely carnivorous and eat worms, insects, spiders, slugs and snails, and occasionally each other. They do so with huge energy as they have to eat every couple of hours in order to sustain their metabolism and consume about 90 per cent of their body weight every day. So a morning without food for them is death by starvation, and on the days when by cruel circumstance I have to miss breakfast, I can share their pain. Although they do not hibernate over winter they do – amazingly – shrink, so need less food to maintain their reduced bodies. This shrinkage extends to their liver, brain and other vital organs as well as their muscle mass.

I occasionally come across them in the garden when I am weeding and disturb one that will skitter away in pursuit of a beetle or other prey. Although their tiny eyes mean that their sight is poor, they have an extremely good sense of smell and are as happy hunting at night as they are during the day. Their saliva contains toxins that stupefy their prey, and whilst they exist mainly on small insects that they can dispatch quickly, tests have shown that this toxin is powerful enough to kill a rabbit in five minutes with a single bite.

Their lives are lived at a frenetic pace. They never move slowly, never pause to reflect or digest. Their metabolism burns furiously, with a heart rate of about 800 beats per minute and the ability to make over ten separate movements per second. It is not surprising then that their average lifespan is about a year and a two-year-old shrew is an example of extreme old age.

This short, rather manic life is made up of a lot of eating, a little sleeping, some fighting to preserve territory – they are extremely aggressive – and quite a lot of breeding. In one summer, they can have four litters of five to seven young, which they will rear in an underground nest. They are good burrowers and spend quite a lot of time underground. The young are occasionally seen in a shrew chain, each one holding the tail of the one in front in its snout, with the mother at the head of this caravan, leading them to a place of safety.

Pygmy shrews are even smaller – about an inch and a half long and weighing about the same as a 1p coin with a long tail. Inside this tiny frame is a spirit that is fiercely bellicose and there are a number of times when I have seen one clinging onto a cat's paw with its teeth while the cat tried to shake it off even though the cat was about a hundred times bigger. Pygmy shrews spend less time below ground than the common shrew and will sometimes climb into bushes and hedgerows after prey.

——

Rosebay Willowherb

By mid-August, the tall stems of the rosebay willowherb are topped with a loose pennant of dozens of magenta-pink flowers and are as tough as steel hawsers. They can quickly blunt the blade of a scythe and reduce strimming cable to tatters.

It does not appear in our garden but on the hillside on the farm, where it is a weed of sorts although not entirely unwelcome. It grows everywhere there is waste land – you most typically see it on railway sidings – but apparently it was quite a rare woodland plant until the beginning of the twentieth century. It is not a native but was introduced to gardens and then, sometime around the middle of the eighteenth century, escaped and started to grow in the wild. But this was mainly in rocky, stony places and as recently as 1888 was described as 'not often met in the wild state but common in gardens'.

Like foxgloves, rosebay willowherb is one of the plants that suddenly appears after a plantation or woodland has been felled, and the huge quantity of timber that was felled during the First World War probably promoted its dramatic expansion. Then after the Second World War, it became a feature of every blitzed bomb site.

Every plant produces tens of thousands of seeds, each with a plume of tiny hairs that help it float in a wispy cloud. Like buddleia, its appearance on railway sidings is down to the seed being sucked along by the draught from passing trains and deposited along the shingly sidings, where it very happily germinates and grows.

It particularly likes sites where there has been a fire and my hillside population – growing where 150 years ago there was oak coppice – probably marks the locations of charcoal fires. As such it is another of the floral ghosts that are found all over the British landscape, especially where woods and hedges have been cleared.

You can apparently make a drinkable tea from the fermented leaves – if you get them before the elephant hawk's caterpillars have eaten them. These are large and look like an elephant's trunk – giving the name to the very un-elephantine but gorgeous pink and gold moth.

———

Dragonflies

It is extraordinary the way that dragonflies appear when you make a pond in your garden. It does not matter how small or simple it is, you can guarantee that within hours a dragonfly will be zipping across its surface adding its jewel-like lustre to the garden.

The larger dragonflies – as opposed to the similar but slimmer damselflies – are divided into two groups, the hawkers that will spend hours on the wing patrolling a stretch of river or pond, and the darters that spend most of their time perched and whipping out to ambush prey before returning to their perch to consume them.

However, very little of a dragonfly's life is actually spent either hawking or darting. The female dragonfly lays her eggs on a plant in water or even directly into the water itself. The eggs hatch into nymphs that look like little beetles that scuttle about the water, where they can remain for up to four years, becoming larger, occasionally devouring each other and gradually maturing. Then, when fully mature, a nymph waits for warmer weather before crawling up a plant and shedding its skin to reveal the young dragonfly lurking within.

It will take about two days for the iridescence of its wings to fully emerge and then it hunts for food for a frantic two months before dying. Its flight can be very fast – faster than any other insect – with speeds clocked at 35 mph.

So what we see is the gloriously speeded-up culmination of a life spent largely underwater. But the ponds in our gardens should have up to four successive generations of nymphs, ready to emerge and shine for their bright, brief time in the sun.

———

Hobby

When I was a boy, my fascination with birds of prey was based not just on the bloodlust of these finely tuned killing machines – attractive as that was (like every small boy of my generation, I was brought up on war comics and films, so birds of prey were easily categorised as another deadly, swooping weapon with which to bash the Boche) – but also on their rarity. I read about them avidly but hardly ever actually saw them. Kestrels were common (alas no more) but all other birds of prey were rare or non-existent. During the mid-1970s, the occasional buzzard appeared as an exotic visitor from the west. But that was about it.

I read about falcons and hawks, harriers, ospreys and eagles as perhaps others read about far and distant lands filled with treasures. I would pore for hours over pictures of these birds and could recite by heart all their individual vagaries of nesting and choice of diet, and the arcane niceties of falconry.

But no bird seemed more fleetingly possible to actually see than the hobby (*Falco subbuteo*). It was, I read, a bird of heath and scattered wood – very different from the chalk and flint agricultural landscape around me. It was, my bird books informed me, a summer visitor and there were as few as a hundred pairs nesting in a small number of suitable places like the New Forest.

I knew that although the hobby could not hover like the kestrel, nor had the jet-plane speed of the peregrine, it was manoeuvrable like no other raptor and could catch dragonflies, swallows and bats in mid-flight, eat them in the air or exchange them at nesting time with its mate. I knew that it had a moustachial stripe, which distinguished it from the kestrel, looked like a giant swift in flight and only called in the mating season. I knew that they laid late, not starting until mid-June, with the eggs hatching in mid-July and the fledglings not leaving the nest till mid to late August. And for 60 years, all this knowledge remained entirely second-hand.

Then a few years ago I was in the garden in late summer, looked up and saw, with a stab of recognition, a hobby. It was flying casually, in a kind of aerial saunter. When identifying birds you always go through a process of elimination, like a flow chart. Is it a bird of prey? Yes. A falcon rather than a hawk? Yes. That narrows it to peregrine, hobby, kestrel or merlin. Too slim and elegant for a peregrine, too big for a merlin and somehow, although the same size and colour, not a kestrel. Longer, more pointed wings. But more than that, there was a certain lazy swagger in its flight that stemmed from supreme confidence like Viv Richards coming in to bat. It owned the sky and nothing was too fast or agile to escape.

It circled a few times, took in the possibilities of the busy martins – which became hysterical and flew in a distracting, convoluted mass before half-heartedly mobbing it. Then it perched on the roof of the potting shed and I saw, as clear as day, his moustachial stripes and splendid orange thighs. I felt blessed.

Since then, the hobbies have come back every year – they must be nesting nearby – and I see them more and more often, although it could never be often enough. They – it is usually only one but sometimes a pair – will return at the same time each day, nine-ish in the morning and then again in late afternoon, and circle the sky like sharks in a bay. Occasionally they will suddenly slice down the sky, diving at a martin or swallow, twisting and following every evasive dodge. I find myself longing for them to succeed in this even though I adore their prey.

They too head south in autumn and return in spring, so are part of summer's riches. Things ain't what they used to be in so many ways and the world is going to hell in a handcart – but I have hobbies that visit me in my garden and that makes up for almost everything.

Bindweed

A number of living things such as slugs, wasps, mare's tail, and bindweed make an awful lot of gardeners ask what on earth is the point of these plants and creatures that seem to only do harm without any balancing benefit?

But of course that is to cast everything in a human-centric mould. The only reason that anything exists is to continue existing. The most successful species are those that best and most readily reproduce themselves, which tends to be a measure of adaptability. If we create an environment where slugs and bindweed can flourish, then we can hardly look for any reason.

There are two types of bindweed, field and hedge. Field bindweed (*Convolvulus arvensis*) has much smaller, heart-shaped leaves with small, button-sized flowers, white with pale pink stripes. The flowers close with a twist at night and in bad weather. Its roots go down over 15ft and it can spread horizontally up to 30 square yards over the course of a growing season. As the name suggests, it grows in arable fields and in cultivated ground in gardens and allotments, where it can become a really difficult weed to remove without resorting to herbicides – which I will not do.

Hedge bindweed (*Calystegia sepium*) was the weed of our Jewel Garden and has fleshier roots that grow less deep but with extraordinary vigour, forming a great mass of spaghetti-like tangles in the ground with individual roots growing 10ft long. The leaves and flowers are bigger and it twines up any plant that will support it, then invariably smothers and suppresses or often kills it by excluding all light. In flower, it is beautiful and were it not so invasive we would celebrate it. The flowers are more robust than those of its field cousin and sometimes a bright full moon will stimulate them to stay open all night, but otherwise twist into a closed cone before reopening into their trumpet shape in the sun. They are pollinated by insects, including bees, and the larvae of the convolvulus hawk moth feed on the leaves.

Hedge bindweed is easy and extremely satisfying to pull out of other plants as it comes away in long ropes. But that does little to stop its spread. The real problem with both types as a garden weed – hedge bindweed is more common in gardens, with field bindweed in allotments – is that the roots are so very brittle. They will snap into pieces as you try and remove them, and then every single piece, however small, will make a new plant. Forking over idly, taking out the odd bits and pieces of root you can see, tends to only make matters worse. You have to be very, very thorough and get every last scrap out of the ground if at all possible. And if the roots were not problem enough, the seeds have extraordinary dormancy, able to remain in the soil for 40 years or more, waiting for the right conditions to germinate. This usually happens when the hard outer coating is damaged or softened sufficiently, with mechanical cultivation suiting those purposes admirably.

The Jewel Garden became infested with bindweed at one stage and eventually we dug out every plant, washed the roots under a hose to remove all soil and every possible scrap of bindweed root, potted them all up and then systematically dug over each of the eight beds, removing every trace of root we could find. Then we replanted. There is still bindweed there of course – we missed some and some was entwined in the roots of the hedges and trees – but at least we got on top of it and now it is manageable.

If it is a comfort to gardeners, neither type of bindweed grows in deep shade or uncultivated ground. If field bindweed appears in a freshly sown lawn, a season or two of mowing will weaken it beyond recovery.

Weasels

Although I see them crossing the road fairly frequently, dashing from bank to bank in the back lanes, I have only once seen a weasel in the garden when a little russet-backed creature snaked out from the back of the border on the Long Walk and skittled into the hedge behind the grass borders.

I saw many dead weasels before I saw my first live one. They were all strung up on the gamekeeper's gibbet at the edge of the woods. There would be rows of weasels, stoats, squirrels, crows, magpies and any bird of prey they could get a shot at. It was something that all gamekeepers did. We accepted it with a shudder, and occasionally crept up to look at them, like peeking at a horror film between your fingers.

In the nineteenth century gamekeepers killed anything that they considered remotely damaging to their business of raising birds for shooting, and this mindset continued well into the twentieth century. In the process, pine martens, wildcats, polecats and red kites were all but made extinct in England. But it is a mystery why stoats and weasels, who were hunted just as assiduously and are potentially just as easy to kill, survived.

It could well be, in the weasel's case, because it can breed so prolifically, often with two litters of half a dozen kits a year if the food supply is good. The kits are weaned at four weeks and can hunt at eight, establishing their own territories at around ten weeks – with males and females having separate territories and meeting only to mate. The female offspring become fertile at three to four months, so can produce a litter during their first summer. In other words, they reproduced faster than gamekeepers could kill them.

I don't think I saw a live weasel until we moved here in the 1980s and I was amazed at how small they are, although the males are always bigger than the females. They say that if you are not sure if you have seen a stoat or a weasel, it is likely to be a stoat because weasels are so much smaller – more an elongated mouse when you see one darting across the road in front of the car than the ferret-like creature that is a stoat. Other indicators are that a weasel, unlike a stoat, does not have a black tip to its tail and no white around its ears. If you are in a position to see it, a weasel's belly is much whiter.

For all their diminutive size, weasels are fearsome hunters, choosing voles above all else but happy to take rabbits, birds and their eggs. Their head is the widest part of the body so if it can peer into a hole, it can get down it – which it will do in pursuit of any burrowing prey. But, given that they prefer voles to all other prey, anything that encourages longer, tufty grass that is ideal for voles will also be good for their predators. Weasels themselves are prey for foxes, kestrels, owls and domestic cats, and there is a high mortality rate, with only about ten per cent surviving more than two years.

———

Harebells

In late August and into September, little patches of harebells start to appear in seemingly random visitations. A few by the side of a track, another little drift in an open field and another tucked just below a dip in the tennis court-sized grassy glade growing above the dingle. They are mauve, pale purple hanging bells of flower on thin stalks and inconspicuous leaves, barely much taller than the grass they are scattered in.

Harebells (*Campanula rotundifolia*) are flowers of heath-grassland, which is acidic and characterised by heather and bilberry with thin grass. Historically most heaths were common land communally grazed, albeit with poor returns. The *ffridd* above the farm is a kind of heath grassland and has been grazed for millennia. Bracken is the great enemy of this distinctive landscape, slowly submerging almost everything under a green eiderdown in summer that becomes a brown mulch in winter.

But little outcrops of flower remain where the bracken cannot grow. The various locations where harebells have appeared all have particularly poor soil in a thin layer above the sandstone. They like this, but clearly not so much that they are spreading a great deal. When we first came to the farm there were just five flowers so our harebell stock has increased tenfold. They are summer's final flowering as all around starts to turn autumnal, and to lie in the grass on the steep hillside next to these delicate flowers and look out across the valley while the afternoon still holds some heat, is a deep draught of the last of the summer wine.

Hornet

I have on the table in front of me, looking like a fossil or a specimen that you might find pinned to a card within a slim drawer, a large hornet. I say large, but in truth I am not sure if it is large for a hornet. I have not bothered to measure them. But compared to an ordinary wasp, it is an absolute whopper.

That is the thing about hornets – we do compare them to wasps, and not favourably. Most people regard wasps as one of nature's bad jokes, so a hornet when viewed as a wasp on steroids is frankly terrifying.

Until recently, you could live quite an adventurous life in the UK without ever coming across a hornet. Part of their frisson of terror was that they were essentially foreign – and not in a good way. If they did appear, they were aliens and certainly did not belong in an English country garden.

However, over the past ten years or so they have become almost common and greater familiarity has bred a measure of respect. We have learned that their size does not mean that they are an extra-dangerous wasp, although they are, technically, a particularly large species of wasp. They are much gentler than the common wasp and not at all aggressive. A hornet sting is, by all accounts, an unpleasant thing but one which you are unlikely to experience unless you sit on a hornet or insist on invading its nest.

The hornet that you are most likely to come across, and the only one that I see here in the garden, is the European hornet (*Vespa crabro*), which is like a huge wasp but more chestnut-coloured. They are attracted to light and I increasingly find them coming through the window at night and buzzing around the light as I am reading in bed. Like wasps, they are carnivorous, feeding off flies, moths, beetles, dragonflies, spiders and honeybees. And like all wasps, hornets can be very destructive predators of bees and cause huge damage to a hive. At the end of summer, when the queens are starting to look for sugar, I quite often find a queen in the greenhouse where the grapes are ripening. But it is only ever one, unlike the swarms of worker wasps gorging on the fruit.

The queen and her workers build the familiar wasp nest made of intricately glued and chewed pulp, and she lays her eggs at the rate of about two a day in April. But whereas the common wasp will often nest in a hole in the ground, hornets usually build their nests in a hollow tree or a loft – anywhere that is dark and up off the ground. Like wasps, they hibernate in winter and I occasionally disturb a very sleepy queen that has tucked herself in the wooden frame of the house.

Rabbits

As a gardener I loathe rabbits but as a countryman and naturalist, I am charmed by them and accept them as a key part of the food chain that makes the wheels of the British countryside go round. And they are country animals and not something the average urban gardener has to deal with.

They do not come to the garden as a friend. By and large, most creatures in a garden, from aphids to moles, have a role to play in the bigger scheme of things, but it is hard to find much to be grateful to rabbits for.

For the first ten years we were here we never saw a rabbit in the garden, so they were not something I gave any consideration to. They were around and about in the hedgerows and the dogs would chase them and the terrier occasionally disappear halfway down a rabbit hole, but myxomatosis had reduced the rabbit population to a rump. Then I started to see the occasional bunny when

I went out into the garden first thing in the morning. This soon added spice to what had been a sleepy potter for the dogs and they shot through the door going from sleep to full hunting mode in seconds – although they never caught anything.

But ever since the harsh winter of 2010, the rabbits have been getting bolder and now they attack everything from crocuses (thousands eaten off) to mature apple trees. Not only are they coming in from the fields, but are now under all the sheds and burrowing in the veg garden and even inside the greenhouse.

I sometimes stand and watch solitary rabbits in the field next door from the bedroom window. They will graze the grass determinedly but warily, keep stopping, look around, twitch their nose, hop forwards a little, graze again, pause, eternally vigilant, more nose twitching and so on. If they think they are in trouble, they hunker down, ears back, hiding in plain sight. Clearly, they have learned that movement is their biggest betrayer but if things get too close – be it one of the cattle, a buzzard or dog – they scuttle off to the nearest hedgerow or, ideally, burrow. But from up above in the house, that habit of lying low, eyes wide open with fear, makes them look terribly exposed, but also makes me realise how many predators need movement to confirm they have found a suitable prey.

One of the reasons that rabbits suddenly became a problem was that the numbers had ballooned. For the first five years on the farm, we never saw even a solitary rabbit, then I would look out of the window in the morning and see a dozen in the yard. But after a couple of years, this population surge was hit again by myxomatosis. That seems to be the pattern – a population boost when the rabbits become resistant to the disease, followed by a crash, after which the population slowly builds up again. Their predators are mainly fox, stoat and buzzards, although weasels, goshawks, kites, owls and, in suburbia, cats, will all take a rabbit if chance comes their way. The predator population fluctuates along with the rabbit population, with buzzards, in particular, suffering from the knock-on effect of the original bout of myxomatosis.

Rabbits were introduced by the Normans and for years were kept as a luxury in jealously guarded warrens. They were farmed for their meat and pelts just as sheep are for their meat and wool. Gradually, some escaped and a wild population grew but did not become widespread until the end of the eighteenth century. This coincided with the rise of game shooting and the gamekeeper, who assiduously destroyed most of the rabbits' natural predators such as foxes, stoats and birds of prey.

They are nocturnal animals, spending their days underground, and can produce up to seven litters a year with around ten in each litter, so, given a steady food supply and lack of predators, the population explosion can be monumental, which it was in the first half of the twentieth century.

Whilst I was growing up in Hampshire, rabbits were everywhere although by the early 1960s myxomatosis had set in with a vengeance. It was introduced in 1954 and apparently reduced the British rabbit population by 99 per cent, from 100 million to one million. It is a particularly revolting disease and the blind, half-rotting creatures were a common feature of any walk in the countryside. But the surviving population evolved to live much more above ground, which limited the spread of the fleas that in turn spread myxomatosis.

When I was a child skinning a rabbit was a rite of passage for every country boy and we ate it often. I can remember rabbits hanging in the butchers, which he would skin and chop up in front of you. But we have become squeamish about such things, although of all the meat you might eat, rabbit is probably the least gory and easiest to prepare.

Ticks

Idly ruffling through Nigel's mane-like fur, my fingers stop and find a hard little nodule on his neck. I know at once what it is. It clearly doesn't hurt him and he is probably unaware of its presence but it is in fact sucking at his lifeblood. It is almost certainly *Ixodes ricinus*, the sheep tick. There are 22 different species of tick in the British Isles, although you or your dog are unlikely to come into contact with most of them. For example, I read that there is one species of tick only found on tortoises, which narrows the field somewhat.

We once had an otherwise lovely holiday in Knoydart on the West Coast of Scotland that was notable not just for the midges that devoured us the minute we stepped outside but also for the deer ticks that attacked us indiscriminately – dogs, adults and children. I can still feel the sensation of them crawling through my hair at night looking for a particularly juicy bit of flesh to attach to. When they did bite, they itched intolerably and, like all ticks, were tricky to extract.

Sheep ticks are very common in the fields around this garden. They like damp, mild weather and used to all but disappear in high summer and winter but climate change is extending their season. Certainly our flat, flooded fields are becoming tick heaven.

Ticks are not insects but spiders, although they do not spin a web and in fact do not do much at all except drink blood when available. They have three stages – larvae, nymphs and adults – all of which will feed on a host, which will include any mammal, bird or reptile, including sheep and Nigel. The nymphs are pinhead-sized and will swell to a little nodule when engorged, but the adult starts out as a hard-bodied little scuttler with visible legs. When it has slated its blood lust, it becomes a pale nugget, like a small bean or seed, in a colour that is best described as taupe. The upside of a big well-fed adult is that it is much easier to remove.

They wait for a suitable host on a blade of grass or leaf – bracken is a favourite – and when any creature with blood in its veins brushes past, it jumps aboard. It will move around until it finds its chosen spot and then bite and gorge itself, its body swelling up with the host's blood.

Ticks are famously tricky to remove because if they sense they are being touched, they respond by digging in and would rather be torn apart than loosen their grip. This results in the head being left in the wound, which can then become infected and generally unpleasant, but I have found on the dogs that if you carefully part the fur around the tick and then make one really fast snatch and grab, it comes away, head and all, and can be disposed of.

There is a dark side to all this which is Lyme's disease. I first heard of it from American friends at the end of the 1990s and it is now in the UK and should be taken seriously. Although the majority of ticks do not carry the bacterium, a small proportion do, so as well as wearing trousers tucked into socks or wellies when walking through places with sheep or deer, anyone finding a tick bite should get rid of the tick immediately. Dogs can get Lyme's disease too, with the main symptom being arthritis but – touch wood – our dogs are so far unaffected. However, a weekly check to remove any ticks is a good idea.

———

Autumn

No other season changes so dramatically in this garden as autumn.

September – certainly for the first few weeks at least – is usually very summery both in weather and appearance. But as the September weeks pass, the leaves fade and thin like an old tapestry. There is a softening of all the edges and a melancholy cast over everything that is reflected in the mistiness of morning and the low evening sun that leaves this lovely month tinted with sweet loss.

October begins still wearing summer's faded gown, but there is a real sense of this being left over from a previous season. Every sunny day is borrowed, and the light – although often the softest and most golden of the whole year – is slipping steadily away.

The berries and fruits that have been more or less ignored by the birds suddenly become aggressively devoured. The seedheads in the borders are busy with small birds.

October 2019 was sodden and flooded and remained so well into spring. This transformed the landscape around the garden. The fields became lakes, with birds floating where the cattle and sheep grazed, and the sky resounded to the calls of geese arriving to their winter home. The other winter visitors – thrushes from Siberia, woodcock from the Urals, goldcrest from Scandinavia

– all arrived in dribs and drabs. On the farm the streams roared and bounded down the hillside and the bracken, now rusty brown, gleamed with permanent damp.

As October drifts helplessly into November the days become sullen, short and unforgiving. The final fireworks of falling leaves can make for a few spectacular days – if it stays dry. But climate change means that frost in autumn is becoming increasingly rare and the alternative – a mild damp that feels colder than a clean hard frost – is always unwelcome. The garden is stripped back to its bones and whereas the hedges and shrubs normally screen and hide all the creatures within them, they are now transparent and reveal another world of life.

SEPTEMBER

Swallows and House Martins Leaving

At the beginning of September the flying patterns of the house martins and swallows change. They take on an urgency. Until mid-August there is a brood to feed but most now have left the nest. It is each bird for itself. The martins dip and bob and fidget in the sky, stalling to adjust, slipping and plunging whilst the swallows swoop and bank and swoop again in long arcing curves, feeding constantly.

I used to think that this was to fatten themselves up for the journey that they know is soon to come, but it seems that much of this behaviour is by this year's young learning the geography of the neighbourhood, imprinting it on their minds rather like taxi drivers doing The Knowledge, so that when – if – they return next year, they will know it as home. It seems that as a result of this frantic autumnal activity they lose fat rather than gain it, which makes flying easier but starvation more likely.

Ahead of them lie the English Channel, the Pyrenees, hunters, falcons, the Sahara and electrical storms (apparently lots die in storms on the journey), and half of the young will die on the way out. Of those that do complete the journey, a fifth will die on the way back. This means that over half of all the hundreds of birds working the sky above the garden now in late summer will not make it through to next spring.

When they are not feeding or reconnoitring the local airways, scores gather on the sunny side of the roof to bask in the late summer heat. There used to be a telegraph wire that ran from the lane to the house and, before we had it put underground, it would sway with dozens of birds perched on it to sunbathe.

Then one day, with no leave-taking, no obvious launching off or decision-making, the swallows are gone, with the martins following a week or so later. Perhaps they always go at night or at the very first glimmer of dawn. I sense their absence before I count it. They leave my skies bereft.

———

Mushrooms

Gardeners traditionally distrust mushrooms, fearing the worst. Mushrooms in any form have generally been seen as a manifestation of trouble lurking beneath the skin of the garden, waiting to erupt. Honey fungus stalks like an underground pestilence and fairy rings ruin the perfect lawn.

But without fungi nothing would grow and not nearly enough would decompose. Although fungi come nowhere near the mind-boggling, astronomical scale of the numbers of bacteria in the soil, in just one gram of soil – about a teaspoonful – you can expect to find around 10,000 species.

These create an infinitely subtle, complex interaction with plants. At their simplest, fungi break down woody material that bacteria cannot digest. That alone makes them an essential element in the natural flow of life, be it in the rainforest or in an old tree stump in a back garden. Nearly 40 per cent of the fungi in a healthy soil are vesicular-arbuscular mycorrhizas, which penetrate the cells of a plant's roots and create a living link between the root and the minerals and water in the soil.

Very few fungi produce fruiting bodies, and only some of those manifest themselves as mushrooms – that are only a small, but visible, part of the fungal world. So what we see, be it on decomposing wood, lawns, or meadows, is the tip of the tip of the fungal iceberg.

I am no mycologist and not even a semi-serious fungi hunter but I do love to eat mushrooms and when they occur in the garden or in the surrounding fields, I gather them avidly.

There are only three that are common with us and which I can identify without any problem – and it is worth stressing that if you have any qualms at all about whether a mushroom is safe or cannot identify it with 100 per cent certainty, then leave it alone. One or two are exceptionally poisonous so it is never worth risking it.

The easiest to confirm is the shaggy ink-cap (*Coprinus comatus*). These tend to grow on waste ground, verges and recently disturbed soils rather than in an established lawn or field and were prevalent for about five years on what is now the Mound. For about 20 years, before we turned it into part of the decorative garden, it was our waste dump and all the uncompostable rubbish, old tree stumps, subsoil and building rubble accumulated there with a bonfire at its centre.

Shaggy ink-caps appear initially as white capsules with a brown top and quickly become scaly, then shaggy and as the stem grows the cap opens and the black gills auto-digest, often dripping black goo until the cap completely dissolves. Once they reach the dripping goo stage they are not good to eat, but if picked when the caps are still closed and cylindrical, they are delicious. They should smell fresh and pleasantly unremarkable. Like all mushrooms, there is no better way to eat them than simply fried in a little butter, sliced or halved. The taste is very mild and subtle but excellent.

Much more common but very erratic is the common field mushroom (*Agaricus campestris*). In some years we could gather barrowloads of these but tend to pick them when we take the dogs for a walk, using a jumper as a basket. As a child I often used to go mushrooming in late August and gather enough to eat for our breakfast, and the combination of chilly late summer mornings heavy with dew and the smell of frying mushrooms, bacon and fried bread with a hot cup of tea is still entwined in my memory and strong 60 years later. Certainly no mushrooms have ever tasted better.

The process of identification is a kind of mental flow chart. Where does it grow? Field mushrooms grow in fields, so if you see what you think is one in a wood or a ditch, it almost certainly isn't a field mushroom. They also do not grow within about 60ft of any tree. What time of year is it? Field mushrooms rarely appear before August and their prime time is mid-August to mid-October. What was or is in the field? Field mushrooms tend to grow in grass and especially where cattle have been grazing so the grass is short and well-manured. You are less likely to find them in fields cut for hay or silage, or in an arable field, although 50 years ago, I gathered huge harvests emerging from under wheat – but that was when commercial wheat had longer straw, so created a more humid environment.

Field mushrooms start out as a pure white, domed button bubbling out of the soil. Then they become creamy, even slightly ochre, and end up as leathery, dirty brown and curled up at the edges. The cuticle often hangs down over the edge of the cap like a fringe. The gills are a rich pink turning to brown as they age. The ideal eating point is when they are big enough to grasp and still more white than tawny, largely smooth and unscaly, and firm to the touch – but we harvest them at every stage. The skin should not stain yellow at all but bruise a faint pink. They smell mushroomy. They tend to grow in scattered, irregular groups and if you find one you are almost certain to find more. I am told that you can identify potential mushroom fields by the visible fairy rings on Google Earth but they are most prevalent after a year or two of drought followed by summer rains. For example, the year of the great drought, 1976, was spectacularly good for field mushrooms.

The third absolutely reliable edible fungus is the giant puffball (*Calvatia gigantea*). We actually see these less and less but have had a few years when there were far more than we could eat. They start about cricket ball size with a fairly smooth skin, but can grow as big as a football, by which time they look like risen dough, often partly folded in on themselves. Finally, they explode, break free from the attached mycelial cord and roll around distributing their spores, after which they turn into brown, leathery, deflated balloons. They are surprisingly firm and you eat them by slicing them into 'steaks', dipping them in beaten egg and frying them. Giant puffballs grow on grass, and can appear, like something from science fiction, on a lawn.

―――――

Nuthatch

I heard unusual chirping amongst the hazels in the little round wood on the farm, and creeping up as quietly as I could watched two nuthatches very busily working up and down a large hazel laden with nuts. A robin appeared, bustling, irritated and clearly cross with them but they kept going, working through the coppice. I waited, crouching, knees screaming, trying to breathe softly and hoping the dogs don't blunder over to see what I am doing and frighten them away in the process.

Black stripe with white above the eye. Blue feathers. Very distinctive call – 'cheep cheep cheep cheep'. I often hear their tapping but nearly always the bird is the other side of the tree, so I rarely get to see them and never before for as long or as close as this.

―――――

Rowan

The intense lipstick-red of the rowan berries comes unseasonably early, as though autumn is gate-crashing summer's party. By the beginning of September the massed bunches of fruits trumpet their wares out against the heavy green of surrounding leaves and a blue summer sky. This is another plant that is practically unknown on the flat flood plain around the garden but is everywhere on the acidic hillsides of the farm.

The blackbirds and thrushes gorge on the berries, especially the fieldfares and redwings arriving from the frozen north in October. The leaves follow in a more timely fashion, turning a pinky orange along with the collective autumnal drift. But it is not just birds that like rowan berries – people have long gathered them to make into jelly, cider, beer or a sloe-gin type spirit. The unripe berries contain sorbic acid, which has anti-fungal and anti-bacterial properties and acts as a food preservative.

In spring, the tree is speckled with white flowers, often at the same time as the hawthorn is in blossom, which is mid- to late-May on the lower parts of the farm and early to mid-June on the higher ground. Rowans are pollinated by a range of insects from bees to flies but are self-fertile, so even in bad weather, when pollinators are not out and about, they can pollinate themselves and produce a heavy crop of berries.

It never gets very large but, for a small tree, has great longevity, with some living to 200 years or more, all of which adds to its spell, for it is a tree laden with magic. It is the witches' tree, the tree whose boughs you hung above the door to ward off evil spirits or bore a sprig of in your pocket to protect against the evil eye. It was used for stirring milk so that bad magic would not curdle it and for the masts of sailing boats to ensure a safe passage home.

Although rowans are much planted as a biddable garden tree, they are wild at heart. This is a tree of mountain and moorland, clinging to rock faces and standing alone, where grazing sheep cannot reach it, on blasted hillsides at 2000ft. Not for nothing is it called the mountain ash.

A large one blew down one New Year's Day, laden with snow that turned to ice, which meant the blasts of wind that followed were too much for it. It lay awkwardly across the dingle, where the sides are at their steepest and slipperiest, making it almost impossible to get at. So we left it for years and new shoots grew from the base and ferns began to grow along the trunk that now bridged the stream. Eventually we got round to clearing it, cutting it for logs and hauling it up the banks with a winch attached to the tractor. Its suckers are now growing well and will soon be bearing their own bunches and swags of berries.

———

New Calf

Walking the dogs in the fields behind the garden as dusk settles there is a lone cow in a field by the river. As I get nearer and come to the hedge I see that she is standing, perhaps ten yards from me, over a tiny calf, umbilical cord still trailing. It struggles to its feet, staggers, reaches for an udder, fails and then drops back to its knees. The cow gently licks its nose whilst never taking her eyes from me and the dogs. I know that she is the most aggressive, dangerous animal you could ever come across in the UK. She would happily and almost certainly attack me and the dogs if she thought there was any danger. Only the gappy hedge and very wonky fence stop this. I murmur soothing words and we beat our retreat.

———

Moths

This morning, there was a huge grey hawk moth resting on a yew outside my front door, its wings characteristically looking like a dead leaf, which made it stand out from the dark green foliage but which – like so many moths – makes it perfectly camouflaged and almost impossible to see amongst leaf litter and scraps of bark.

PREVIOUS PAGE By early October the light is slipping through a thousand chinks amongst the thinning leaves of a large beech on the farm.

TOP The path that divides the hazel coppice in the garden. We leave fallen leaves on the ground if the weather is good because they look beautiful.

ABOVE Climate change now means that the fields around the garden flood every autumn.

OPPOSITE From mid-autumn our cattle are fed hay made from the wild-flower meadows.

OPPOSITE We leave seed heads in the borders for the birds and hollow stems for the insects.
TOP LEFT The grass borders become a lovely tapestry of ochres and browns in autumn.
TOP RIGHT The lovely cidery tang from thousands of apples in the orchard
runs through the whole garden in October.
ABOVE LEFT Fig leaves turn a brilliant yellow before falling.
ABOVE RIGHT Whereas the fields around the garden flood and become still lakes,
the streams on the farm roar and tumble down the mountainside.

ABOVE From October through to April the roar of falling water is a constant background
on the farm – and after heavy rain, very much to the fore.
OPPOSITE In the garden the floodwater lies still and wide, the only sound
a gentle lapping against the flower beds.
OVERLEAF The low autumnal light across flat fields around the garden
make for wonderful sunsets.

I confess I find it hard to feel terribly enthusiastic about moths. Butterflies, wafting through the garden like flying flowers, are easy to love. Pausing to sip at a plant's nectar, before flitting to another with a delicate aerial dance, they add another dimension of colour and delight to any garden. But moths have a crepuscular, slightly sinister quality that makes them much less accessible. Mind you, there are those obsessed by moths with just the same intensity and passion as any butterfly fancier. I used to employ a gardener who set moth traps in our borders and she would come into work in the morning almost bouncing with excitement at the various anonymous grey and brown moths that she had caught – and then, once noted, duly set free.

The best time to see moths is at the end of summer, when they start to become really noticeable at dusk and have the nasty habit of bashing into you as you are trying to read in bed. But they are harmless, attracted only by the light and what they really want is to be out in your garden.

There are more than 2500 species of moth in the British Isles and almost all the caterpillars that you are likely to come across in your garden (other than the dreaded cabbage white) are those of moths rather than butterflies. Some of these caterpillars are huge – those of the privet hawk moth, that feeds on lilac, ash and privet, will reach 4in.

Although the caterpillars munch through a huge amount of foliage, moths perform a really useful role in pollinating flowers that have evolved to attract insects at night, when the competition from other plants is much reduced. Night-scented plants such as jasmine, honeysuckle, evening primrose, tobacco plants and night-scented stock depend upon moths and you should include some such plants in your garden to increase the richness of insect life and shore up the steady decline in moth numbers.

Moth caterpillars are the main source of food for nesting birds such as tits, wrens, robins and blackbirds. It is estimated, for example, that the blue tit chicks of the British Isles consume an astonishing 50 billion moth caterpillars every year. Cuckoos are one of the few birds that actively seek out hairy caterpillars such as those of the garden tiger moth, and one of the factors contributing to the loss of cuckoos is the shortfall in caterpillars of this declining moth. Bats, frogs, toads, shrews, hedgehogs and spiders eat many adult moths, too. In short, moths may not have glamour and may even be slightly creepy, but they are an essential link in the food chain of our gardens.

Old Man's Beard

The only clematis native to the British Isles, *Clematis vitalba*, or old man's beard, grew everywhere around my Hampshire home, festooning the hedges and trees along great stretches of lane and road. Like all clematis it loved the chalky, alkaline soil and individual plants could grow enormous, with a massed tangle of stems like jungle vines and its fluffy seedheads – the old man's white beard – covering miles of hedgerow.

It is also known as traveller's joy and baccy plant. The latter name derives from the fact that the stems could make a substitute for tobacco. I discovered this when I was about eleven and immediately tried it out. I was told by an old boy who worked as a farm labourer in the village – this was over 50 years ago and he would have been well into his seventies, so he was talking about a world around the time of the First World War – that if they ran out of tobacco they would cut a plug of old man's beard for their pipes and smoke it. 'Bit harsh like, but better'n nothing.' He said the secret was to cut a piece between two knuckles, as he called them – what horticulture calls nodes, or the points at which leaves or buds grow from the side of stems before they become woody vines.

We duly did this, making cigars from the clematis, peeling off the outer bark and lighting up. It was very effective. Within the otherwise bare, woody stem were a series of hollow tubes through which we could inhale the smoke. It burned well, too, not too fast, and rarely went out. Over time, we would choose our stems carefully, mulling over different thicknesses like a connoisseur in a St James's cigar shop deliberating between panatelas, coronas or perhaps, a short, fat robusto. For about three years, before we graduated to Player's Number 6, we used to puff on them whenever we took the dogs for a walk, which was most days. If anyone under 40 is reading this and is shocked at children smoking, well, we all did back then. I smoked cigarettes from the age of twelve to 20 and was even allowed to do so at home by otherwise very strict parents from the age of fifteen.

The seedheads of old man's beard have become a kind of flowering and are the most distinctive thing about the plant, but the actual flowers, which are small and have a mass of needle-thin petals like little anemones, are very attractive to pollinators. Although hardly ever grown in gardens, it belongs to the group 3, late-flowering type of clematis, which means that all its flowers are produced on new growth.

This is why the seedheads are so visible, as they are invariably at the very top of the plant, above the hedges, walls or trees that it has sprawled over, and is why the lower lengths of the bines steadily get thicker and thicker and woodier and woodier. It also means that it can be cut back really hard by flail or axe and will happily resprout without any damage to the plant itself.

Finally, surely Woodbine cigarettes were named after *C. vitalba* that makes for such a satisfying smoke?

Sparrowhawk

Bowling down the lane in my Land Rover, a male sparrowhawk leaves its kill on the road and skims ahead of me, inches off the ground, like a sinuous hovercraft. After perhaps 400 yards, he veers off into the gateway of a field. This is not uncommon but breathtaking every time I see it, and I rejoice. A minute later he is back, overtaking me with a sinuous manoeuvre, and flies in front as close to the road as a raised shoe, until he slips sideways into a garden.

———

Brambles

Brambles are villains for eleven months of the year but heroes for one, when their blackberries are ripe. They grow through the holly hedge by our front gate and snag me every time I pass until, outraged, I sever the offending thorny spray with my pocket knife, gingerly holding the stem between thorns. It is a vindictive and rather pointless – not to say inefficient – process because it barely halts them growing. And I don't want it to because, other than the thorns that catch me, these brambles are, by September, smothered with blackberries.

There is a large clump near the back door that we leave uncut as it provides such good winter protection for the small birds that come to eat the food we put out on the table nearby. Without it, the sparrowhawks can zoom in at will and pick a dunnock or finch for their winter breakfast.

The hedgerow around our boundary is completely brambly, as are all the hedges in the fields around. Blackberries then, are easy pickings. But I remember as a child going blackberrying as a kind of hunting expedition, which at times was tediously slow, and not allowed to return with less than a full bowl – so blackberries must have been scarcer then.

I grow a thornless variety trained against wires that has exceptionally large berries and it is strange to think that in Elizabethan times, blackberries were cultivated as a domestic fruit and raspberries were gathered from the wild. One of the idiosyncrasies of blackberries is that they have developed many natural hybrids, or micro-species – over 400 by some accounts – all with peculiarities and distinctions of size, texture and taste.

The berry at the very end of a shoot is the largest and sweetest and the first to ripen, so the epicure trawls along a hedgerow, picking these special first-comers. The fruit lower down ripens later and smaller but is excellent for jam, crumbles or pies. Bramble jelly made from freshly gathered blackberries is heaven and blackberry-and-apple pie, a seasonal feast.

But leave a piece of ground empty and untended for a while – barely a year – and the brambles mound and spread in unholy spiny snares like barbed wire in a battlefield. Any attempt to clear them leaves you bloody, exhausted and very bowed. However, this thorny, bulky barrier has its uses. Plant a young oak sapling and surround it with brambles, and rabbits, sheep, cattle or deer will not be able to reach it, thus giving it a fighting chance of growing to maturity.

―――――

Martins Cutting it Fine

The nest just jutting above our south-facing bedroom window still has young martins in it. It is getting terribly late for them to leave for the long journey south. Their chances of surviving must be very slim. I lie in bed and worry about them.

―――――

Little Owl

Little owls always look cross. Although they mostly hunt by night, they are one of the few owls that are often out and about in daylight. I sometimes see one sitting on a post by an old, half-collapsed pollarded willow just beyond the garden edge, usually in the late afternoon and usually making its distinctive, high-pitched, indignant call.

If it sees me – and the old adage that if you can see a bird of prey, then it has already seen you, seems to be almost always true – it bobs uncomfortably, like a middleweight boxer feinting and ducking under imaginary blows.

It is very small and squat – perhaps the size of a song thrush – with a flat top to its head and a permanent expression of indignation and annoyance. Occasionally, it will dart down from its perch after a worm or beetle and then return to eat it. Like tawny owls its diet is very varied, living off insects, earthworms, moths, voles and even young rabbits that are easily as big as itself.

Little owls were only introduced to this country in the 1870s and started to breed in these border counties around the end of the First World War. Given their southern European and Asian provenance, the greatest danger to them is exceptionally cold winters and certainly after the winter of 2010/2011, my own sightings – and soundings – became less frequent.

But they are still there, and in the quarter of a century I have been noticing them I always see them in the same spot, just beyond the Spring Garden, near that old willow. Obviously these are not the same birds – little owls live for about a dozen years, although infant mortality is high and the average life expectancy is only about four years. But I like to think that they nest inside the hollow body of the willow or perhaps in a hole in one of the big old ash trees by the river. This would be consistent with their preferred nesting sites. It would also be consistent with their loyalty to a site from one generation to the next. Their territories are small and they are a very parochial bird.

They are not apparent on the farm, preferring lowland, mixed agricultural or suburban countryside with lots of hedges and woodland edges. But in the garden, especially in spring, I often hear that querulous, urgent call out in the dark hedgerow beneath our bedroom window, and picture that bobbing, suspicious hostility as a little owl seeks out a juicy moth or scurrying mouse for supper.

———

Damsons

I love the arrival of damson blossom, usually at the beginning of April, sprinkling a white froth along bare hedgerows. It has none of the opulence of pear or apple blossom but is a brave, heartening sight, and damsons are part of the landscape here. Almost every hedgerow has a few scruffy little damson trees in it and our boundary hedge is no exception.

Damsons, for all their idiosyncratic taste and colour, are really just a form of wild plum. It came to Britain from its home in Eastern Europe and the western fringes of Asia. It was also grown in the Middle East, from where it was brought to Italy over 2000 years ago, from Damascus, hence its name.

As trees, damsons don't have a great deal of charisma and are often hardly more than a scrawny, overgrown shrub. Yet the taste of the fruit has more intensity than almost anything you can put in your mouth. Despite this, you rarely see damsons for sale. They are not a (super) marketable fruit. But damson jam is the richest and best there is, and damson cheese is a voluptuous luxury. It certainly has the most intense colour that garden and kitchen can muster. That intensity was used to make commercial dye for wool and leather; in the nineteenth century, when every well-dressed woman had a pair of leather gloves, dyeing leather with damson juice was an important, small rural industry in these parts, with a factory devoted solely to dyeing gloves damson-red.

When we came here, the southern boundary of the Walled Garden was made up of a suckering hedge of damsons. Other than the large hazel growing beyond the back door, this was the only indicator of gardening of any kind that had survived. However, I later found out that the Walled Garden was the vegetable patch and clearly damsons, and to a certain extent plums – for which damsons act as a reliable pollinator and which were often added to an orchard for that reason – were nurtured carefully. There is also a bullace growing that leans over the wall and drops its round fruits onto the cars of the film crew that park under it. Both damsons and bullace throw up a thicket of suckers that we pull and cut every year but never get rid of entirely.

_____

Spiders

Every year, some day in September, I go downstairs at first light and let the dogs outside to the front garden, which is filled with eighteen large yew cones. These were planted in 1993 and, although clipped tight every August, have steadily grown bigger and bigger, as all hedges and topiary are wont to do. On this one September day, year after year, around the second week, these yews are strung with tens of thousands of cobwebs, a gossamer filigree around the curving surfaces of the cones and also strung between them in impossibly fine hammocks. It is always a morning heavy with dew, the air just slightly chill, a touch of mist, and yet the sun already starting to burn through, making these countless threads sparkle and glow. It is a magical moment.

The reason why the cobwebs suddenly appear in such profusion has to do with the life cycle of the garden spider (*Araneus diadematus*). They hatch in May and a huge number are eaten throughout spring and summer by birds. Those that manage to avoid this fate do so by lying low. But if they make it through to late summer they are big enough to start spinning webs and, if female, laying their eggs which they wrap in a woven silken cocoon to protect them over the winter months, before she is killed by the first frost. The webs are made by ejecting a liquid protein that hardens to a polymer on contact with the air. They are, of course, flytraps and the spiders sit in the centre, rushing out to bite their tangled prey and inject them with a venom before consuming them.

I love the fact that some birds – notably in the tit family – use cobwebs to bind their fragile mossy nests together.

Spiders are not insects but part of the same family as mites, ticks and scorpions. There are 650 species of spider in Britain, of which the average garden might host over a hundred, although only about 20 are common.

I know that arachnophobia is, like all phobias, genuinely distressing, but I like spiders, which is just as well because our house is full of them and the garden even fuller. However, it is a perfectly rational phobia. Spiders used to be considered universally poisonous, even to touch, and whereas bees gathered pollen from plants, spiders were said to gather and store poison. The Saxon name *attercop* means poison head (with the word 'cobweb' deriving from *copweb*). Spider is a less damning designation, coming from the Saxon *spinnan*, meaning spinner.

Although all spiders are carnivores and hunt aggressively, only a dozen British spiders are large enough to bite humans and none are dangerous. Having said that, a spider's bite is extremely painful and can become very irritated and make you feel unwell for a while. Some spider bites are appreciably worse than a wasp or bee sting because they last longer. However, most of their energy is devoted to biting and eating each other as well as a wide range of insects, woodlice and even frogs and young birds.

Their consumption of insects is staggering. It has been calculated that an acre of undisturbed grassland can accommodate more than a million tiny money spiders, each eating at least a hundred insects a day. Garden spiders are reckoned to eat around 500 insects a day each and – for lovers of arcane statistics – it has been calculated that British spiders consume more insects by weight every year than the combined weight of the whole of Britain's human population. For gardeners, this means that spiders are your best friends in controlling the insects that would otherwise be feeding on your precious plants.

———

Two Goshawks

Two goshawks circling – quite slow and low – over the garden at about 5 p.m. Very pale, almost dove-grey, barred, broad wings, full, heavy body.

Sarah and Adam see the same pair the next day a couple of miles away on the road to Dilwyn.

This year's young? Seem to match all the descriptions. This implies there was a nest nearby. Given that we see goshawks here increasingly often it suggests that they live here rather than just visit.

———

Meadow Saffron

On the road between garden and farm, just across the border into Wales behind Hay-on-Wye, there is a dark mountain road, overhung with trees. In September, a stretch of about a quarter of a mile is thick with the flowers of meadow saffron (*Colchicum autumnale*). This is nothing to do with the saffron crocus (*Crocus sativus*), nor the autumn crocus (*C. nudiflorus*) but is, confusingly, a member of the lily family. The pale pink and lavender petals rise naked from the bank, the leaves having grown and died back before the first hint of flower. It is an astonishing display for its otherworldliness, these bulbs appearing almost like mushrooms in late summer, when there is nothing else like them around – let alone here, high in the dark tunnels of the roads winding up the hillside.

They also grow a mile or so along the hillside at the bottom of the slope of a small meadow invariably cut for hay, and unlike the roadside ones that are banded thickly along the strip of bank, these are dotted around the grassy field like wild daffodils, leaping out like a surreal burst of spring at the fag-end of summer.

The reason they grow in both places is because, unlike the true autumn crocus that does have foliage alongside the flower, these will happily grow in damp shade. The trees along the road provide plenty of shade and a Welsh hillside will always be damp. And, being at the bottom of the sloping meadow, the water runs down to them. They grow there, too, because they are poisonous to stock and are often got rid of by farmers. But they are safe along a road and a hay meadow is cut late in this part of the world, so the aftermath will not be grazed until after the flowers have gone. These subtleties of meadow management allow them a brief window of opportunity.

They can self-pollinate but their seeds do not appear until the following spring, along with the broad, strappy leaves, and are then dispersed by ants. In meadows, the hooves of cattle grazing over winter will create patches of bare soil for them to germinate in, whilst in woodland, they germinate in the litter of leaves and twigs. But meadow saffron is becoming increasingly rare due to the decreasing habitats and deliberate removal due to its toxicity. However, the Welsh Marches – exactly the territory between garden and farm – are its main stronghold. So my two displays that I invariably see for a week or so every year, is a rare instance of me being in exactly the right place at the right time.

———

Hazelnuts

Hazelwood is the main source of bean and pea sticks, and all the fencing at Longmeadow is woven from coppiced hazel. But at this time of year the hazels exist for their nuts. Growing nuts for harvest is rare in modern gardens, but until the Second World War, a nuttery was a feature of many gardens large enough to accommodate one. The biggest nuts are produced on old wood, so – unlike coppicing – the hazels are pruned of young growth to get the right amount of light and air to them, fixing them into a perpetual maturity.

Most trees do not cross-pollinate, so natural hybrids, although not unknown, are rare in the tree world. However, hazels cross-pollinate easily between different versions of themselves and as a result, there are many hybrids. But although they cross-pollinate, they do not come true from seed. So, plant a nut or, as I did 25 years ago, transplant seedlings as they appear, and you might get any permutation of filbert or cob.

The wild hazel of woodland is *Corylus avellana*, or the cobnut. It carries its nuts in clusters of two to four, the squat nut sleeved by a short husk. 'Cob' comes from the Old English *cop*, for a head, and the word 'hazel' derives from the Saxon *haesil*, meaning a headdress – which must surely come from the appearance of the nut in its ragged bonnet.

The filbert is *C. maxima* and has longer nuts completely enveloped in the surrounding husk. In our Jewel Garden, we have four purple hazels that are *C. maxima purpurea* and they have nuts with a lovely pink husk as well as being one of the best purple-leafed foliage plants for any garden.

Christians named filberts after St Philibert, a seventh-century Benedictine, whose saint's day is 20 August – which is about the time when the nuts start to be edible.

To get the best nuts, hazel, rather like fig, needs to be grown on poor, stony soil. If the ground is too rich and damp, the goodness will go into the wood rather than the fruit. Hazelnuts will store until Christmas if kept in their husk, which stops them from drying out too fast. If collected whilst still green, leave them in a dry place and they will ripen by about November.

But the reality is that most years, the squirrels take the vast majority of nuts from the trees before they ripen, and in mid-August, the ground is littered with green, unripe nuts. However, the summer of 2019 produced the heaviest hazel crop I have known and we had all we could eat and more, the squirrels grew fat and there were still enough left over for hundreds of seedlings to flourish in years to come.

_____

Earwigs

At this time of year, it is very common to find the dahlia petals chewed and nibbled, and sometimes reduced to rags. The culprits are earwigs, who have a distinct penchant for what is – to them at least – a juicy and delicious dahlia flower.

Conventional horticultural advice is to trap the earwigs over-night by placing an upturned pot or matchbox on a cane by the dahlia and stuffing it with straw. The earwig goes into this at dawn to rest up, thinking it a convenient safe haven, without realising that you are going to extract it from its strawy bed before doing something very unpleasant and probably terminal.

But the common earwig (*Forficula auricularia*) is a fascinating creature and does not rely upon the dahlia alone for its daily diet, being pretty much omnivorous and eating other insects that gardeners often consider as pests. They thrive in mild, damp conditions which makes the UK almost ideal for them, and can most readily be found under loose bark or in any woody crevice in great clusters – attracted to each other by scent pheromones that they release. The females lay about 30 cream-coloured eggs in underground nests in the new year and the nymphs hatch out in April and go through a number of cycles, during which time the female will protect and feed them until they are large enough to foray out on their own.

They seem to like dahlias because the massed petals of the flower heads provide ideal shelter and, once ensconced, they nibble a little at their surroundings.

Common earwigs have wings and are able to fly but rarely do, whereas there are three other native species of earwig that fly much more often. I – or more accurately, the lamp by my bedside – have frequently been buzzed by earwigs as I read in bed. All earwigs can use their pincers to pinch and one way of telling the difference between the sexes is that males have curved pincers whereas those of the female are more or less straight.

———

Common Oak

How many people plant an oak tree in their garden? Not enough, for sure. They are lovely from the first and give enormous pleasure as they grow. I say this from experience as I have planted two and watched them develop from slim saplings that fitted easily into the boot of our car to significant trees, one tall – perhaps 50ft now – and slim, and the other shorter but stocky and somehow more robust.

One, the slender, elegant one, we know as Becky and the other, stocky and powerful, is Peter because the trees were presents celebrating the wedding of our friends Peter and Becky, over 20 years ago. Giving each guest at a wedding an oak tree to plant is a wonderful idea. Nothing could be a better symbol of enduring hope and promise in the future.

Oaks like our rich Herefordshire clay and they grow both magnificently broad and spreading and, if managed appropriately, as tall and straight and good for building as any in the land. Our house is constructed around a framework made from hundreds of oak trees, each of the beams squared from the trunk of a single *Quercus robur* – the English, or common oak. Oaks cut for building are between 50 and 100 years old, the best beams squared off from the entire trunk. After this age, the upwards growth of the main trunk slows and the branches spread more.

There still persists the canard of oak-framed houses being made from old ships' timbers but that is extremely rare and only ever in ship-building towns. The cost and labour of transporting the timber was far too great for this. But what was very common – also to save on the huge cost of transportation – was the reuse of timbers from older, demolished nearby houses or barns. So our Tudor, timber-framed house is a jumble of beams ranging from the thirteenth century, through major rebuilds at the end of the fifteenth and sixteenth centuries, to our own contributions and repairs made from oak trees cut at the end of the twentieth century.

Cut into a centuries-old oak beam and your saw blunts in minutes. The wood is astonishingly hard and strong. I have defrassed beams honeycombed with woodworm, removing the outer 2in or 3in with an axe, whilst the inner core is untouched and as strong still as any steel girder.

And in the ground no other tree is so resolutely able to adapt to and seemingly survive near-total decay. Last year a huge oak tree blew down from the hedge that bounds the edge of our farm. Its true size was only really apparent once it was lying on the ground. I counted the rings on one of the branches fairly near the top of the tree and got to 102 before my eyes gave out. The tree itself was probably four or five times that age, which in oak time, is middle-aged. This fallen hulk had seen the monastery down the valley dissolved and abandoned, seen beacons lit to warn of the Armada, was already tall during the Civil War, and had provided shelter for those building the barn just down the slope in 1702. It was as much archaeology as lumber.

It was a 'stag-headed' tree. At first glance it seemed more dead than alive, with most of its branches leafless and worn like antlers – hence the name. But a second look showed that there were healthy leaves sprouting from a collection of smaller branches lower down the tree, rather like a bald man preserving a tonsure of hair circling his otherwise egg-smooth scalp. The bark and sapwood of the upper branches had rotted but these oaks – and it is not at all uncommon – grow a new and completely healthy crown and they can remain stripped back, seemingly clinging to life through a few leaves although the vast majority of the tree is a gaunt skeleton.

Whilst it was stretched out on the ground like a toppled giant it was fascinating to see just how many holes and hollows there were right up the trunk and throughout the larger branches. Each one of these would have been a potential home for birds or bats, let alone for the mass of insect and fungal life that lives in and on the bark and leaves.

And in the garden, no other plant is nearly so good a host to such a quantity or range of wildlife. It is reckoned that an average common oak supports over 280 different insect species, 200 different species of caterpillar and over 300 different forms of lichens, as well as moths, birds, bats and fungi. To put that into context, the introduced (and lovely) holm oak (*Q. ilex*) supports only one solitary species of insect!

The acorns of the common oak have stalks attached to their cups, making a ladle, and are much more plentiful than in the sessile oak (*Q. petraea*). This is our only other native but less common oak, which is more likely to be found on acidic and upland soils. The acorns were much valued in medieval times for feeding pigs ('pannage'). The pigs would be put into the woods in autumn to fatten on the fallen acorns before being slaughtered to provide what was very often the only source of meat over the winter months.

We think of oak trees as statuesque, mature individuals, crowning a landscape or standing alone in a field, but ancient oaks were rare in medieval times and usually only found in woods or where the timber was too awkward to extract. Almost all were grown as 'standards', with one or two trees per acre of coppice, or pollarded every 30 years for smaller lengths of fine timber, coppiced for charcoal, or grown in plantations for harvesting every hundred years or so as building material for houses and, from the mid-seventeenth century, ships.

One medieval plantation a few miles from the garden survives and is still in active use, the hundred-year-old trees as straight as arrows and ready for cutting. It was from this plantation that the beams of St George's Chapel at Windsor were taken, and when it burned down in 1992, it was to this same plantation, 600 years later, that they came for the replacements.

I shall not be cutting down either Peter or Becky because they are beautiful and the sylvan presence of two dear friends. But perhaps, in 50 or 100 years' time, when a new beam is needed for the house, someone will look at Becky's straight trunk or Peter's powerful girth, reckon the savings of transportation with such fine trees growing less than a hundred yards from the house, and take them to join the others that have created the building I am writing this in so that it may endure for another 700 years.

Clinging to Summer

A flock of perhaps 20 martins spent an hour or two above the garden this morning, obviously from much further north and on their migratory way south.

More at dusk as I return from a walk. Feeding, swirling, swooping – it must be like this all the way south – filling up when the pickings are easy (which is a credit to the number of insects in and above this garden), and then on. And on and on for such a very long way.

Daddy Longlegs

At some point in the middle of September my garden (and house) becomes alive with daddy longlegs. I cannot say that this is a joyous moment but it manages to stay just on the right side of creepy. Craneflies – to give them their proper name – have six long, hair-thin legs that dangle beneath them in flight. These legs seem to have no practical purpose other than to act as tendrils and stabilisers for their slim bodies.

I was amazed to discover that one fly in ten is a cranefly. The largest, *Tipula maxima,* is easily the biggest British fly but it is less likely to be seen in gardens than on the margins of streams and damp woods. However, the common cranefly (*T. oleracea*) is present in pretty much every back (and front) garden.

They descend in September as a kind of insect invasion, especially if there is plenty of long grass. They are then greedily devoured by a wide range of birds, bats, spiders, fish (especially trout and craneflies – real and fake – are the best bait for trout fishing) and some mammals.

The September influx of so many daddy longlegs is due to the hatching of their larvae, which gardeners know only too well as leatherjackets. These feed on the roots of grass and can create bare patches, so are hated by the more ardent cultivators of lawns. The larvae of the spotted cranefly (*Nephrotoma appendiculata*) are also feared for the way that they devour potatoes and the roots of young cabbages. The best way to treat leatherjackets is using nematodes that will devour them from within.

Despite the damage that they cause, leatherjackets are an important food source for rooks and starlings, great flocks of which can be seen picking over playing fields, meadows and lawns after rain, which brings the larvae to the surface. Leatherjackets also eat a great deal of decaying organic matter, recycling it and thereby enriching the soil.

However, once the leatherjackets have hatched, the adults hardly feed at all, mating and hatching eggs within 24 hours of emerging from the pupae. So, daddy longlegs exist only to reproduce – and to be part of the infinitely complex food chain that unifies all our garden wildlife, however damaging one single aspect of it might seem to be when taken in isolation.

Snipe

I only ever see the back of snipe. This is because they are invariably half-gone before I am aware they are here, bursting from the ground beneath my feet and dashing away fast and low in erratic flight before dropping down again.

For years I thought they were the common snipe (*Gallinago gallinago*) because I did not know any better and because they more or less conformed to the limited knowledge I had. But the bird that I see whizzing away from me a foot or two above the ground is, in fact, the much rarer jack snipe (*Lymnocryptes minimus*). It is smaller with an appreciably shorter bill – albeit, given that the snipe's bill is proportionately the longest of any British bird, still on the long side. It is an autumnal visitor here, appearing around September and then gone by mid-March.

They like the stubble in the field next to the orchard when it is there, which is only once every three years as it has had a tripartite crop rotation – oilseed rape, followed in turn by wheat and then potatoes – for the past 20 years. The ground is ploughed and drilled with the fresh crop of wheat and rape almost immediately the rape and potatoes are harvested in autumn but the potatoes – which follow wheat – do not go into the ground until spring, so the wheat stubble is left unploughed all winter and the snipe seem to love this. Every time the dogs and I walk through the coarse, scratchy stubble, a jack snipe or two are put up and skittle away erratically down the field.

I also see them in the low-lying pastures that are half-flooded most of winter. The snipe rise out of the ditches that appear in every hollow and runnel that summer grass obscures, flying so fast that even Nell forgoes to chase them.

Photographs show them to be a mini version of woodcock, with the same rather curious head shape and long straight bill for probing into soft ground in search of earthworms. But unlike woodcock they have the charming characteristic of constantly bobbing up and down as they feed, as though their legs are made of springs.

Then, at the end of winter, as the daffodils open and the farmer looks for the first opportunity to plough the wheat stubble to plant his potato crop, they vanish, making their way back to Scandinavia and the steppes of Siberia.

———

OCTOBER

OCTOBER

Wild Apples

This part of the Welsh Marches is apple country. It is the home of cider and arguably has the best cider orchards in the world, as well as growing apples for eating.

Not only do I love the fruit, raw and cooked in any and every way, but I adore apple trees and have planted over 70, with over 60 different varieties of cooking and dessert apples in the garden, as well as a dozen crab apples. Some of these are cordons and espaliers, a few are low step-overs but most are large trees, grown as standards or vigorous rootstocks. I have seen these grow over the past 30 years from whips to large trees big enough to climb and hang a swing from, and we harvest enough fruit for both eating most days of the year and for juicing. These mature trees are now bedecked with great bunches of mistletoe and a dozen or more host great swags of rambling roses. The orchard has become a place rather than just some trees in grass, and I am as happy and proud of it as of any other part of the garden.

However, there are four apple trees that I did not plant – that nobody planted – that I love even more and which are on our land. These are all *Malus sylvestris*, the native crab apple, growing in the woods on the farm, mixed in with hazel, alder, willow, hawthorn and ash, their wild tangle of branches and straight, sturdy trunks looking quite unlike any of the trees around them. They are smothered with blossom in May and drop thousands of tiny apples in autumn, carpeting the ground beneath them and which are then eaten by foxes, badgers, hedgehogs, mice and birds but none by us as they are mouth-shrivellingly tannic.

These are handsome and immediately distinctive trees, at least 30ft tall and wide, with thick trunks 2ft to 3ft in diameter, quite unlike the much smaller crab apples in my garden.

The Anglo-Saxon and Welsh charters, which defined tracts of land, largely by naming the trees that marked out the areas, have apple as the third most common tree after thorn and oak. This implies both that it was a common hedgerow tree and was immediately recognisable. Certainly each of ours is more than just recognisable, but touched with magic.

———

Swan Family Procession

The dogs and I are walking across the fields when I see two swans sailing in a flooded field ditch ahead of me. Only their necks and heads are visible above the grassy groove that is made into a temporary canal by recent heavy rain. They look surreal, as though they are swimming through the short, cow-cropped grass.

The swans see the dogs and clamber out of the water to get away (the ditch is a cul-de-sac, the truncated remnant of something more effective) and start walking across the fields towards the river. Then, from the ditch, unseen till now, come seven large cygnets – the size of peahens, their feathers a stained, pale brown – slowly and awkwardly stepping in single file after their parents. It is an extraordinary procession, ungainly but oddly moving. They head for the safety of the river but are blocked by the fence that the Environment Agency put up to stop cattle treading down the banks and silting up the water when they go to drink.

For a moment the parents turn and realise they are trapped and their young in possible danger. But the dogs and I pass quickly on, heading away from them, to stop the birds panicking and tangling in the wire fence and also because I know how aggressive a defensive parent swan can be.

Later I see the family sailing serenely on the water, in the same single file, having found a suitable gap in the fence. I feel like someone in a crowd lining a street watching a royal cavalcade go by.

————

Hops

By the end of summer, the hedgerows around this garden and all along the lanes and fields nearby are wreathed with long strands of hops (*Humulus lupulus*) twining amongst the hawthorn, dogwood and blackthorn.

These are the ghostly descendants of the hop yards that once occupied a few fields – and sometimes nearly all – on every farm in this part of Herefordshire. (Herefordshire hops are grown in a field called a 'yard' whereas in Kent, the identical set-up is known as a 'garden', and we have hop 'kilns' whereas they have 'oast houses'.)

When we moved to this part of the world in the mid-1980s, there were thousands of acres of these yards, with their grid of poles held by wires and strung with tens of thousands of strings to support the hop vines. Hops climb heroically and will put on 15ft to 20ft of growth each year before dying back completely in winter.

The coarse twine that supported them came in great balls like striated pumpkins. They were taken to the hop yards by the hundreds loaded high in trailers, and we would buy them for about 50 pence each. They were – are – beautiful objects as well as incredibly useful and for years, I used the same twine in the garden for stringing out new areas and for tying everything and anything. Nowadays, the hop yards have nearly all gone and the twine sells for 20 times that amount or more as a decorative lifestyle accessory.

I am writing these words in one of the two hop kilns attached to this house, which, until 1990, was a working farm. The kilns were last used before the First World War and the interior was left to slowly decay. I write in the upper part, where the hops were spread to dry and below me, in what was the furnace with its brick floor still stained dark from the fires, is where the garden tools are kept.

The golden hop (*H. l.* 'Aureus') is the tamed, domestic version but it, too, produces the cone-like female flowers that can be brewed. They can also be used as an aid to sleep when stuffed into a pillow. Hops are native to this country, although they were not used in brewing until the sixteenth century. Until then 'ale' was made without hops which meant that it did not store so well so had to be brewed more often and did not have what we regard as the characteristic bitter 'hoppy' flavour. 'Beer' made with hops quickly grew in popularity and since about 1600 has been more popular than ale – albeit the two words are now used interchangeably.

My father brewed his own beer and the distinctive smell of hops ran through my childhood. He would stew up the brew once a month on the stove, filling one of my mother's stockings with fresh hops that he draped into the simmering pan of malt, yeast and sugar. The resulting intense mixture was then watered down and decanted into old two-pint cider bottles made of thick brown glass that were screwed tight and taken down to the cellar to mature for a few weeks. Occasionally, there would be an explosion and one would burst, leaving a hoppy smell lingering in the cellar for months.

Skein

The geese are coming back. Skeins in perfect arrow formations flying low over the garden. A strike force.

Pheasants

A few years ago, on a lovely May afternoon, I was weeding in one of the Jewel Garden borders, when a hen pheasant exploded out of the middle of a large clump of grass. (The grass was, with poetic appropriateness, *Anemanthele lessoniana*, better known as pheasant grass.) Inside the clump was a nest, with a clutch of a dozen olive-brown eggs about the size of ones from a bantam hen. We had cleared, weeded, mulched, put up stakes, planted and propped in that border over the previous weeks but somehow she had chosen that busy site and remained undetected all the while. I left them and tried to stay well out of the way but she abandoned the nest and gradually the eggs disappeared, probably to magpies, crows, rats and hedgehogs, all of which will eagerly predate pheasants' eggs.

We often have cock pheasants in the garden, strutting around nervously and then rising in a cackle of alarm and a noisy whirring of wings, which Nell in particular finds intensely exciting and will rush round the garden to see if it might be hiding somewhere long after the bird has flown at least two fields away. At dusk, the receding 'cock cock cock' of the males, answering each other across the fields as night falls and they head to their roost, is deeply evocative of my childhood and, in its own way, is as beautiful as waves of cooing from wood pigeons.

Pheasants are almost entirely a rural bird but where there are any at all, there tend to be lots. But although they are so common around us, they are still an extraordinarily gorgeous and dramatic bird – at least the male is. The hen is much paler, drabber and altogether less conspicuous, albeit the size of a chicken. But a cock pheasant in his full rig is a splendid sight, with his iridescent green-and-indigo neck, bright red wattle and face mask, little round yellow beady eye, white collar and rich chestnut-speckled plumage ending in a hugely long tail. He is made to be seen, a hulking bird of paradise, a popinjay and, above all, a target.

For pheasants exist primarily to be shot. They are bred by the million and then released into the countryside at the end of summer, ready for the shooting season, which begins in October and lasts until the end of January. Around here almost every piece of land is part of a shoot, and twice a week in the season, there will be a barrage of guns from first to last light. Personally, I choose not to do this but I happily eat pheasant and other game, so it would be deeply hypocritical to be offended by the sport.

Pheasant shooting literally shaped my childhood as it has shaped much of the English post-war landscape. This is because a shoot requires cover for the birds to be reared and roost, so needs woods, spinneys (slithers of wood, originally of thorns, between fields), coppices and hedgerows.

It was the invention of the breech-loading shotgun that really brought about the passion for shooting and hence the dramatic increase in the pheasant population in the mid-nineteenth century, and soon there was a whole social code of shooting parties, gun dogs and gamekeepers, with even the appropriate clothing bound up into it, all of which remains today.

But after the Second World War, there was a huge demand to increase agricultural productivity, initially driven by the threat of starvation by the U-boat blockade in the early years of the war and the determination that this should not happen again – but also in pursuit of profit and, for the first time since the 1870s, farming began to make money. Thousands of miles of hedge were ripped out, machinery got bigger and bigger, and the spinneys and woods were seen as unprofitable land to be grubbed and ploughed up.

Only the love of pheasant shooting by wealthy landowners held this agricultural rampage in check and in the second half of the twentieth century, pheasant shooting steadily increased. One of the corollaries of this was that gamekeepers had immense power in areas where there were shoots, and as children, we lived in terror of gamekeepers because they were known to shoot dogs that chased their precious pheasants. They also shot anything and everything that they thought could possibly predate on them and the gamekeeper's gibbet, with its rows of dead birds and mammals strung up on barbed-wire fencing or gates, was one of the gruesome facts of country life.

Amongst the many ironies bound into this thread of rural life is that, had pheasant shooting been banned, just as fox hunting has been, there is no doubt that a whole host of wildlife, from songbirds to mammals and insects, would have been dramatically affected by the loss of habitat – and the pheasant would have quickly become a rarity. So pheasant shoots – which I grew up hating and believing a blight on my rural life – were, in fact, preserving many of the things I loved. As ever, life is complicated.

In truth, pheasants are not well adapted to living in the British countryside. They are heavy and slow, and originally came from Asia – probably introduced to Britain by the Romans. It is a bird of woodland edge, seeking protection from woodland cover. Its wings are short and wide and adapted to explosive flight over very short distances and low altitudes. This makes them ideal for escaping a predator within the confines of a wood but also a perfect target for shooting with a shotgun when out in the open.

Over 20 million birds (some figures say double that number) are reared every year, which is a significant part of the British bird population. It is a substantial business. For example, in 2015, it was calculated that over 560,000 tons of grain per year were provided just at feeding stations for game birds. Game birds actually only consume about half of this, so other birds (mostly pigeons and corvids) and small mammals are the unintended beneficiaries. It has also been estimated that around 220,000 acres of cover crops are specially grown and then ploughed in at the end of the shooting season.

About 60 per cent of the birds released into the wild are shot. Additionally, many are killed on the roads – in this part of the world you cannot drive a mile without seeing a dead pheasant – and many die of natural causes or are predated, especially as chicks. Their life expectancy averages about one year.

Despite pheasants being, above all, birds of farmland, we hardly ever see them on our farm because there is no shoot in the valley, and the hillside weather, along with the depredations of foxes, sparrowhawks and pine martens, is too harsh for them to survive long. But, although they peck at the primrose and crocus flowers in spring, I like them in the garden and would feel honoured if one chose to nest in a border again.

––––––

Fieldfares

You know winter is round the corner when the fieldfares and redwings arrive from their summer quarters in Scandinavia or even as far afield as Siberia. They are heralds of the season just as surely as summer is certified by the first swallow.

But the swallows arrive with a kind of soaring familiarity, re-forming an intimacy with the garden and the precise details of the house, like a child returning home after some weeks away. Fieldfares (*Turdus pilaris*), on the other hand, are a curious mixture of awkward truculence and shyness. They look like large thrushes with handsome grey heads held upright and tall, chestnut back, black tail and spotted underparts, but they are always seen in flocks whereas the resident song thrushes are much shyer, more solitary birds – and have a much sweeter song.

Fieldfares rise in a clucking, chattering cloud if you so much as appear within their sight, yet are always pushing aggressively forwards as soon as they think your back is turned. Everything about them is harsh and jerky. Yet they are of the season.

They like the apples left in the orchard best of all and will fiercely defend a tree with windfalls from other birds. They also do a lot of good for the gardener, eating snails, leatherjackets and caterpillars. They were once caught by the thousand and eaten with relish and it has been reckoned that in East Prussia alone, wedged on the Baltic coast between modern Lithuania and Poland, over a million fieldfares were killed each year for the table.

They leave us around the end of March, scurrying across the spring sky as though running out of time, gathering their belongings. And then, like all migratory birds, there is no leaving, but when you walk out one morning just their absence.

Redwing

Whereas the fieldfare has a mauvey-grey head, the redwing is less distinguished, smaller, daintier and altogether less intrusive. In flight you can only really tell it from a song thrush by the red flash under its wing – although its tendency to flock, like the fieldfare, is also a giveaway. In the dead of the country night, in an otherwise silent absolute blackness, I sometimes hear their thin, rather ghostly flight calls as they pass overhead.

In the day, they are flighty and endlessly alert, alarmed by any sudden movement or shape, flitting from tree to bush to orchard floor in a fidgety flock, restlessly hunting berries, stripping holly, hawthorn and rowan from woods and cotoneaster from gardens or picking over the fields, hopping cautiously, heads cocked, looking for invertebrates.

Then, one day in March, they are no longer there, gone in the night to their Arctic homes in Russia, Finland or Iceland to breed.

———

Lords-and-Ladies

Few plants have so many names as *Arum maculatum*. Cuckoo pint, lords-and-ladies, Adam and Eve, parson in the pulpit, devils and angels, willy lily and many more local and much bawdier variations. But most relate to the explicit sexual imagery of the opened hood of the spathe with the spadix standing erect inside it.

There is not much use being coy about it in this garden because as a weed it pops up everywhere. Sarah and I agree to disagree about it. She loves it and would allow it unrestricted access to all areas – albeit shady ones because it does not grow in full sun – whereas I try and keep it under some control, removing it, often surreptitiously, from most of the borders. However, it is ever-present in the Spring Garden, the seeds brought in by the flood and the plants loving the rich, alluvial soil and the shade of the trees.

Despite its rapacious spread, it has many virtues. It is, for example, pollinated by the owl midge. This spends most of its life happily buried in a cowpat but when the spadix at the centre of the plant is ripe and ready, it warms up and gives off a faint faecal aroma. This is irresistible to the owl midge, who finds the plant and delves into the tubular centre where the female flower is hidden. Thus pollinated, the spadix begins to wither and die, revealing the familiar spike of bright vermilion berries that appear in late summer – and which are poisonous. In fact no part of the plant should be touched as it can irritate bare flesh.

The first signs of the plant are as early as December and certainly by February, with small, pale green, matt leaves, which mature to become arrow-shaped, big and glossy, often speckled with black.

These die back after their first year and are replaced the following spring by the spathe and its smutty spadix. Then these undergo their transformation and are replaced in late summer by the bright orange fruit on a stick, like a granular lolly. Not many birds eat these although pheasants will have the occasional nibble. Mice will nibble at the spadix before it withers, probably attracted by the heat it emits as much as by the odour of cow poo.

Stoats

Sarah and I once watched a stoat going round and round a solitary hawthorn in a field. Presumably it was chasing something that had taken refuge in the tree but although stoats are excellent climbers, it remained on the ground, circling perhaps four or five times, and then disappeared.

But I used to see stoats most often on the gamekeeper's gibbet. The keepers considered them vermin – along with hedgehogs, any bird of prey, magpies, crows and – we knew – our dogs, who occasionally chased and even killed a pheasant. Gamekeepers still trap and kill stoats because they undoubtedly do catch game birds, their eggs and chicks, but whereas this used to be blithely accepted as the way of the privileged world, there is now a growing sense that the life of a natural predator is just as important as any bird reared solely to be shot for sport by a tiny handful of people.

Many years later, I saw my first ermine stoat – pure white other than his (or her) black-tipped tail, on the cold February hillside near the farm. Stoats are easier to see than weasels because they are bigger, but there is not much difference. They share the same russet back but their undersides are cream, not white, they have a black tip to their longer tail and sometimes white on their ears – and of course, in winter, they can turn pure white, which no weasel ever does.

Rabbits are their preferred prey even though a fully grown rabbit is much bigger than they are. They also eat rats, squirrels, mice, voles and ground-nesting birds and their chicks and eggs as well as climbing to take birds in a nest in a tree or on a wall.

They have an unusual sexual cycle. They will mate in May but then the fertilised egg cells go into suspended animation for nine months with gestation not beginning until the following March, followed by birth just 25 days later. The litters are very large with about a dozen kits. Then, soon after their birth, the mother will mate again – and the fertilised females will then give birth a year later.

Females mature much more quickly than males, the females being fully mature at about six months whereas the males do not reach maturity and full size until a year old. Stoats can live to be five years or even more, but many die in their first two years.

Leaves

The ash leaves are suddenly falling and the field maples turning orange touched with purple. It has been slow to arrive, but autumn is most certainly here now.

Worms

I can guarantee that every autumn I will receive a flurry of letters asking how to deal with worm casts on lawns, and even some asking how to get rid of worms. I always answer in the same vein – far from being a problem, worms are the gardener's best friend.

There are 27 species of earthworm in the UK, although most are rare. They are divided into three groups. The anecic worms include the most common, the lobworm (*Lumbricus terrestris*) and can reach populations of up to 40 per square yard in a healthy lawn. They make vertical burrows up to 10ft deep and have a profoundly beneficial effect on the soil, both fertilising it and digging it. As they burrow, they swallow mineral particles and small amounts of plant material, which then gets mixed up inside them and is excreted as the familiar 'casts' on the surface. The lobworm is pinky-red tinged with blue and has a pointed head and much flatter tail.

Endogeic worms are paler and make horizontal burrows, often quite deep underground, and rarely appear above the surface, whilst epigeic worms live on the surface and include brandlings – the red worms found in a healthy compost heap.

Worms move and digest soil on an incredible scale. Charles Darwin is best known as author of *On the Origin of Species* and for his theory of evolution, but he spent his lifetime studying worms and estimated that there can be up to 40 tons of worm casts per acre incorporated into the soil. These casts are invariably richer, finer and less acidic than the surrounding soil, containing around 50 per cent more calcium, nitrogen, phosphorus, potassium and bacteria.

Worms also till the ground remarkably effectively and will move between 100 and 200 tons of soil per hectare per year – which is more than any plough can do. Whether we appreciate it or not, the earth is literally moving beneath our feet.

Worms prefer alkaline conditions to acid and this is why brandlings – the red worms found by the thousand in a healthy compost heap – are a good sign that the compost is making well because acidity deters bacteria action and slows down decomposition. Lots of worms in your soil does not just mean it contains plenty of organic matter but also that its pH is in balance.

Earthworms come out at night to travel along the surface of the ground to harvest leaves and plant debris. If you walk in your garden on a dark, wet evening you will sense as much as see hundreds of worms disappearing into the soil as your torchlight precedes you. They avoid the light of day whenever possible because they are extremely sensitive to ultraviolet rays, which are present in uncomfortable amounts for them, even on an overcast day.

They move by pulling themselves along using short, stiff bristles the length of their body. Although invisible to the naked eye, these bristles are extremely powerful and mean that the worms can climb as well as haul themselves quite long distances over ground.

Worms also pull fallen leaves and plant debris into their burrows, which adds organic material to the soil, improving its structure and fertility. If you are short of compost, a mulch of leaves, preferably chopped up, will dramatically increase the worm population in your soil and therefore its health and fertility.

Worms are an essential food for shrews, moles, hedgehogs and foxes, as well as for birds ranging from robins to buzzards and a healthy soil contains enough worms both to feed any amount of predators and improve your soil.

———

Nest

As I cut back a clematis in the Jewel Garden, removing the thick tangle of dried stems from the supporting tripod of hazel bean sticks, a bright green ball was revealed right at the heart of the densest thicket of last summer's growth. It was a nest, the size of a large orange, and made entirely from moss. There was a little hole at the top and when I eased this open, it revealed an interior lined with feathers and hair – that looked very much as if it had once belonged to Nigel. There was no evidence of broken shells or droppings.

I am not sure what made or used it – or even if it was used at all. Because this was a late-flowering clematis – *Clematis viticella* 'Purpurea Plena Elegans' as it happens – the growth would not have been developed enough to hide the nest or to attract a bird needing a secluded spot until well into May or even June. That is very late. Was this a second nest for a second clutch in July? Swallows can have three broods and robins often have two, but this was not for either of them.

Male wrens make a number of nests to entice a female and then only use one of them. They also often have two broods in a summer. I suspect that this was a nest lovingly constructed by an ardent male wren some time around midsummer for a second family, but for some reason it was rejected by the female and never used. I wonder how many other rejected wrens' nests there are around the garden every year, representing hundreds of flights gathering material for these extraordinary creations.

In any event, the Jenny wren's final choice last July must have been a very des res indeed for her to have passed on this exquisite little mossy home hidden in amongst the entwined strands of the clematis.

———

Skull 2

On the table before me is a skull. It is small, about the size of a dessertspoon, slightly muddy, incomplete, the lower jaw missing. The eye sockets, as always with skulls, seeming disproportionately huge, the brow and back of the head low and curved as though hunched. Only one long front incisor remains, stained brown and surprisingly sharp and dagger-like, whereas the rest of the teeth, set much further back in the jaw, are tiny. In fact, only one tooth remains but the holes for the others are a double row of dots, like empty seed casings.

There is something bird-like about this skull, the upper mandible almost a beak from above, and the skull aerodynamic and yet heavy. But it never belonged to a bird and rather than a beak, there once was a snout ending in a round nose that hid that nibbling, gnawing incisor, for this was once the bone beneath the skin of a grey squirrel.

Lying upside down it has the extraordinary moulded complexity and efficiency of any skull, with its holes for veins and flanges for muscle and the crazy graph lines bones join. It has a beautiful sculpted curve below the eye sockets to the snout, big enough to hold a pair of strong jaw muscles. The chewing teeth might be small but the initial bite was fierce enough to cut through nuts and seed shells to the soft flesh inside.

I found it in amongst leaves and rotting wood at the heart of the hazel that stands beyond the back door in the Spring Garden. The rest of the skeleton was not there, no doubt disposed of by magpies and crows.

———

Elms

English elms (*Ulmus procera*) all but disappeared as mature trees from the lives of most people in the summer of 1976, although I was astonished to find myself filming amongst a small wood of them in Ipswich in 2016 as part of the Big Dreams Small Spaces series, and discovered that Dutch Elm disease had somehow passed them by.

When we came here in 1991, there was a very rotten section of trunk down in what is now the Damp Garden – but was then just at the edge of the open field. It was all that remained of a large elm that had died in 1976. I have a picture of it taken in the 1960s, with the familiar tall outline of an elm that so dominated the

English countryside of my youth, heavy with leaf, cattle standing in its shade. All that remains now are the nettles that still come up from that potash-enriched soil – the result of years of cattle manuring the ground beneath those branches.

But although almost all the wonderful large elms have gone, the lanes are full of immature ones and we have one growing yards from our back door. It is now on its third incarnation, part of the reliable pattern of growth that has become established since the 1970s. Elms grow, look healthy and happy, have the yellowest of all yellow autumnal leaves and then, when they get to about 30ft tall, which is around twelve years old, they start to produce patches of yellowing and dead leaves in summer, and within six months they are dead. Then they start all over again as suckers from the roots.

This is because the elm bark beetle that spreads Dutch Elm disease flies at about 30ft, so it ignores any young trees smaller than that. This is almost certainly nothing to do with the height of the tree but with the thickness of the bark. When the bark is thick enough, the beetles can burrow under it and lay their eggs. The resulting grubs leave the tell-tale tracery of grooves that I got to know so well when I sawed up dozens of affected large elms in the 1970s.

But the hedgerows from which these novice elms are growing remain healthy and strong, and there are miles of them running through the county. Although kept trimmed and low, these hedgerow plants are often as old as mature trees. They throw up suckers that are exact clones of themselves, so an elm hedge is really the same plant reproducing itself from its roots. From these came the once very common large hedgerow elms, which were really just outgrown members of the hedge.

For many centuries elms were the dominant trees in agricultural landscapes, growing along the edge of fields and standing alone in the middle of pastures. They are not a woodland tree and need a rich soil to grow well. This means that they have a special place in my own – and folk – memory because they were usually seen against sky, unlike woodland trees that often could not be properly seen for the wood, whereas the whole outline of an elm was visible, skeletal in winter, majestic in summer.

Elm used to be used a great deal as timber. The roof trusses on part of our house are made of elm and dated 1761. There is evidence that these were put in after a fire that burned the original medieval oak roof down, leaving just the gable ends that are dated about 1470. This either indicates that oak was becoming more scarce as building timber by the mid-eighteenth century or that elm was considered equally good for the job.

Elm wood was used for all kinds of applications where the wood might get wet, as it is very slow to rot if kept permanently moist. So it was used for groins, underwater piles and the sides of wharves, as well as for coffins or bored out for water pipes. Elm was the main timber for weatherboarding and because it will not easily split, was used for flails, for the sides of barns that get kicked by cattle, chopping blocks and for the seats of chairs because it resists splitting even when drilled to take the legs and spokes of the chairback. But it makes poor firewood, burning at a smoulder, and is a nightmare to split into logs. In the winter of 1976 I had to saw up and split six large elms that had died that summer. It was weeks of deeply unrewarding work.

Whilst we have hedgerows of English elm in the lanes by our house, on the farm we have a few wych elms (*U. glabra*). Elms are noxiously prone to variation, which has led to much dispute as to what makes a separate species or a hybrid, but *U. glabra* is distinctly different from other elms, whilst retaining all its elmy characteristics. The leaves are large and very pointed, a little like a hazel but less round and with a distinct point or tail at the end. By early March the flowers appear as a purplish fuzz along the branches and are wind-pollinated, with male and female parts in each flower. The resulting seeds are flat and winged. It is a good tree for insects and will support over 80 species of invertebrates. Whereas the English elm grew most in the agricultural lowlands of the south and Midlands, wych elm is much more common in Wales and upland areas.

English elm is upright with short horizontal branches, but the wych elm is a spreading tree, with a trunk that curves and forks and has no suckers. The name 'wych' refers to its flexibility as a wood, which made it very suitable for longbows, and was considered inferior only to high-quality yew. Having made a bow from our own yew, I must now do so from our own elmwood.

———

Grouse

Back in October 1979 I earned some much-needed money (£5 a day and a bottle of beer to wash down my sandwiches) 'bud drivin'', which was the North York Moors term for grouse beating. Myself, Sarah and about a dozen local farmers were marshalled by the gamekeepers to stretch out across the moor and clatter our sticks, wave our arms and flush the grouse out of the heather into the line of fire of the guns that were waiting in hides on the horizon. It was October, the weather and company were good, and I soon saw that not many birds got shot despite the enormously expensive guns, dogs and tweed outfits of the shooting party. It was a fine way to spend a week out on the moors and get paid for the pleasure.

And I loved the red grouse (*Lagopus lagopus*). This will surprise and dismay all those opposed to game shooting but without shooting there would have been far fewer grouse. It also has to be said that if there was no grouse shooting there would have been more predators such as hen harriers, but that was not an issue much addressed 40 years ago.

I like grouse as much for their call as anything else. For someone who had spent his entire life in the wooded lowlands of North Hampshire, the bleak expanse of the moors, corrugated with dales, was intoxicating. I loved them. I rode across them every day, the agreement being that I did so to keep Countess, the large Cleveland bay owned by our landlord, fit and looked after in lieu of rent. The grouse would explode up in front of us with their distinct 'go back go back go back' call as we cantered down the narrow peat tracks and this would be augmented by a whirring, chirring throating call, as though winding themselves up.

Anyway, for many years I thought grouse, bud driving and the moors – even horse riding – were all part of my distant past. But the much smaller moorland on top of the Welsh valley where the farm is has a few grouse butts and there was some grouse shooting within living memory – albeit on a very small scale and none in the last 20 years.

Without the attention of gamekeepers and the management of the heather by burning, the grouse population inevitably falls because the older heather is woodier and less palatable to the birds, who feed on the heather's new shoots, flowers and seeds, as well as bilberries and grass. In ten years I never saw a single bird.

But one fine October morning, I was lying in the bath, when I heard a loud 'go back go back go back' call and that coiling, throaty, whirring sound. Grouse!

I leapt out of the water, went to the window and on a track no more than 20ft from me were three red grouse, squat, rather matronly birds, picking their way along like neat chickens rather than wild creatures of distant moors. Scared away by the apparition of a dripping wet, naked man at the window, they took flight and disappeared up the hillside.

I have never seen any grouse on our land since and don't know why those three decided to come so low down from the moor or whether there are often grouse around more often but I never notice them. But it was a nostalgic link to those romantic, carefree days on the North York Moors so many years ago.

————

Crack Willow

The garden is less than 100 yards from a stream and a river and countless ditches that run through a wet plain on the wet side of a wet country. Plants of all kinds that like to be damp do well here. Two trees, in particular, that flourish along the banks are alder and willow, and of the willows, crack willow (*Salix fragilis*) is by far the most common, although there are also some large specimens of white willow (*S. alba*).

Both produce fluffy catkins with male and female on separate trees, the female ones pollinated by bees. These form wispy seeds, which are blown by the wind. They will only germinate if they fall on wet soil, so willows tend to be found alongside or near rivers and streams and the roots, always reaching towards water, provide a home for water voles, kingfishers and otters that can safely burrow into the river bank within the tracery of willow roots revetting it.

Superficially, white and crack willows are hard to tell apart, as both can make large trees reaching over 100ft with similar foliage and this is made more complicated by the fact that they hybridise freely. However, crack willow has smooth leaves with a serrated edge whereas white willow has hairy leaves and a smooth edge. Also, if you try and snap a branch of white willow, it will probably bend, whereas a crack willow will break with a satisfying snap. Crack willow has also usually been pollarded, whereas many of the white willows have been left to grow into large, truly magnificent trees.

Moth caterpillars like both species and a whole range of birds nest in the hollowed-out trunks, which get bigger and bigger whilst the pollarded growth remains eternally young.

Pollarding protected the new shoots from grazing cattle and sheep but it also stopped the tree from splitting, which it is very prone to do. We now tend to think of willow as being not much use as timber other than for cricket bats – made from a particular kind of white willow – but farmers used willow a lot in pre-barbed wire days, harvesting the shoots on top of the trunk on a regular seven-year cycle. They used these poles as fencing stakes when laying a hedge, as light but very strong gate hurdles, and as handles and thatching spars. Cleft willow, split into thin strips and then steamed to shape, is still used for making garden trugs and was once employed for a whole range of baskets.

We have an old crack willow at the back of our compost heap which is split right down the middle, although still grows very strongly. I made a tree house there for the children when they were little – actually more a tree village than house because it stretched and meandered all over and along the almost horizontal branches – but we have pollarded it twice since then as one of the largest branches snapped off in a storm, taking a great chunk of trunk with it. Crack willows do that, breaking apart with a noisy brittleness unmatched by any other British tree.

Until 50 years ago, the sight of pollarded willows along a river's edge was absolutely normal and it is significant that the original drawings for Kenneth Grahame's *The Wind in the Willows* show the pollarded willows rather than the Chinese weeping willows which were garden escapees of a later date and often used in the illustrations of modern editions.

Unfortunately, since barbed wire became ubiquitous, which is only really since the Second World War around this part of the world, too many of the old pollards have been left and the weight of the top growth has split them apart. The large branches then reach the ground, where they root, producing new growth, and these are quickly grazed by cattle before they have a chance to establish. In this way, the original tree, which could have been preserved for centuries if regularly pollarded, dies.

———

Berries

The hawthorn and rosehips, elder and dogwood (white) are all very good this year as are the damsons and nuts of all kinds. Really spectacular. The only real disappointment is the apple crop – the worst ever. This is probably due to the late frost whilst I was away filming in America.

———

The Red Kite

In the year I was born, 1955, there were seven pairs of breeding adult kites that managed, between them, to raise just one solitary surviving young. Those are the statistics of extinction.

All seven nesting birds were centred around just the one site, near Builth Wells, in mid-Wales. Despite these terrifyingly low numbers, these birds actually represented something of a triumph for conservationists. The kite had been exterminated in England by 1870, was gone from Scotland by 1900, and by 1905, there were reckoned to be as few as just four or five breeding pairs in Wales.

The reason that they were so rapidly wiped out after being as common in the mid-eighteenth century as they are today, was the rise of intensive game preservation, their proximity to humans which made them easy to shoot and snare, and their predilection for carrion, making them easy to poison. In short, they were a soft target, although given the opportunity, they are comparatively long-lived birds, often reaching double figures and one has been recorded in Germany at 26 years old. This longevity was probably one of the major factors that enabled the tiny residual Welsh population to cling on.

Their survival, reintroduction and flourishing is one of the great wildlife success stories of the late twentieth century. Now, in 2020, you cannot drive from London to Oxford through the Chilterns without seeing kites, they are common as far south as Brighton and have almost reached East Anglia.

When we first moved to Longmeadow in 1991 I saw a kite perhaps every other year and then only after a storm had blown it eastwards from its Welsh stronghold 40 miles to the west. Now I see them daily. When we bought the farm in 2005 they were seen less often than peregrines or goshawks and now one will follow the tractor every time I top a field.

Nevertheless, I still stop and stare at their size and mastery. They are beautiful birds. Because of their remote Welsh base for much of the twentieth century, I had associated them with mountain and moor but they like open, lightly wooded countryside and will eat almost anything that they can get hold of – literally. Carrion makes up about half of their diet and on the Welsh hillsides that means dead sheep, although there is no record of a kite taking even the smallest lamb alive as they have comparatively weak feet compared to many raptors. Pellet analysis shows that voles, rabbits, rats, moles, crows, magpies, pigeons, fish, insects, worms and reptiles make up the bulk of their prey.

They are sociable, gregarious birds, and driving along the M40 I have counted up to a dozen birds hunting together. They often roost together in winter and, unlike most other birds of prey, their nests are often as close as a few hundred yards from each other. These are often adorned with plastic bags, wool, bits of cloth and scraps of paper, and it seems that a pair will rotate favoured nesting sites from year to year, returning to an old one as much as five years later. Perhaps this is an aspect of their longevity.

But it is the solitary visitor over the garden, deep V-shaped tail, wings bent slightly back, mewing call not unlike, but thinner than, a buzzard's, that still surprises and thrills me. A distant descendant, perhaps, from that solitary surviving chick in the year of my birth.

————

Dogwood

It is not often that one can credit the rise and rise of particular plants to the Thatcherite enterprise culture but dogwood – and particularly *Cornus alba* – became ubiquitous as a vegetative fill for the front of business parks, service stations, company HQs and shopping centres. It grows almost anywhere, has nice bright stems in winter, inoffensive foliage in summer and makes a really good autumnal display as its leaves turn orange. It can be pruned back brutally hard if required and will spring back with unabated vigour and, best of all for the grower, it strikes ridiculously easily from cuttings, so costs almost nothing to propagate and grow.

Cornus are still the mainstay of any so-called winter garden, where coloured bark of all hues contributes the most significant elements – although I would strongly argue that clipped evergreens make by far the best gardens in mid-winter. I have a number of *C. alba* growing down by the pond, where they relish the regular flooding. But in the hedges flanking the roads and lanes around this garden is the real deal, our native *C. sanguinea*. In autumn, the leaves turn red and then deep purple with black berries held on crimson stems, and the lanes blaze for a few weeks as the light fades, and then the burning leaves fall.

The name 'dogwood' has no canine connection but is derived from *dag* meaning a skewer. The blood-red straight stems were used both for butchers' skewers, arrows and goads – and when every vehicle was drawn by horse or oxen, there was a demand for such things.

Oliver Rackham, whose 1986 *The History of the Countryside* changed my life as much as any other factual book I have read, points out that dogwood is not a good coloniser and was almost never planted in any hedge after 1800. It tends to be the fourth or fifth species within a hedge – and it is generally accepted via Hooper's Rule, that a rough-and-ready guide to dating a hedge is to count the number of woody species in a 30-yard length and multiply that by 110. So the hedge running down to our house has hawthorn, ash, dogwood, elm, blackthorn, hazel and field maple. It also has elder but that is not part of the calculations because it is such a ready coloniser. Apply the rule and that gives you an age of 770 years, which means that the hedge goes back to 1250. That seems very probable given the history of the area. The cornus would not be that old however, unless the hedge had been deliberately planted as a mixed selection, which is unlikely. Planted hedges tended to be hawthorn, with everything else slowly joining in across the centuries. Given that dogwood is a late coloniser it probably appeared as recently as the sixteenth or even seventeenth century. A positive parvenu.

What matters is not the game of precisely dating hedges – although it is one I play at every opportunity – but that our hedgerows, filled with 'ordinary' plants, are manifestations of deep history and should be nurtured and treasured for their historical importance as much as for being habitats for wildlife. Every landscape, however apparently mundane, hums with history.

Read any book about this dogwood and it will say it is a plant primarily of chalk. But I grew up on chalk and cannot recall seeing it, whilst this part of Herefordshire has no chalk at all but is uniformly heavy clay. All rules were made to be broken.

————

Rats

Given the lengths that mankind goes to try and get rid of them, you would think that rats would avoid people as much as possible. But the opposite is true. Wherever you have people you will find rats, and their spread is almost entirely down to their ability to coexist with people and feed off our waste. We have only ourselves to blame.

Rats and gardens are an unhappy combination but our local rat catcher (OK, Pest Control Operative – and he will happily deal with wasps' nests, moles, mice and anything else that you deem a pest, but rats are the main thing) tells me that garden sheds are the most likely home of rats, followed by compost heaps. Rats dislike disturbance and underneath a garden shed is likely to be as free of disturbance as anywhere else. But an undisturbed compost heap is likely to be one that is neglected or misunderstood. There are a lot of half-hearted attempts at making compost which quickly go wrong and the compost heap is either abandoned or vaguely poked at intervals. With its supply of half-rotted food and its insulation against bad weather, it is rat heaven.

There are a few simple rules of composting that will almost entirely remove the risk of rats. The first is to exclude any fats, meat or cooked food because these will break down slowly and attract rats. The second is to add bulk – lots of brown matter, like dried stems or cardboard. The third is to turn the heap regularly – certainly at least every two months and ideally every few weeks. Remember, rats hate disturbance and a turned compost heap is a very disturbed and disturbing thing.

In cities, rats live in buildings and sewers but in the countryside, a lot live in the fields and hedges, feeding off grain, seeds, young birds – anything and everything. These field rats invariably head towards buildings and people after harvest and, as the autumnal weather worsens, we always see one or two in October. Before combine harvesters, all grain was stored indoors in barns or silos separately from the straw. The sheaves would be stacked either in barns or outside in ricks that were built up to the size of a small house and then thatched to keep the rain out. In spring, these ricks would be taken apart and the sheaves thrown into a thrashing machine to separate the grain from the straw. I can just remember, as a very small child, a threshing machine threshing sheaves of corn from a rick of wheat to provide long straw for thatching. As the great wooden machine, with its layers of sieves driven by a huge flapping belt attached to a tractor, shuffled and creaked, the men pitching the sheaves had string tied under their knees to stop the rats running up inside their trouser legs, and three or four terriers patrolled the outside of the rick as it got lower and the rats inside broke cover.

The size of a fully grown brown rat is always a shock but although I would rather not share my space with them, there is something almost amiable about a rat pottering about, looking for food. They don't dart or sneak so much as investigate and explore. They do not seem to me to be a lot worse than a squirrel – but then I was brought up to believe that squirrels were rats with bushy tails, so maybe I am just a bit confused.

My (limited) benignity is entirely restricted to rats' presence in the garden. I do not like them in the house. Fortunately this is rare. But when we bought the house, in the autumn of 1991, it was riddled with rats and the evidence was that it had been for a very long time. That evidence came in the form of a deep litter of rat poo under the fifteenth-century floorboards and the Victorian ceiling that fell on me as I exposed the Tudor building hidden beneath layers of nineteenth- and twentieth-century gentrification. When I had wiped myself down, there was a layer on the floor inches deep that I had to shovel into a number of wheelbarrow loads to clear away. It was historic, archaeological rat shit, some of which was hundreds of years old – but somehow not made any the more attractive for that.

And there were very modern rats, too. The house originally had no electricity (or mains water, toilets, bathroom or drains, other than one soakaway), so I would work until it became too dark to see and then walk across the fields to the cottage that we rented for a year whilst we made the house habitable.

One day I was easing away modern floorboards nailed to Tudor rafters, when I came across the body of a freshly dead large rat. It was getting dark and if I was going to have to contend with rats under the floorboards, I wanted at least to have good light to see them. The next morning I returned and found the body of the rat had been completely devoured, leaving only its skin and bones. I confess I became more tentative lifting floorboards after that.

A few years later, the children – who were still all little – called me excitedly to point out that there was a large but very woozy rat behind the sofa in the sitting room. I was wondering the best way of dealing with it when our Jack Russell terrier, Poppy, appeared and dispatched it in one quick move. I suspect it had been poisoned and wandered in through the front door that was always left open on sunny days. Not your average visitor.

The last manifestation was when I was filming recently in America. I spoke to Sarah on the phone and, amongst other things, she said, 'We had a rat in the larder. It was hiding behind a tray leaning against the wall but its tail was sticking out.' I replied, 'What did you do?' 'Oh,' she said, completely unfazed, 'called the dogs, shut the door and they got it.'

This was six months ago now and the dogs are still tremendously excited every time we go outside to the larder.

———

Field Maple

It always surprises me how keen people are to grow exotic species and varieties of maple from Japan and America and yet rarely select our own native maple (*Acer campestre*), despite it being a good garden tree, having incredible yellow autumn foliage and making a robust hedge as well as being remarkably trouble-free and easy to grow – which can hardly be said about most other kinds of maple.

But gardeners tend to spurn the obvious and the native probably because it reflects less well on their skill and ingenuity. However, I planted scores of field maples in this garden over a quarter of a century ago and, whilst most make up a long hedge, about a dozen are now really good-sized, beautiful trees.

Unlike some introduced and more glamorous garden trees, field maples are a good host to a wide range of wildlife, with aphids and many species of moth feeding off the leaves, the flowers providing pollen and nectar for bees, and the seeds, with their typical winged sails that take them twisting to the ground, eaten by small mammals.

Field maples appeared as part of the wildwood that grew after the last glacial period, arriving quite late in its waves of colonisation alongside ash, hornbeam, holly and beech, and coming from warmer parts of the still-linked European continent.

Most specimens are small, either because they have been coppiced or pollarded or because they are growing in shaded woodland. Given time and the right situation, they will make mature trees that will reach 80ft or 90ft, with a grooved and fissured trunk that becomes knobbly and sprouts clusters of shoots. Some of the field maples I planted as saplings in 1993 are already half that size.

The wood is dense, good for firewood and turning, and was used to make mazers or ceremonial wooden bowls. The leaves, whilst recognisably maple-shaped, are small and dense, and cast a deep shade. It was often used as part of general coppiced woodland, with the resulting wood used as fencing stakes or firewood.

Many of the plants formerly intended as hedgerow trees that could be pollarded have now been cut back, like so many hedges, into uniformity by the flail. If you see field maple in a mixed hedge, it is a pretty good indicator that the hedge is at least 200 years old and probably more, as it was seldom planted as part of the enclosures and divisions of open fields.

———

Flood

Returning from the heat and constant sun of California after two weeks' filming, I have to wade waist-deep the last quarter mile home from the airport, my luggage abandoned at a kind stranger's house up the road. Floods are not unusual here but this is a big one and, as homecomings go, this is a first.

The garden is half underwater and beyond the fence cattle are stranded on a slither of dry ground with just room for them to stand bunched together miserably. Swans drift across the fields. The rain falls constantly and at night I can hear the water lapping into the back yard.

———

NOVEMBER

Bird Table

When the clocks go back at the end of October, it is the signal to set up the bird table. This is in the back yard and is a large, single salting stone about 6ft by 3ft. These were once a fixture in every farmhouse in Herefordshire – and probably across the country – until around the 1970s, when people gradually stopped keeping pigs and salting their own bacon. It has a groove running round the outer edge leading to a lip so that the excess salty water could drain. We did keep pigs here once, in the orchard, which they trashed with astonishing efficiency. In fact, the pigs are responsible for the current orchard beds because the grass never really recovered from their groundwork that summer ten years ago. I made bacon from their meat and was astonished at how much liquid the process created. Hence the need for the groove.

On this stone table is a shallow stone bowl filled with water for the birds to drink and wash in, a mossy, rather rotten log, and a piece of driftwood. Both are deeply fissured and weathered. I pour the bird food over the wood so that seeds, nuts and little pellets of fat lodge in the crevices and grooves.

We have a large dustbin in the larder filled with my own custom bird mix. Nothing particularly original but it is a combination of husked and black sunflower seeds, mealworms, niger seed and suet pellets. I don't put out grain as only the sparrows and pigeons really eat it and they drive away other seed-eating birds. I have another dustbin filled with peanuts and three or four hanging wire tubes are replenished with these daily. Finally, I also use fat blocks and fat balls in protected wire cages. This is all extravagant but I consider it as important to the garden as the potting compost and horticultural grit that I spend much more on.

The upshot is that none of the smaller birds go hungry in winter, so they then are fit and healthy to breed in spring as well as to hunt and feed their offspring. It is an investment into a healthy, self-sustaining garden.

Well, that is the formal, slightly pompous explanation. It also gives me huge pleasure watching them feed at the table every day. I love it and that alone is sufficient justification. Winter is the best time to watch garden birds because they are easier to see, less busy with the all-consuming business of mating, nesting and rearing young, and the weather means that a garden is often a safe port in a storm.

We stop feeding in mid-April, clean the table, put the logs aside, and the stone slab goes from bird table to display stand, covered with pots of pelargoniums whilst the birds, many of whom happily ate the seeds and nuts in winter, turn to a carnivorous diet to feed their young, eating caterpillars, aphids and spiders from the garden.

———

Wagtails

Wagtail names are perverse. With its white face and black bib, white belly and grey back, the pied wagtail looks grey. Whereas the grey wagtail, sort of grey-brown on top but its bright yellow chest and belly make it look predominantly yellow. If that were not bad enough, the yellow wagtail, which is admittedly very yellow underneath, is greenish on top.

Here in the garden we see pied wagtails all day long. There is one, right now, pecking away at the skylight 20ft above my head. It is at the very top of the cone of the hop kiln, where there is a Perspex bubble – an oculus – and the flies find their way up there to the light. The wagtails then pursue an endless process of frustration, pecking vainly at the outside of the bubble to get at the flies sidling less than half an inch beneath them. I once had a carrion crow land there and looked up to see this enormous beak hammering on the Perspex. I seriously expected it to break through like a pickaxe on thin ice.

The pied wagtail is, as its name suggests, always in movement, its tail flicking and bobbing constantly, and scampering along the ridge of the roof or on the ground after insects. Its flight is characteristically jerky and undulating, like a woodpecker's, slowly rising and then falling back down again before rising into another climb.

It feeds almost exclusively on insects and thus hardly ever comes to the bird table, so a hard winter can be very difficult for it. One of the reasons why they may be so common in the garden is that they prefer wet sites to dry, being happiest in mud and bog and sodden turf – which pretty much describes this garden in all but drought. Its nest is likely to be on a ledge or somewhere open on one side, rather than tucked into a hedge or cavity. Away from wooded areas or reeds, the nests are sometimes chosen by cuckoos to foster their eggs.

However, I have never seen a grey wagtail in the garden but do so frequently on the farm 30 miles to the west, even though they are much rarer than the pied. This is not so much an attribute of geography – although for a long time they were the preserve of the south – but of landscape. They love fast-flowing mountain streams and we have three of those on the farm, one of which flows fast and hard all year round and winter rains turn it into a torrent.

With its yellow breast like a mustard waistcoat under a grey morning coat, and brilliantly yellow rump beneath an extra-long grey and white tail that flips and juts and rhythmically flicks, the grey wagtail looks like a pied wagtail dressed up in party clothes. It feeds exclusively on aquatic insects and will nest next to a stream in amongst the rocks or hollows in stream-side trees like alders.

I see it mostly in the ford that leads to the wild-flower meadow, standing midstream on the wet stones, flicking and bouncing its tail and shining bright yellow against the dark, rushing water.

———

Canada Geese

The geese honk mournfully across the evening dark. They are flying around a lot at the moment, circling the flooded fields, sometimes in pairs but occasionally as many as seven or eight in a 'V' formation, the huge birds dominating the sky by their sheer presence and disciplined aerial display.

But it is their call that is so distinctive and so much a part of the winter months here. It belongs to Canada geese. They were introduced from America in the seventeenth century as exotic wildfowl but now are probably the most common of all British geese.

In an urban park, they can be a nuisance, badgering to be fed and grazing the grass excessively, resulting in widespread and voluminous droppings. But here above this rural garden they remain mysterious and liminal, if not exactly rare. We are on the edge of their habitat, only really suitable when the floods rise, and they are on the edges of ours, flying heavily over but always feeling like visitors, even though, unlike in North America, where they are migratory, they remain very limited to their chosen territory, never moving far from it from birth to death.

So these birds calling dolefully from a home that seems far away to the north are doing so with a Herefordshire accent and are just as local as me.

———

Pine Marten

We were on a picnic with friends near Drimnin on the Morvern Peninsula overlooking the Isle of Mull when our Land Rover broke down. Waiting for assistance, I idly walked to the edge of a steep escarpment and saw an animal moving amongst the trees. Recognisably not a squirrel, nor cat, it was smaller than a fox, larger than a stoat and with a chocolate-brown body blazed with an ivory throat and bib, upright ears and long tail. I realised with a shock that it was a pine marten.

The shock was because at the time – over 25 years ago – pine martens were still incredibly rare and those that were around were very secretive and nocturnal. The chances of ever seeing one were minuscule and there it was, pottering around in the middle of the day with a couple of families on a jaunt just 50ft above – albeit in one of the more remote corners of the British Isles.

Since then the pine marten has made something of a comeback, but is still one of our rarer mammals. Although there are reckoned to be a few thousand spread across most of Scotland, wherever there is woodland cover, in England and Wales they were all but exterminated by gamekeepers and deforestation but have returned thanks to the efforts of conservationists. Between 2015 and 2017, 50 pine martens were brought from Scotland to mid-Wales and are being monitored.

I only learned about this project a few months ago but in 2017, I was fixing a fence that ran along the edge of a deep gulley when, out of the corner of my eye, I saw a chocolate-brown creature slip through the bracken with a flash of creamy yellow fur. My brain immediately registered pine marten – although I believed that there were none in this part of Wales and if there were, they would more likely be found in deep coniferous woodland. But I had seen one before, and the image, although fleeting, was strong. However, I did not count it as a sighting and accepted that wishful thinking might have been involved.

Then last year I was talking to my son on the phone, going through the work he had done that day on the farm, when he said, almost by the by, 'Oh, I saw a pine marten today', and he described it exactly and unmistakably. To share our space with this elusive creature that was considered extinct earlier in my lifetime, is an astonishing gift.

For a creature that is so rare, pine martens are adaptable and are apex predators. They are long-lived, too, with an average lifespan of eight to ten years. They eat small mammals including grey squirrels, birds, eggs and carrion, and in autumn and winter, a lot of berries, nuts and fungi. But they do need a big territory. This can range from a couple of square miles if the habitat is rich in food up to ten square miles in highland forest.

The only time two martens ever come together or tolerate another's presence at all is for mating. The females are not mature until their third year and have a litter of one to five kits in early spring in a den in a hollow tree or under a rock. The young are reared exclusively by the female and will leave and become independent in early autumn.

Finally, one factoid about pine martens – they have semi-retractable claws, which means they are excellent climbers and scamperers high in the branches of trees and will rob the nests of corvid eggs and young such as crows and jays.

———

Teasels

Goldfinches love the seeds of teasels and at this time of year I often see these brightly painted little birds clinging to the conical, bristly seedheads, greedily extracting each seed from its little sleeve. The flowers are tiny, with both male and female on the same plant. They open as small lavender-coloured tubes in rings around the conical head, from which the bristles are formed of tiny hooked spikes like Velcro.

Sarah loves teasels and encourages them to grow wherever they will – and they will almost everywhere – whereas I have an ambiguous relationship with them. I love the way they look, the way that they are so good for birds and that they choose to grow so freely in this garden. In winter, the leaves brown and crumble to dust leaving just the bare stem beneath the seedheads so they are sculptural and dramatic – as well as so good for the birds. But – and here's the rub – by early spring, the leaves start to regrow and have the knack of scratching me to ribbons whilst simultaneously drenching me. It is quite a party trick.

The scratching – and clearing teasels always results in my arms running with blood – is not from the spiny seedheads but from the leaves and the stems that are punctuated along their length by razor-sharp short spines. These do not detach and stick into you like thorns but simply rip through your skin like a sharp rake. The soaking comes from the cup that is formed at the base of the leaves where they join the stem, where there is a membrane that holds rainwater funnelled down the leaves. By the time the plant is mature the leaves nearest to the ground can hold a lot of water – perhaps half a pint – which the plant can use at times of drought. This water is said to have restorative powers and people still use it to bathe tired eyes. These cups of water are also traps for insects that drown and rot and the partially carnivorous plant absorbs their nutrients as they biodegrade in the mini water-traps.

This is a key to its favoured growing conditions, because although it seeds in all sorts of nooks and crannies, it is happiest in damp ditches or boggy bits of ground – which is why we have so many growing in the garden and in the ditches of the surrounding fields.

The softly spiked seedheads have been used for centuries for carding or teasing out the pile of woollen cloth. Brush one over a woollen scarf or jersey and the fibres will be gently collected and lifted as it passes but never pulled out or torn. The best teasel for this is fuller's teasel (*Dipsacus sativus*), which differs from the wild teasel – confusingly called *D. fullonum* – mainly by its spiny bracts that curve up around the flower head like elaborate moustaches.

————

Barn Owls

I wish I could say I regularly saw barn owls here but I have not done so over the past 30 years. However, about ten years ago, for about a month, I would see one about half an hour before dusk, flying in exactly the same line and height along the edge of the garden, heading out to the tussocky, half-grazed fields that would have been its best bet for voles.

But I do quite often see one from the car on my way to the farm, around the same half-mile stretch of road, flying at hedge height in the last light of the day before dusk.

In my childhood, one of the standard party tricks was to take visitors 'up to see the owls'. This involved a mile-long walk with the dogs up the muddy lane opposite our garden to a deserted farm. My mother remembered when the farm was working and the farmer's daughter would walk down these lanes to the village school, a daily two-mile, cross-country solitary trip for a seven-year-old.

But that was before the war and by the 1960s, the ceilings were falling through, elder grew from the top of the chimneys, windows were smashed and weeds grew through the concrete of the milking stalls. However, in both an upstairs bedroom of one of the two cottages and high up in the lovely old barn, were barn owl nests. We would creep into the big open door of the barn and look up above the bales where we would hear a sneezing, wheezing, snoring sound and sometimes see three or four young owlets looking down at us, and in winter one or two adults, who would silently slip away through a gap in the wall. They were a fixture. It was where they lived and we treated it like making a social call.

But even as a very young boy I was aware of the specialness of them, the beauty and the slight fear, their utterly silent flight and ghostly whiteness, and the curious sounds they made. We also were well aware of the kudos attached to being able to summon them on cue.

That was over 50 years ago. Since then, barn owls have suffered, not least through the loss of breeding sites like that derelict farm which has now been razed. Of almost all British birds, barn owls are the most dependent on barns and unoccupied buildings for nesting.

They hunt with a slow, quartering flight, searching for prey – especially voles – on the ground. This slow, almost silent flight comes from their very low wing loading, meaning that the bird has exceptionally large wings in proportion to its weight. On top of that, their feathers are very flexible, which aids manoeuvring at slow speeds, and the silence is due to a comb-like structure on the leading edge of the outer primary feather and soft fringes on the trailing edge of the flight feathers. The combination of these seemingly small details reduces the ultrasonic sound that small mammals are particularly sensitive to. In other words, the owls have evolved in a particularly precise way, with slow, low almost completely silent flight to give them an advantage over very specific prey. However, one disadvantage of this slow, very low flight is that far too many barn owls die on our roads, hit by cars as they drift out in front of them.

Despite their ghostly reputation, they are not, of course, white but a lovely blend of ochres, gold and russet feathers on their backs and face, and a much purer pale colour underneath. The females are spotted with ochre and the males are pure white, which is what you see as they fly. The facial disc is very distinctive with the beak emerging from feathers that makes it look like a nose between the two absolutely black eyes.

Barn owls are birds of open country and numbers have steadily increased as the woodland cover has dropped from about 50 per cent in the Bronze Age to today's five per cent – the level it has been for the past 700 years. They flourished in the countryside of the sixteenth to the mid-nineteenth centuries and were regarded as the most common of all British owls, but modern agriculture has affected them badly and they declined steadily throughout the twentieth century. They are very responsive to fluctuations in vole populations, which in turn tend to boom and bust and are affected by harsh winters.

They are not garden birds and our farm is too wooded to be their natural habitat, although they hunt on the top of the hillside on the open, exposed landscape of thick grasses, heather and bilberries. They are tied closely to man's use of grasslands, and one of the ironies of the current desire to plant billions – no trillions – of trees, go vegan and stop all meat and dairy production, is that one of the earliest casualties would be the beautiful barn owl. The more you study and learn from nature, the more complicated and qualified interventions by humans become – however well-intentioned.

———

Yellow-necked Mice

Everyone, including me, is squeamish about rats, but mice are a worse problem because there are so many of them in our houses and because, unlike rats, they are more or less incontinent. They pee as they go.

We have house mice, and occasionally far too many of them, but now and then we get visited by a rarer species – a better class of mouse if you like. I first saw a yellow-necked mouse in a trap that I had set under the sink in the house that we rented whilst this one was being made habitable. In fact, that house was infested with rats and the trap was destined for them and was – in every sense of the word – overkill for the poor mouse.

But even in the extreme violence of death, this mouse was like no other I had seen. It was quite big, with large ears, a distinctly yellow bib below its throat, a white underbelly and pale chestnut fur on its back. I discovered that it was *Apodemus flavicollis*, the yellow-necked mouse.

It is found in the south-east, East Anglia, across the Welsh Marches and into the Midlands, and is associated with ancient woodland – although it is common in gardens. They are an arboreal species, feeding on tree seeds, making their nests in tunnels amongst tree roots or in hollowed trees. They are good climbers and leapers, being able to jump – it is said – fully 3ft into the air. Unfortunately, this one under the sink did not jump quickly enough.

The truth is that I only ever encounter them as corpses – as cat kill or one found dead in the garden that was probably owl kill. But, as with roadkill, at least it means that they are about.

———

The Wren's Song

Out of the half-bare undergrowth, as many leaves now on the ground as still clinging to the branches, a little bird appears, moving more like a mouse than a bird, creeping, crouching, body a ball of brown feathers, beak pin-sharp and surprisingly long tail cocked high. Then it flits off to another branch, inquisitive, eager and always busy. It is a wren (*Troglodytes troglodytes*) – one of our most common and best-loved garden birds. The name Jenny wren is a tribute to our familiarity with them.

On a number of occasions we have had a wren come into the house in winter and stay indoors for a few days, flitting and scurrying around the furniture and behind cupboards, probably feasting on the spiders and enjoying the relative warmth. Then, when it had eaten its fill or got bored of our company, it takes the first opportunity to dart off outside again.

Gardeners often talk about the way a robin will accompany them as they work outside, feeding on worms and insects uncovered by digging or weeding, but I am as often aware of wrens around me as I garden. They are much less brazen, more wary and furtive, mostly keeping low but never far away, and never frightened of human company. The best time to see them is in winter, not just because the lack of leaves reveals them more easily but also because numbers in gardens rise in winter as they seek shelter and food.

They love the fallen leaves and untidiness of autumn and spend as much time flitting in and amongst the debris on the ground as in the branches of the hedges and shrubs. However, they suffer badly in cold weather and many will die in a really hard winter. To counter the cold they will have communal night-time roosts, often in unused nests of other species, with as many as 60 birds recorded crammed like sardines into one nesting box. However, mild winters have helped them and now there are reckoned to be over eleven million pairs in the UK – making it our most populous bird.

They will nest in a whole series of imaginative and unlikely places, with the male building a series of nests to entice a mate. We often have them nesting in amongst the stacked pots and seed trays in the potting shed, and the regular removal of these and our coming and going does not seem to bother them in the slightest.

Wrens are rare visitors to a bird table because their long, very pointed beak is adapted for snaffling insects rather than opening seeds or nuts. But if you do not see a wren as often as a robin, you are sure to hear it. Its song is high-quality, extraordinarily loud for such a tiny bird, rounded and rich but very treble, and so fast as to become a blur of sharp music. But listen to a slowed-down version and it is transformed into a deeply melodic, fluting, sound, combining the haunting tones of a whale's call and a night-ingale's song. Its vocal range – lost to the human ear when heard at normal speed – is extraordinary, using over a hundred notes at a rate of over 700 per minute. All of this is beyond the human ear or hand. It is music played in another dimension.

If you live in a town, then the song will be even better and even louder. Urban wrens are on average one-third louder again than their rural cousins, with more complex songs, higher frequencies and longer notes – all of which seem to be a development as a result of the greater background noise. Their songs are mainly territorial, although in spring they are used to attract a mate, and will always end with a final flourish in the form of a long, strong trill. It is just noticeable to us but is a positively soaring final aria to the listening female or potential male intruder.

————

Sparrowhawks

Sparrowhawks have fared very well in my lifetime. When I was younger and obsessed with birds of prey, I was as likely to see a sparrowhawk as a nightingale. They were there, but only just and very hidden. However, they, and almost every other raptor other than the kestrel, have dramatically increased since the mid-1980s.

The decimation of British raptors was a combination of game-keepers killing them and the effect of organochlorine pesticides such as DDT, but gamekeepers got a longer run at sparrowhawks than at other birds of prey. Whilst the Protection of Birds Act, 1954 gave legal protection to all wild birds, it omitted sparrow-hawks, who were considered fair game for persecution until they were included in 1963.

It took longer to stop organochlorine use, which built up a residue in insects that, in turn, built up in the songbirds that ate them and that, in turn, built up in the raptors that predated on them. The result was eggs that had shells so thin they were not viable. Despite the warnings of environmentalists – most notably Rachel Carson in *Silent Spring*, published in 1962 – organochlorine pesticides were not banned in the UK until 1984, at which point, bird populations started to increase.

It was ironic that the first sparrowhawk I ever saw, when I was 33 and had moved to Herefordshire, was flying high in the sky. Normally the sky is as good a place as any to start looking for birds, but sparrowhawks spend most of their time skimming low to the ground or over hedgerows, making lightning raids on prey and then twisting and flicking away through the branches of a tree and out of sight. They never swoop down from the sky or fly away up into it but seem to emerge almost from within the ground, like sharks breaking water – and just as deadly.

But in spring, the male will claim his territory by high, looping aerial displays. The male – the musket – is not a big bird and at four to six ounces, weighs little more than a mistle thrush. He does not fill a large space up in the sky but is distinctive enough through the nature of his flight and through his characteristic broad wings and long tail. What you cannot see when he is up there are his orange breast and slate-blue back and wings, or his half-crazed orange eyes. For a murderous killer, he is a very handsome bird.

The female lays her eggs in May and they hatch just over a month later – which used to coincide with the period of maximum availability of fledgling songbirds, which the male catches and delivers to the nest and which the female dismembers and dishes out in suitable portion sizes. However, there is evidence that climate change means that leaves are opening earlier, so caterpillars are emerging to feed on them earlier, and songbirds are responding by breeding earlier to take advantage of this main source of food for their young. Sparrowhawks however, are still breeding at the same time with their young hatching between the middle of June and early July. The knock-on effect of this is that in their third week, the growing fledglings are increasingly running out of food and then larger young will sometimes kill and eat the weakest.

The young are fledged and leave the nest after about 28 days, which is usually about the beginning of August. They stay within around ten miles of the nest and if they survive their first winter will pair and breed themselves the next year. About two-thirds of the young die, mostly of starvation and mostly within a month or two of leaving the nest. One-third of all adults die each year, too, with the highest mortality, again from starvation, in early spring. Others are preyed upon and eaten by goshawks, peregrines and tawny owls, and it is not unknown for females to attack and eat the much smaller males.

The female is twice as heavy as the male and 30 per cent bigger, with a brown-and-white barred chest, brown back and heavily barred tail. Both males and females have noticeably long, yellow legs, designed for plucking small birds from hedges or the ground. They feed almost exclusively on small birds, although the female will take a wood pigeon or small duck, eating it where it falls as it is often heavier than she is.

But if you want to see sparrowhawks at their best, doing what no other bird on earth can do, then the best vantage point is from a car on a country lane. Surprisingly often, a sparrowhawk will be disturbed from a kill in the middle of the road and take off in front of you, never leaving the road and never rising more than an inch or two above the surface of the tarmac. Instinctively you slow down to avoid collision and have a better view, but invariably you find yourself speeding up to keep up with the bird. It can fly for up to a mile at this ridiculous, impossible, insane altitude at 30 miles an hour, twisting to follow every bend in the road. Then, when you fear this cannot be right and that surely, *surely* the bird is suffering, it will twist and rise over the hedge or through the bars of a gate and be gone.

I must have had this experience a score of times and each one feels terrifying, triumphant and exhausting.

They are woodland birds and they have evolved to appear from cover into a clearing or glade, grab their prey before it knows what is happening, then disappear back into the trees. Their broad wings and long tail mean that they have exceptionally good control as they twist and manoeuvre through trees and undergrowth. If a bird evades the first pass or flies into open sky, the sparrowhawk rarely gives chase. They appear to fly like lightning but they are sprinters and over any distance longer than a few hundred yards they are not actually that fast – a wood pigeon can outfly them with ease. Their most effective weapon is surprise.

The number of predators is always controlled by the number of prey – not the other way round. If you want to see sparrowhawks in your garden the best way is to have a bird feeding station near a hedge or wall or some bushes. Songbirds such as blue tits and great tits, sparrows, blackbirds, robins and starlings – all good sparrowhawk prey – will come to feed and sparrowhawks will come to kill and eat them. Not many though – each male eats only about two tit-size birds per day, not enough, as studies have shown, to affect songbird numbers, but sufficient to help maintain a sparrowhawk or two. And if you feel squeamish about this, heaven forfend that you should ever own a cat.

Squirrels

When we first moved here, there was just one tree in the garden, which was a very old and rather gnarled hazel (*Corylus avellana*). This bore a quantity of nuts every year although most would be snaffled by squirrels before they were ripe enough to be gathered and eaten by us. But after a year or two, I noticed hazel seedlings popping up. These were nuts that the squirrels had gathered and buried and then forgotten about. They had then germinated and become little hazel saplings.

So I started to dig them up and pot them. After a few years I had about a hundred, so decided to plant a small hazel coppice. Now, a quarter of a century later, this provides us with all our bean sticks, lots of nuts and is a beautiful part of the garden, filled with spring flowers like primroses, anemones and bluebells.

I suppose I should thank the squirrels for this, although it is hard to find a gardener – and especially a forester – who has a good word to say about them.

The first grey squirrel (*Sciurus carolinensis*) was introduced into this country from its native North America at the end of the nineteenth century, when ten were released at Woburn Abbey in 1890. They were first considered charming novelties but within 50 years, they had driven out the native red squirrel (*S. vulgaris*). This is the Squirrel Nutkin of Beatrix Potter with its ginger fur and tufted ears, and was generally considered a charming addition to woodland and garden fauna, whose worst crime was to steal a few nuts.

However, it soon became apparent that wherever the grey squirrel took residence the red was quickly driven out or killed. There are a number of reasons for this. For a start, the bigger grey can lay down more fat and is therefore much better adapted to coping with cold winters and periods of food shortage, so when there was intense competition for food between the two species, the grey invariably came off best. This was primarily because the greys will eat a wide range of nuts and seeds, as well as eggs and young chicks in spring, whereas the red will only eat smaller seeds such as pine and spruce nuts.

The grey also carry the squirrel pox virus which, although they have developed an immunity to it, kills red squirrels. The upshot is that red squirrels are virtually extinct from the south save for a very few areas such as the Isle of Wight, and are reduced to a few areas of large coniferous – mainly pine – planting in the north and in Scotland.

But grey squirrels are everywhere and dig up bulbs from gardens, eat young songbirds and do huge damage to forestry by gnawing the bark of trees. They also invariably find a way to steal peanuts and seeds from the bird feeders however ingeniously you hang them, returning again and again with their own brand of acrobatic furtiveness.

———

Crows

If you keep sheep, sooner or later you are going to have a bad experience with crows. Any sheep, young or old, that is sick, trapped or injured is likely to have its eyes attacked. I have seen a crow perching on the head of a lamb whilst it is still being born and pecking its eyes out. This is repulsive and hard to think of as anything other than a particularly cruel form of torture. But we do not object to thrushes eating snails or a heron eating a frog or fish, or a sparrowhawk plucking a blackbird out of the air. This is nature in its reddest tooth and claw but the crow cannot be blamed for finding easy pickings. The brutal reality of life is that the first rule is to eat and the second not to be eaten. The third is to successfully procreate. Everything else is a bonus.

In fact, the carrion crow is an exceptionally clever survivor, able to eat almost anything, dead or alive, and to live almost anywhere. Their diet will vary from carrion, seeds, insects, fruit, worms, shellfish, rats, mice and birds, and they will even hunt and catch quite large birds – like a pigeon – in mid-flight. Although they can form flocks, crows rarely do and if you see a rook-sized bird flying alone or in a spaced pair, then it is likely to be a crow, especially if its beak is black (rooks have a distinct grey patch at the base of their beak). Their 'kraa' is hoarser and coarser than a rook's call and without that deep honk of the raven.

Their propensity to take game chicks and eggs meant that for years they were fiercely persecuted by gamekeepers and lines of crows would adorn their gibbets, strung up by their neck on barbed-wire fences. However, crows are now protected and cannot be killed without a licence. Anyway, they are not easy to shoot because they are extremely wary and vigilant and will take flight if at all suspicious. Their cleverness has been much studied and has been put on a par with that of dolphins and chimps. They can learn, use tools and plan.

We have them on the farm, their nests a big construction of sticks, wool, baler twine and bits of plastic high up in a tree. They do not reuse last year's nest even if it survives the winter storms but often build a new one in the same area. They have not nested yet in the garden – and I would not expect them to as there would not be enough privacy for them – but they do visit, sitting high in a tree, cawing, fidgeting, taking stock and then, seeing that I have no gun and pose no threat, rise nonchalantly into the air, remarkably easily for a big bird, as though pulled up by a string.

Bats in the Afternoon

A pipistrelle bat hunting above the house at 3.30 p.m. and another, heading off in the opposite direction, at 4.15 p.m. I suppose they are hunting whilst they can – no rain, wind and quite mild – before hibernation and whilst there are some insects about. But strange to see in broad autumnal daylight.

Wood Pigeons

Hubris will always find you out. Ten years ago, in an article for a Sunday newspaper, I wrote, 'Wood pigeons pose no threat to my garden whatsoever.' Ha! How times change. They threaten me now alright and they seem to have multiplied tenfold in those ten years. Pigeons are now a perfect nuisance, eating peas, brassicas, lettuce and all kinds of young seedlings waiting to be planted out.

Columba palumbus, the common wood pigeon, may be a pest but it has one of the most evocative and soulful calls of all birds. Its sifting waves of cooing, throaty song are the perfect lullaby and the gentlest way to wake to a new day. I am happy to pay the price of a ravaged veg patch for the beauty of that song alone.

They are one of our commonest birds, with over ten million breeding birds in the UK. Climate change and the introduction of thousands of acres of oilseed rape – which they love – has meant that they can survive winters much better than they could, and their numbers are still rising, especially in urban and suburban areas. In the last 30 years, they have gone from being primarily a rural bird to one that is as at home in a city as in a field.

They are prolific breeders and, weather permitting, are one of the few birds that can and will produce clutches round the calendar, although most will produce their two or three broods between April and October. For the past couple of years, a pair has determinedly tried to nest in the potting shed, building a nest of twigs on top of the shelves where we store pots, and clattering frantically out of the door every time we go in or out until they give up – until the next time.

The young are fed on 'crop milk', which is very similar to human milk. Pigeons are one of the very few birds that do this – the others are flamingos and emperor penguins – despite the emperor penguin not having a crop. It is actually formed in the wall of the gut and parents produce it as a result of hormones stimulated by egg production and store the 'milk' in their crop. It is rather like cottage cheese, with up to 35 per cent dry matter and enormously rich and nutritious with a very high protein and fat content, although no carbohydrates or lactose. It is the only food the young get for the first few days after hatching, then it is supplemented by other food that is gradually introduced over the four-week fledgling period. This means that the young are effectively weaned just like mammals and that the squabs grow very big very fast.

It was this that made pigeons such a good source of winter food and why there are so many dovecotes around the country. This house used to have one but it has almost disappeared. The only sign of it is when we have a drought and the octagonal footprint of the foundations show clearly in the field just next to the house.

When disturbed, they clatter away noisily – a deliberate device to confuse a predator and buy them a second's advantage. They are strong and rather beautiful fliers, whether skimming through trees or high in the sky. They are also the favourite meal for peregrine falcons – so more pigeons means more and healthier, happier falcons. It all seems a fair price to pay for the loss of a few peas and cabbages.

———

Woodlice

Woodlice are the only species of crustacean on this planet that inhabits dry land as opposed to watery places. I have always had a soft spot for them. As children, we always called them 'chiselbobs', which humanises them and gets rid of all the distasteful associations that go with lice. They are perfect for children, rolling into tiny little armadillo balls when picked up, unwrapping quickly when put down and then dashing for cover, which makes them ideal for racing. We raced chiselbobs a lot. Our pleasures were simple.

I had never heard anyone else use the name until I discovered that other people knew them as 'cheesy pigs', 'chisel pigs' and 'cheese logs' (amongst many other names), all of which are surely variations of chiselbobs. It seems that there are hundreds of vernacular names for *Porcellio scaber*, which is always a sign of human affection. The Latin name translates as 'rough little pig', which seems to come from their similarity to another kind of louse that lives on pigs. The 'bob' name comes from the extraordinary practice of swallowing the lice like a round pill or 'bob' to alleviate indigestion. I have no idea if they worked or caused further harm but people certainly believed them to be very effective.

So it is strange that I get so many letters from people wondering 'what to do' about woodlice. The 'what to do about' letters are always a sign that people fear something and suspect it to be the root cause of a whole host of problems in their garden. A plant dies or fails, woodlice are found under or in the pot, and two and two are added to make five.

The truth is that woodlice are an important cog in the eco machine that recycles decaying vegetation. However, they can occasionally nibble seedlings in a greenhouse, where they are attracted by the warm damp – although they much prefer decaying wood and leaves. The best defence is to keep the greenhouse tidy and plants moving.

But they do far more good for the gardener than harm, eating decaying wood and leaves that would otherwise house potentially much more harmful fungi. Woodlice have enough to contend with without humans trying to harm them as they have a range of predators such as toads, centipedes, spiders, millipedes and wasps – hence their defensive strategy of forming a tight little armoured ball until danger passes.

—————

Woodcock

The leaves are mostly fallen and the hillside has become a soggy, dank place. The dogs rootle and rustle amongst the fallen leaves and bracken at the edge of the wood, running the ditches, breathing deep of the new strangeness of autumn. The bracken is now auburn and russet, meaning great swathes of hillside that have been green since May are now a feathery brown.

For much of October, enough of summer remains to cling to but there is always a point, perhaps at the end of the month, perhaps early in November, when every trace of summer has left and we are beached on winter's shores.

Then a bird flies up from practically under my feet, silent, twisting as it flies, quite big, as brown as bracken, as brown as the fallen leaves. I just catch sight of a long, straight beak and then it disappears in low, slightly corkscrewy but fast flight before it finds cover again. It is a woodcock, my first sighting of the season.

The woodcock is not a garden bird, unless your garden is large enough to include secluded bits of woodland and parkland, but they like the farm because there is plenty of cover and the soil is rather damp and soft, so they can dib for worms with their long beaks.

They are superbly camouflaged amongst the fallen leaves and bracken, and spend their days hunkered down on the ground, their long, straight beak looking twig-like and their eyes set high and wide, almost on either side of their head rather than in front, practically able to detect 360-degree movement around them. Stillness is their best protection and when they do lose their nerve and break cover, they seek it out again as quickly as possible. The camouflage hides it from foxes – and my dogs – and its twisting, rapid flight is designed to deter peregrine falcons or even, I suppose, in their northern fastness, gyrfalcons. The irony in modern Britain is that the successful increase of urban peregrines over the past 25 years means that woodcock are more likely to be caught migrating over a city, amongst its street lights, than out here in wild countryside.

They feed at night, using that long beak to push into the rain-softened earth for leatherjackets and earthworms, like the shore waders that they are related to. They then hoover these up from underground, like a child sucking spaghetti. If the weather turns cold and the ground freezes hard for a week or more, they can weaken and even starve to death.

The vast majority of woodcocks are winter visitors from much colder areas, with around a million birds visiting between late October to March from eastern Europe, Scandinavia, the Baltic or from even deeper in the wilder tracts of Russia. There are some resident breeding birds – about 50,000, with that number quadrupling when all young have fledged – but numbers are steadily dropping, mainly due to the decline of suitable woodland.

'Suitable woodland' includes dense tree cover with plenty of undergrowth but also includes rises and glades, where the birds can do their courtship, or roding, displays. I have seen this roding but it was many years ago. You are as likely to hear as see it because, as the bird circles high above the trees, it utters a mixture of high-pitched whistling squeaks and frog-like croaking grunts designed to entice a mate, whilst the atypical flight is territorial. But of course, only resident birds do this and they are few and far between.

Woodcock are considered game and shot, but apparently there is no evidence that this is contributing to their decline. That is because shoots manage woodland so it is ideal for pheasants and also suits woodcock. Where there is not an active shoot in action, you are likely to have less managed woodland resulting in fewer woodcock. It is a good example of the moral complexity of wild-life management, where easy fixes simply do not work.

I confess I have eaten woodcock. I was given a shot bird and prepared and ate it according to an eighteenth-century recipe – roasted whole, on toast. It was delicious.

———

Lichen

About once a year I receive a letter from a worried gardener asking how to get rid of the scaly fungus spreading over their apple tree – and should they cut it down before it spreads? Invariably, they are referring to lichen which, as well as being beautiful, is a sure sign of clean air, since lichen is especially sensitive to sulphur dioxide from coal or acid rain and will not harm its host, whether of plant material or stone.

Lichen is one of the success stories of the past 50 to 100 years because as coal has ceased to be the main fuel, both industrially and domestically, the air has become much cleaner and lichen now grows in towns and suburbia, whereas even in my own lifetime it used to be a feature of remote graveyards and hillsides. Now, the trees in the garden and on the farm are encrusted with its huge range of rich but delicate colours and textures and should be treasured.

Although often lumped in with liverworts and mosses, lichens are a partnership between fungi and algae, and have more in common with the algae on the surface of a pond than with the moss on the stones at its edge. This fungi/algae association is extraordinarily successful, resulting in over 15,000 lichen species, many of which thrive in situations where neither fungi nor algae would survive alone. They have a huge range of colours and forms from the familiar, slightly crusted, almost paint-like stain on stone or wood, to mossy, fibrous growth that hangs from branches.

Back in our jewellery days we once designed a whole collection based upon the colours of lichens – the yellows, oranges, slate-blues, greys, and powdery greens that so beautifully adorned the stones of the Hebridean islands we had visited that summer. It did not do terribly well, being out of kilter with the glitzy brashness of the early 1980s. But that lack of appreciation did not lessen the beauty of those colours.

————

The Goshawk

I first read *The Goshawk* by TH White when I was seventeen. It was a life-changing experience. It felt that I had opened a door into a world where everything was both familiar and endlessly fascinating. It was partly the idea of White living alone in a game-keeper's cottage in a wood, partly the solipsism and isolation, partly deep fascination with the natural world and corresponding alien-ation and dislocation from the human – and partly the hawk itself, Gos, with his berserk, murderous wildness.

For those who have not read it – and I urge you to do so – White, living alone in a gamekeeper's cottage in a wood in Stowe Ridings with his beloved dog Brownie, determines to train a hawk using a seventeenth-century textbook as his guide. The process was not only archaic but unnecessarily arduous and almost maso-chistic. This was 1936 (although the book was not published until 1951) and goshawks were to all intents and purposes extinct in Britain (and remained so until the 1980s) so a young bird arrives from Germany, taken from the nest.

The relationship between the bird and White is sado-masochistic with the bird not only tormenting his body with lack of sleep but ultimately breaking his heart by escaping. It is a strange, unnerving book with only two main characters – a deeply troubled man and the wildest of all animals.

This, of course, was irresistible. From that day on – and I read it in one sitting and then reread it almost constantly for the next ten years – the goshawk was my symbol of true wildness and untamed beauty. I longed to live alone in the woods with my dog and hawk and seriously planned and intended to do that. I also read everything I could lay my hands on to do with falconry, went to every display and was set to do a course and get my own bird when I won a place at Cambridge so felt I could not keep a bird – a falcon rather than the much more tricky goshawk – until I left. With hindsight I could easily have done so – I kept a dog and six hens and the outside loo that doubled as the henhouse could easily have served as a mews. Then I met Sarah and for the first time there was someone that I wanted to be with more than myself and we flew away together.

In the years that followed, although I obsessively scanned every sky for raptors and came to know quite a lot about them, not only did I not own or train a goshawk – I never even saw one. They had become, in my mind, the rarest of all living things that might enter my world – even though I knew I should instantly recognise one.

Then – after over 30 years' wait – I did.

I was driving my tractor up a steep slope on August Bank Holiday in 2006, cutting the bracken, when a buzzard-sized bird flew across the hillside above me. This bird looked like a sparrow-hawk but was bigger than the biggest female sparrowhawk could possibly be. In the half a millisecond that my bird-identifying brain took, I realised that it was a goshawk, but – and this really threw me – it had a very pale, almost-white unstreaked chest. All my images of goshawks had the female brown with a distinctly streaked chest and the male grey-blue, with a grey-streaked body. But I could see no streaks. The body and underside of the wings, viewed from my tractor, looked almost white. I have since learned that goshawks vary quite a lot – as indeed do most birds of prey – and that the young tend to be much paler, with the mature plumage only establishing after the first moult. This bird was probably one of that year's fledglings, fully grown but very immature.

It was probably in my sight for two seconds at most, flying from a group of trees across the slice of hillside to the dingle. I was ecstatic but did not have a phone and nor did anyone else within half a mile. So, wildly excited and triumphant, I carried on cutting the bracken.

Later that afternoon I saw it again from my tractor, the same bird, crossing a field on the same hillside. You wait a lifetime to see a goshawk and then see two – or at least one twice – on the same day.

Since then, goshawks have become frequent – if still heart-stoppingly thrilling – visitors to the skies above this garden and the fields around. I don't suppose many twenty-first-century seventeen-year-olds now read a book about a distinctly troubled and odd man failing to train a goshawk in the 1930s. But I am infinitely grateful that I did, and thanks to it, the goshawk remains for me the measure of all that is truly wild and untamed.

Clothes Moths

We insulated the farmhouse with recycled fleeces. We sheared our sheep, sent the wool off to the recyclers and they came back as rolls of great thick woolly insulation – albeit almost certainly not made exclusively from our own wool. No matter. It was all a very eco-friendly experience and superbly efficient. The house is snug and the heating – entirely fuelled by our own wood

– is minimal. Works a treat. However, after a few years we noticed that clothes moths were living in – and presumably eating – the wool insulation and, looking to expand the limitations of their diet, emerging through the floorboards and roof spaces to tuck into our clothes.

Clothes moths evolved to live in birds' nests, eating feathers and other detritus as well as carcasses. They are one of the few creatures that can digest the keratin found in feathers, skin, wool and silk. We have always had to contend with them to a degree as we have always lived in old houses which have more environments for them to comfortably inhabit. But now their depredations had become farcical, expensive and occasionally heartbreaking as a favourite jersey would be taken out of the drawer, only to resemble a string vest.

If you only wore or furnished your home with rayon, nylon, polyester or any other man-made fabric, you would barely be aware of the existence of clothes moths. They feed exclusively on wool, fur, silk, feathers, felt and leather, which covers most of my ward-robe – although my assortment of feathered outfits is a little scant. Any sweat, blood, other bodily fluids or food or oil stains add to the attraction, so if you are careless with the soup spoon, it makes matters a lot worse.

There are two types of clothes moth, the case-bearing clothes moth and the webbing clothes moth, although the case-bearing one is likely to be doing the damage. The moths are small – about half an inch long – and anonymously beige. They dislike exposure to light, air or cold, so clothes crammed into a drawer or on a rail are their ideal habitat. It is the larvae that eat our clothes. As soon as they hatch, when only about a millimetre long, they burrow into the fibres of clothes and start eating. It can take between three and nine months for them to pupate into moths and all that time they are steadily munching.

As a child, my granny always put mothballs made from naphthalene in her clothes drawers to deter them. We use scented bars of soap, which helps a little. It also pays to keep clothes as clean as possible, to wash them using the hottest temperature the fabric will take and to put clothes into a freezer for a week or so to kill the eggs before storing them for any length of time. Additionally, clean your house as much as possible, don't use central heating, don't store clothes for more than a week or so without airing them, and finally, sad to say, however good an insulator sheep's wool is, or how satisfyingly green its credentials, do not use it as insulating material in the roof or under the floorboards.

———

Ravens

I remember going to the Tower of London as a small boy in my best school-grey flannel suit and cap. There were only two things that I really wanted to see – the swords and the ravens. I was fascinated and terrified by their black immensity and the size of their beaks with their bristly whiskers, and the knowing intelligence that shone from their eyes.

The next time I saw a raven was when I was 21 and on a trip to Snowdonia, climbing and camping with friends. We were watching the ravens at first light in a tumbling acrobatic display that was doubly remarkable given that it was performed by those heavy, muscle-bound birds I had seen as a child.

And then they turned up here. I cannot remember the first one I saw but I suspect if I hunted through my diaries, it will be there. But certainly as recently as the last five years, ravens have increased to the point where we expect to see them daily.

They are the top of the corvid tree, with crows, rooks, jackdaws, magpies, jays and choughs beneath them. In truth, they are top of every tree and although the eggs, nestlings and newly fledged young are sometimes taken, not even a golden eagle will risk a head-on clash with an adult raven.

Their deep croaking honk is instantly recognisable and they are to a crow what golden eagles are to buzzards – much bigger, with broad, splayed wings, a wedge of a tail and a longer head that noticeably sticks out in flight.

Above the farm, they patrol the skies, hunting for food, marshalling the airways like black-clad militia. It will eat almost anything from carrion to young lambs and anything edible in between, be it a worm, rabbit or bird. But, like the crow, it is always attracted to carrion and historically, it was the bird of the battlefield and gibbet, where it would take the easy meat on offer. But today, their most likely habitat is upland areas with grazing sheep, because sheep have a habit of finding ingenious ways to die if left to their own devices. So if a sheep dies on our hillside (which they do, often), it is picked clean astonishingly quickly and you can guarantee that ravens got the first pickings.

But their presence above the much more domesticated landscape around the garden is an indication of their success and expansion over the past 20 years. They were once reduced to about 1000 breeding pairs, mainly as a result of persecution by gamekeepers and the effect of pesticides, but since then they have increased as much as tenfold. There seems to be no direct reason for this increase other than the lack of persecution and the availability of food, which means that they have spread from their strongholds in the mountains of Wales and Scotland.

As ever, conservation is a complicated and emotionally fraught business. Increased numbers of ravens mean increased attacks on ground-nesting birds like lapwings and curlews, as well as a possible reduction in birds that are already endangered. But in nature, survival rules and the answer lies not in policing the numbers of individual species but in preserving habitats for specialised breeders and feeders. Birds like ravens that can feed on anything will always survive unless persecuted, but niche feeders or nesters need their niches zealously protected.

Ravens are birds of death and fear, but also of wisdom. Their intelligence and longevity (they will live for ten to fifteen years in the wild and some of those at the Tower of London have lived for over 40 years) make them good pets, although I regret to say I have yet to come across one as part of any household I have visited.

———

Winter

Winter is bleak in this part of the world. With the days getting shorter – so that by Christmas it is not light until 8 a.m. and then dark again by 4.30 p.m. – there is a real sense of life of all kinds closing in and hunkering down for the duration.

It is, above all, a wet season and increasingly so as climate change has meant we have far fewer days of frost or snow. When we first came here thirty years ago, we would reckon on half a dozen days when it went down below −10°C and at least a month's worth of frosts averaging about −5°C. The ground was hard and the skies clear, and the cold was clean and dry and invigorating. It was a good time to get things done because you could move around without mud. But the winter of 2019/2020 was one of the wettest in living memory and certainly the wettest of my life, with all the fields flooded for months on end and the garden also often underwater.

But there are compensations. The fields become lakes and attract a wide range of birds that we do not see so much in the summer months. Swans, geese, ducks and herons are common, both in the wet fields and circling the grey winter skies. The leafless trees have a stark beauty and you can see so much more in and through their bare branches.

But the greatest pleasure of the winter months takes place outside our kitchen window, where we feed the birds from mid-October until May. Standing at the kitchen sink we can watch sparrows, four kinds of tits, various finches, dunnocks, blackbirds, thrushes, woodpeckers, starlings, blackcaps, robins, chaffinches, warblers, magpies, jays, pigeons, doves, and the occasional mouse, squirrel and rat, which visit the various feeders all day long. It is a source of endless fascination and pleasure as well as an investment into a healthy self-sustaining garden because a strong bird population means that the predatory balance of the garden will result in fewer pests in the spring and summer.

DECEMBER

Mistle Thrush

Unlike the song thrush, which is modest and surprisingly small, the mistle thrush, or storm cock, with its barrel chest and generally greater heft, is loud and proud and appreciably bigger than its singing cousin. The spots on its front are just that – spots – as opposed to the linear freckles of a song thrush. Its wing and back feathers are brown but unlike the chestnut of the song thrush, are washed with pale grey so it seems altogether paler. Although their distinctive size and upright posture makes them easy to recognise, they are much rarer – five times rarer – than song thrushes.

One often sings his song from the top of a tree in the corner of the Walled Garden when the branches are bare and bleak, the sky heavy and snow forecast. This is meat and drink to the mistle thrush and he sings on regardless, the notes loud and rich but the tune suffused with melancholy.

They like to take their vantage point from tall trees and are birds of parks and woodland rather than small gardens. They are very partial to holly berries and one of their renowned habits is to take possession of a particular holly in winter and see off all comers who might try to share the berries.

Their song is not just loud but beautiful and mellifluous and stands out at a time when very few other birds are singing at all and never in such a sustained performance. When alarmed they have a loud rattling call. I see them more on the farm than I do here in the garden, which fits their general pattern of behaviour since they prefer open, wooded countryside to the more tightly packed features of gardens that song thrushes and blackbirds prefer.

They get their name from their liking for mistletoe and are responsible for some of its spread by eating the berries but not digesting the seeds, which pass through their digestive tract and are deposited later on another branch with a helpful dollop of poo to fertilise them.

They will nest behind ivy on a wall or high up in a tree, with early nests tending to be within evergreen cover and later ones higher in a tree or shrub once there is a canopy of deciduous leaves. A few years ago a pair nested behind the cattle skull and horns nailed to the gable end of one of our sheds and reared their brood in full view of us down below. They will defend a nest site aggressively, attacking quite large birds and swooping at golden retrievers who dare to get too close.

One of the oddities of their story is that until about 1800, they were only seen in the south but for some reason that no one has been able to work out, they then quickly spread right across the country except for the extreme northern Highlands and Islands of Scotland.

———

Pike

A pike is marooned in a pond made by the flood just the other side of our fence by the Mound. I suspect that this is actually an old fishpond and the depression is a relic of the days when the water was managed with greater sophistication for fish, pasture and drainage. It is huge, a great barracuda of a fish over 3ft long, the body grey with touches of olive refracted through the shallow muddy water, suffering the indignity of these reduced and undignified circumstances, like a baby shark in a goldfish bowl. Its size means it is almost certainly a female, as males are much smaller, rarely exceeding 10lb, whereas a large female can often reach four times that.

We used to see pike quite often in the shallows of the brook that runs into the river. Perhaps it was this same one, because pike can live for over 20 years. They lurk in well-vegetated shallows and then burst out like a crocodile to grab their prey, be it another fish, frog or bird as large as duck, and drag it back under. When little, the children used to tell each other that the pike would catch them as they went down to the river's edge. We all half-believed it.

We used to have fishermen who came regularly to the river and they occasionally caught pike but discarded them as not being table-worthy, although in medieval England they were valued above salmon and turbot and are still prized in much of Europe. But by and large, we have lost interest in freshwater fish in Britain. I blame the Reformation. So we asked that next time the fishermen caught one, they would give it to us to eat. Soon we were presented with one about 18in long, with a long, flattened jaw rimmed with teeth. We cooked it and ate it Eastern-European style with hot horseradish sauce and beetroot. It was good, if awkwardly bony.

The stranded pike died as the water drained and evaporated and it was left high and dry. The carcass was picked over by birds and left bare-boned until the spring grass grew and the cattle grazed around it.

Silver Birch

There is just one silver birch in the garden, a seedling I was given that I planted in the far corner in the boundary hedge by the leaf mould. Out of the way and, if I am honest, out of sight. But on the farm we have one birch tree in particular that is magnificent. It is a large tree with a splayed, buttressed trunk, silvery mottled bark with a deeply 'ropey' effect, where the trunk has stretched itself into twining corrugations, and a broad, generous spread of branches. It is set in the middle of a field like a park tree, holding its own against any of the other mature trees in the valley. Of course I cannot take the slightest credit for this. It was there when we arrived years ago and was wonderful then. But its size and position tell a story.

Birch is an early coloniser, saplings establishing and growing fast. The tiny winged seeds will be blown long distances by wind so it will appear without any apparent parent tree in the vicinity. Rather than the great tangled forests of Disneyfied folklore, the first wildwoods would have been mostly birch, aspen and sallow – before pine spread about 10,000 years ago, replacing the birch. So throughout most of the last 1000 years birch was fairly uncommon except on upland ground or heath.

But in the twentieth century, it increased greatly. Where woods were felled and sold off for timber, especially after the two world wars – when the timber on an estate was often more valuable than the house – birch, with its ability to get in first and colonise bare ground before other trees, quickly seeded and grew.

It is the archetypal 'weed tree', along with ash and holly, and starts popping up all over the place, given light and space. If you see a forestry plantation that is cut down with a large area suddenly exposed, it will invariably start sprouting birch within a year or two. Also, the myxomatosis epidemic in the 1950s and 1960s meant that large areas of rough grass were no longer grazed by rabbits and became scrub – which is where birch takes hold.

The 1880s six-inch-to-a-mile Ordnance Survey map of the farm, which is accurate down to each and every significant tree, shows the slope above our mature birch as rough woodland. Later maps show that this wood was grubbed out about 80 years ago, during the Second World War. So it is highly likely that birch recolonised that slope and for some reason, this specimen was allowed to stand as an individual tree. So it is the ghost of secondary woodland that replaced ancient woodland, all within living memory.

It is used for besoms, those glorious brushes that are the archetypal witches' broomsticks with their long handle and great splay of long, twiggy branches. Birch wood was also used for a multitude of small tools, ties, hoops and domestic utensils and, when well-seasoned, it is an exceptionally tough, hardy wood.

But I have an especially soft spot for besoms, and when I rule the world, I shall ban all leaf blowers and issue besoms instead with mandatory lessons on how to handle and use them properly. They were intended for brushing dew off lawns in spring and summer and for gathering leaves in autumn, and they are still the most efficient and sustainable tool for the latter job even if dew-brushing has rather lost its urgency in most households nowadays.

Although we have a number of smaller birches, our one particularly fine specimen must be near the end of its days. Birches are short-lived and 70 is a ripe old age. But it has lived to see the slope above now replanted by us as a wood – of which, for so many years, it was the sole reminder.

———

Mink or Polecat

I am of a generation brought up to think of mink primarily as a symbol of ostentatious luxury, of trophy wives or film stars draped in fur coats assembled from scores of pelts harvested from mink 'farms'. But the animal itself as an individual, wild creature, was too remote, too foreign to be reality.

That changed when we moved here. Wild mink were spreading fast from farm escapees and had become more common than otters. From the very beginning we kept poultry – chickens, ducks and guinea fowl – and because we live so near the river, mink became something we had to protect the birds from. Birds were being attacked both in the run and, on one occasion, inside the

PREVIOUS PAGE The King of the Valley surveying his wintry realm.
TOP LEFT A weather-gnarled hawthorn growing at 1500ft right at the top of our land.
TOP RIGHT Flood and sky merge, and we have the gift of a lovely lake on our doorstep.
ABOVE The high rainfall on the hillside means that moss flourishes.
OPPOSITE A full, fat midwinter moon rising as I walk the dogs.

OPPOSITE Climate change means that clear, crisp frosty days are
becoming rarer – and all the more lovely for that.
ABOVE Frost riming every branch, twig and blade of grass.

TOP Our Black Welsh Mountain sheep are very hardy, but they must be
fed daily and occasionally dug out of snowdrifts.
ABOVE Winter fields in the valley.
OPPOSITE Nigel always loved the snow.
OVERLEAF Nigel. The last picture.

henhouse at night, when half a dozen birds were killed, although only one was eaten.

Mink are members of the weasel family and all the wild British population are escapees from mink farms. The first got out in the 1930s, they started to breed in the 1950s, and in the 1970s, the population exploded.

This coincided with the demise of the otter and caused the almost complete extinction of the water vole. These, although largely ignored by otters, became easy prey for the mink that, unlike otters, were small enough to enter and catch the voles inside their burrows.

Mink are fierce and effective hunters and will kill and eat a wide range of prey, including fish, shellfish, small birds, amphibians and domestic poultry. I would see them occasionally as a flash of chocolate fur by the river and the mink hounds hunted them for years until the foot-and-mouth epidemic of 2001 stopped access.

But then I stopped seeing mink or any evidence of them about ten years ago. They seemed to have disappeared or gone elsewhere.

Then one night there was an attack in the henhouse, with the only possible point of entry through a tiny hole at the corner of the door. Inside was a horrific scene, with slaughtered birds huddled and twisted all over the floor. All six of my lovely ducks were killed and five hens. Given the tiny hole and the mass carnage, I assumed it had to be the work of mink. I went to the game shop and bought a humane trap. This is a galvanised wire rectangle with a pressure pad that closes the door behind any animal that steps into it, thus containing but not harming it. The man who sold it to me said the secret was to bait it with sardines. 'Your mink cannot resist a sardine', he assured me.

So I did as I was told and that night set the trap, duly dripping with sardine oil. At first light I went to check and saw what looked to be an angry and very alive mink that had made the mistake of opting for sardines rather than chicken as his first course.

But when I got nearer, I saw that it was not the pure dark chocolate-brown coat with little white goatee of a mink. Although the coat was dark brown, it had an under layer of cream and the face was cream with a dark brown mask over its eyes and cream tips to its ears. It was not a mink, but a polecat.

I was delighted on two accounts. The first was having caught the little bastard and stopping him killing any more of our lovely and utterly harmless birds, and the second was that polecats are much rarer than mink and it was fascinating to see one here in the garden alive and relatively well – albeit very, very cross.

Many years ago I kept a ferret that I called Roger Ditchley. Roger had polecat colouring although was fairer and I used him to catch rabbits, although he was pretty useless at it. In the end, when I went away to university I gave him to a more dedicated ferreter than myself. Roger was often called a polecat but although polecats and ferrets are closely related, a true polecat is the original thing, with ferrets probably a domesticated version.

Polecats used to be common but were aggressively hunted down by gamekeepers. In the late twentieth century, they re-established themselves from the remnant population in Wales and from there have spread with a strong foothold here in the Herefordshire border country. Their preferred prey are rabbits but a flare-up of myxomatosis had reduced the local rabbit population and obviously my birds were a very acceptable alternative.

I carried the trap back down to the house to show the children, with the furious animal doing its best to get at me through the bars. I had no intention of killing it but did not want it to come back and finish off the rest of the hens, so I drove about ten miles to remote woodland and released it. I hope it went on to live a long and happy life, albeit one that did not include hens or ducks – or sardines.

———

Water

I was told many years ago that you should never try and dig out a spring because then it will move. I tried it once and it is true. I dug down into a field where the water was seeping out, creating a puddled hole to not much effect, but I intended to put stones in and around it to make it more identifiable, more permanent, not least so the sheep and cattle could drink from it. The next day it had dried up. Gone. And then a few days later, water began to seep ten yards away. The spring had moved.

So we accept springs on the farm where they are, for good or ill, and work around them. Then when the wet weather passes, most dry up and disappear until next time.

But it is not the biggest that remain. There are two or three very small springs, scarcely more than a cupful bubbling or even quietly overflowing, whatever the weather. These are the ones that we can tap into for a sure supply of water when the rest of the country is undergoing severe drought.

As I write this, the water is lapping round and into the garden, roads are impassable and the local floods are the worst ever known. Climate change means that this is probably the face of winters to come – milder, wetter, stormier. Last night I lay listening to water lapping against the trees and hedgerows, like a lake, where in a month or two's time, cattle will graze. It is strangely calm and unthreatening although the calamity of flooding is real for people just down the road. And 30 miles away due west, across the border, I know the water will be rushing and roaring down the dingles, bubbling out of new holes in the fields and bouncing on the mossy rocks, restless and even violent. It is the sound of water slowly eating into the stone of the mountain and carving the dingles deeper, the sound of slow time shaping the wild hillside.

———

Herons

Sometimes, after a flood, there can be half a dozen herons standing stock-still or slowly stalking the muddy fields on stilted legs, the grey of their folded wings merging into the grey of a winter's day, their long beaks ready to stab into the soft grass to extract a worm or frog, beetle, mole or vole driven too close to the surface by the wet.

Herons will eat almost anything living that they can catch in water, in the ground or even pluck out of the air, although they like eels and fish best of all – as any gardener with a fishpond sooner or later finds out.

Although I have never seen one land in this garden, herons fly over so often and land so regularly in the fields around us that they are part of our landscape. Walking the dogs through the low-lying water meadows will often disturb one, rising out of a grassy ditch as though from within the earth. They are instantly recognisable. Other than swans, they are the biggest British bird, flying with their long legs stretched behind them, head and beak held horizontal on a bent neck, and huge 6ft wings flapping in slow but steady undulations.

Apparently, heron flesh tastes unpleasantly fishy, but around the time that this house was built in the 1470s, it would have been served at banquets as a delicacy and, being an honorary fish and therefore not the proscribed flesh of a Catholic Friday, was allowed to be eaten on 'fish days'.

But herons' real claim to fame was as prey for the biggest and boldest of falcons such as peregrines and gyrfalcons, and for your bird to catch a heron reflected well on your manhood and status. Thus, whilst falconry remained the sport of kings and nobles, herons were fiercely protected.

When Hamlet proclaims that he is not mad because he can 'know a hawk from a handsaw', he is not comparing a bird of prey to a carpenter's tool but is saying he can tell a falcon (hawk) from the heron (handsaw) that it is chasing. Shakespeare's audience would have known and appreciated the difference between the dashing, arrowhead silhouette of the diving peregrine and the lumbering flight of the *hernshaw*, or young heron. But when sporting guns became established and birds could be shot out of the air, falconry became arcane and archaic. Then fishing took over as the universal country sport and the heron's predilection for fish became a nuisance so they were shot to protect fish stocks.

I have never found out where they nest locally. Given that the nests are very bulky and usually in the tops of fairly large trees, they are easy to see, so the herons that come and visit us must be doing just that – visiting from potentially miles away. Their feeding territories, which for an individual bird will be around 50 acres in size, will be fiercely defended and can be as much as ten or more miles from the nest. When they are feeding the young, they will hunt day and night and I sometimes hear their idiosyncratic, harsh 'fraarrnk' call shattering out of the soft summer darkness.

Gorse

Gorse is not at home in our fat Herefordshire loam but it is a main feature of the acidic, thin soil on the hillside above the farm. *Ulex europaeus*, known commonly as furze in the south and whin in the north, grows on the acidic soil in great prickly, swathes in the strip above the grazed fields and below the high tops, where only bilberries, heather and the purple moor grass of the *rhos* pasture can survive the icy winds.

By the end of the year the bright chrome-yellow flowers start to appear and continue right on deep into summer. Then the western gorse (*U. gallii*) takes over but both varieties can, and often do, flower sporadically the whole year round.

The spiny evergreen leaves carried on woody stems are impenetrable and provide important cover for linnets, yellowhammers and warblers, and rabbits burrow beneath its protective shade. Bees love the flowers and gorse pod moths eat the seedpods.

For us it is a plant that we tolerate in the corners that we cannot cultivate or cut, but on the mountainside the gorse quickly takes hold and can become a problem, engulfing the tracks, or *rhiws*, that cut diagonally up the hillsides and have been used by man and beast for centuries.

It is controlled by burning, leaving acres of blackened hillside amongst the surrounding bracken, but it invariably grows back with lots of new, more vigorous young plants since the heat stimulates the seeds of western gorse to germinate.

However, until relatively recently, gorse was valued and nurtured for a number of uses. It was traditionally the best fuel for a bread oven and was cut and gathered into faggots for this. I have tried it in our bread oven here and the oily leaves and wood burned with a frighteningly fierce blaze that left little ash – both ideal qualities for a baking fuel.

Gorse was also used as a highly nutritious winter feed, especially for horses. The prickles have evolved to deter grazing animals but the gorse would be cut and then milled by feeding it into a spiked metal drum that crushed it and made it palatable. There are reports from areas where modern tractors have used a flail to cut gorse, leaving the smashed material on the ground, attracting mountain ponies who come and eat the residue. Cutting the gorse whilst it is still relatively young – less than ten years – leads to healthy regeneration and a constant supply and some farmers carefully cultivated it, with, according to one late eighteenth-century Scottish account, an acre of gorse being enough to keep six horses for four months.

———

Hen Harrier

About ten years ago we started to see a new bird on the hillside above the farm. Not often, and sometimes tantalisingly briefly, but we all reported separate sightings and they all matched to indicate only one possible bird – a hen harrier.

Hen harriers have been a bird of rarity, trouble and great controversy for all of my life and for most of the twentieth century. Gamekeepers have persecuted them – which hardly singles them out – but for hen harriers, it has been catastrophic. The persecution was not personal. It was strictly business. The result was in my opinion morally and practically wrong, but – to an extent – understandable.

It was based on the following.

On the upland moors that they like best, hen harriers feed on grouse, and in particular young grouse when they are feeding their young. This reduces the grouse that are available to be shot later in the summer and autumn, which has a serious effect on the viability of the shoots. This, in turn, damages jobs and the local economy. Thus gamekeepers saw harriers as vermin to be eradicated if possible, just as a shepherd will shoot a fox that steals his lambs or a forester will shoot deer to protect his trees (and over half a million deer are shot every year for this reason).

The gamekeeper's job was made easier by the way that hen harriers hunt – slowly, with their long wings and long tail enabling them to glide low over the ground with just a few wing beats as they scan for prey. They make an easy target. They also nest on the ground and are reluctant to leave the nest if threatened – making the gamekeeper's job even easier. As a result, hen harriers stopped breeding in England in 1997 and although there are some accounts of a return – kept very secret – they are still vanishingly rare.

Now that there is growing social unease with shooting as a sport, there is, to my mind, no justification for killing them. But the fundamental issue is, at what point should we protect a species for the sake of society at large – even if that means a local population suffering? If there is no game shooting, then real people – and in some areas a significant proportion of the local community – lose real jobs. However, there may well be good justification for providing financial support to gamekeepers and communities for *not* killing game. Those of us who want to enjoy harriers should perhaps be prepared to pay for the privilege rather than expect local communities to subsidise our pleasure.

The solution to this problem, as always with wildlife conflict, comes not from people many miles away expressing outrage, but from the local community that is actually affected. Those that know the harriers and their environment most intimately, and are in the best position to preserve them, are the very gamekeepers that are currently the harriers' nemesis (albeit often under heavy pressure from their employers). But people are finding ways to conserve harriers *and* maintain grouse moors. It is happening.

Outside of the breeding season, when hand-reared grouse are not readily available and with wild grouse very thin on the ground, harriers hunt mainly for meadow pipits and voles but will take any ground-based bird or mammal they can find. Voles and pipits only thrive in grass and if the heather spreads (which it is encouraged to do on grouse moors as heather is the grouse's main food), the harriers must eat grouse or go elsewhere – if there is an elsewhere to go to.

Anyway, I am seeing harriers up on the grouse moors that span England and Wales and this is exhilarating. However, I have never seen more than one at a time. Is there just one? Could I be seeing the same bird? In any event, I have only seen a female, chestnut-brown with pale underwings and long barred tail. I once saw a male in Normandy and he is strikingly different – pale grey with black wing tips. My son has also seen one right by the house, flying across the farmyard, just 20 yards from where he and his wife were walking on the hillside.

What we do not know is if they are breeding on 'our' hillside or anywhere within ten miles or so. We may just be seeing winter visitors or young birds too immature to breed (females breed at two and males at three years old). Adults can live to fifteen or more, although few get older than ten. But every time I look up to the skyline, 1000ft above the house, I now instinctively scan for harriers – although ironically the two best sightings I have had, close, clear and quite long, have been from the car when driving back to the garden.

Yew

Twenty years ago I wrote, 'To cut an old yew down is vandalism of a shocking order, although it will almost certainly regrow. To grub one up is inviting catastrophe.' But five years after publishing those words, I cut down an ancient yew and then grubbed its roots out so it could never regrow. Catastrophe? I hope not. But certainly guilt, as if I had shot an elephant or bulldozed a historic building. Yet I think it was the right thing to do.

It was a large yew planted right up against the side of the farmhouse. It had been cut down to the ground at least once – the last time probably about a hundred years ago – and was now multi-stemmed, with each of the dozen or so new growths the thickness of a gatepost rising from a trunk 6ft wide. That is modest. There are yews alive that measure 30ft or more across.

The roots of ours were growing into the building, and the bank it was on was covering 6ft of the house wall, which was sopping damp. The only way to dry it out was to dig out the bank and that meant removing the tree. But it was a solemn thing to do.

It was the only yew we had growing on our land and although I have since planted many others as inadequate reparation, all those years cannot be recompensed. The debt will take hundreds of growing years to repay.

I grew up in yew country. It grows very well and widely on the chalk downland of southern England but is less happy on heavy clay, so not many grow wild on the Herefordshire lowlands. The much lighter, sandier soil of the farm is better for it. The reason it copes so well on that exceptionally wet Welsh hillside is the drainage created by the slope. A lot of water comes, but a lot of water quickly goes away.

Yew has become such a feature of European gardens that it is sometimes easy to forget that it is a wild tree – and the oldest, wildest tree that there is. People tend to confuse the incredible age that yew can reach with the speed of its growth. For the first hundred years or so, they grow quite fast. I have planted yews in the garden for hedges and topiary that grew to be 12ft tall and a dense 4ft to 5ft wide within ten years. After that, it is just a question of keeping them in check by clipping once a year.

But once they get to about 400 years old, their growth rate slows and after 1000 years, becomes very slow indeed. They take their time because they, above all living things, have time to take. It is appropriate that one of the oldest wooden artefacts in the world is a 250,000-year-old spear found in Essex – made of yew.

It is also easy to misjudge the age of a yew because height and grandeur do not come with age. Unlike oaks, beeches, limes or the giant redwoods, it never becomes very tall. Until about 500 years old, it grows in a neat but unremarkable mop-headed shape and then, with true venerability, it sprawls and swells, and the branches grow out and then down to the ground. Age gives it mystery rather than majesty.

There are yews growing in this Marcher country between England and Wales that are over 4000 years old and look set for a lot longer. At Discoed, about 20 miles from here, near Presteigne, the yew is reckoned to be over 5000 years old and is arguably the oldest in existence (although Fortingall in Scotland also claims that trophy). That kind of longevity becomes geological, and outside any human frame of reference.

There are subterranean fungi that are tens of thousands of years old and cloned groups of trees, growing from suckers that are over 40,000 years, but the only individual tree specimens that can challenge the Marcher yews are the Bristlecone pines of California and Nevada.

However, yew ages are contentious and good authorities put them at less – much less. Despite this, we know that there are hundreds of yews that are older than 1000 years. In global tree terms, this is not that exceptional, but it represents mere middle age in the potential span of a yew's life.

So, an ancient yew in a churchyard is likely to be older – much older – than the church. Near here is the Peterchurch yew, known to be 3000 years old and a sprawling, hollowed, dark presence with a trunk like molten wax, growing near the entrance to the church door.

It follows that the church was built near the mature yew, perhaps because of it, rather than the other way round. When the church was built 1000 years ago, the yew would have been the oldest living thing in the landscape, and not just living but evergreen and vibrantly alive even in the dead of winter. It is easy to see, then, how the yew became a venerable symbol of eternal life – and, therefore, magical – which is why you might want one near your church. And the oldest and most magical yews in the world all grow along this border country and into Wales.

Yew has two qualities that make it exceptionally able to live a long time. The first is that it will regenerate from a completely bare stem or stump. Cut an old yew hedge back to its central stem and it will sprout a fuzz of new green growth that will become a neat, tight shape after just a couple of years.

The second is that it is composed of two kinds of wood. There is the outer sapwood, which is very elastic and the inner heartwood which is enormously hard and strong and resists compression. This combination of being able to simultaneously stretch and compress and then return to its original shape with enormous force is why the English longbows that dominated medieval warfare were constructed of yew.

The two types of wood that make up the yew also mean that when the tree is afflicted by fungus that rots away the interior wood, the thin shell of heartwood has sufficient tensile strength to hold the whole large tree upright and together for further huge stretches of time. Of all British trees, only the yew can do this and continue to live healthily for so long.

Even if the whole thing were cut down, it would regrow perfectly happily as the same tree, although one factor that makes dating yews impossibly difficult is that they sucker and although these suckers are genetically identical to the parent and grow in the same spot, it can be argued that they are not the same tree.

I kept all the wood from the yew we cut down. Some I have carved into bowls. Some stands in the dry, iron-hard, waiting. My neighbour, who has farmed this land for all his 85 years, told me that yew made the best gateposts of all. He said this as though speaking of some great luxury. Perhaps I should use a couple of the straight boughs for that. There is honour in that basic utility on this harsh, unforgiving hillside, where things that work reliably well are indeed a true luxury.

———

A Visitation from the Moors

Taking the dogs for a walk in the 4 p.m. dusk in the Long Field and a falcon flew out of the large ash tree near the far end. Too small for a peregrine and nothing about it seemed remotely like a kestrel. It flew low over the field, skimmed, rose, dipped down again, crossed the field and then rose up into one of the trees at the far side. It couldn't be a hobby at this time of year – they don't arrive before May or even June. Merlin? By a process of elimination that seems most likely. I have seen a merlin here before about ten years ago but this is not home territory. It is a stranger, a visitation from mountain and moor to these soggy midwinter fields.

———

Field Mice

Standing at the kitchen sink on 22 December, the Winter Solstice, I notice a mouse dart out of the stone wall around the back yard. It rushes forward, sniffs suspiciously, grabs a seed from the bird food I had scattered just moments before and nips back into the wall. Then a moment later it reappears, takes more food, scurries back. This goes on for about five minutes, with the mouse never stopping to eat but always taking its trophy back into the wall where, presumably, it has a nest.

From my viewpoint at the sink it was quite hard to identify accurately. It certainly was not a shrew and its ears and eyes seemed too big for a bank vole – although that might live in the wall. It was not the distinctive yellow-necked mouse or a harvest mouse, and certainly not a dormouse. It could have been a house mouse (*Mus musculus domesticus*) but there was something about its anxious, scurrying speed that was more feral than the average house mouse, in my experience, ever displays. We have house mice in the barns and occasionally in the house and they will happily potter around in daylight. So it was likely to be *Apodemus sylvaticus*, the field or wood mouse.

Field mice are essentially nocturnal so coming out at all during the day was an unusual and scary thing to do, driven probably by the floods. They live mainly in hedges and dry-stone walls or walls like ours, which have lots of mortarless cavities that make a safe, dry and reasonably warm home for small creatures.

I rarely see them at all now but I used to, albeit nearly always dead. When we had our pair of identical twin Burmese cats, Stimpy and Blue, Stimpy would often leave the half-eaten body of a field mouse on the doorstep or at various points around the house. Their white tummies and rather subtle rusetty-ochre colouring were distinctive despite their mangled bodies. Thankfully, now the cats have gone, the grisly depositions have stopped.

However, I do still find evidence of their nocturnal feeding. Like voles, they love hazelnuts and the Spring Garden is littered with nuts with a neat round hole gnawed into them by the mice. There are nice distinctions to be observed from the details of these holes. A field mouse will leave toothmarks around the edge of the hole and sometimes on the shell itself so that it has a ragged edge, whereas a dormouse makes a smooth hole with the toothmarks only on the interior of the shell. I once got convinced that we had dormice and studied the fine detail of toothmarks on scores of nuts but realised that I was deceiving myself and that, in fact, we just had lots of hungry field mice. For the record, bank voles also make a round hole on the side of the nut but never leave toothmarks on the surface. You can see where confusion might arise.

Field mice will clamber over and through hedges, seeking out the seeds and berries they love, but always at night and almost always unseen, except by owls for which they make an important prey. But I did once see a whole family of rats, two adults and perhaps a dozen young, running in a row along the top of a hedge like rodent topiary.

———

Hollins

In a little wood at the very far corner of our patch of land is a large holly. I sometimes disturb a tawny owl that uses it as a daytime roost, hidden within its dark recesses from the mobbing of small birds. The recesses are dark partly because of the density of the branches and evergreen leaves, but also because it is simply huge, the main trunk being fully 6ft across and a mass of straight branches splaying up from it like a woody explosion.

Holly grows well here on our light, acidic soil, and spreads easily by seed so will pop up all over the place – and in particular on the banks of the dingles. I planted quite a few in the hedgerows, mixed in with hawthorn and hazel, but unless they were fenced off they were always the first to get eaten by sheep and rabbits.

Farmers on the hills of the border country between Wales and England have used this willingness to eat holly to provide winter feed when thick snow or an iron frost means that there is no grass at all to be had for weeks on end, and the hay has to be rationed. Often there were a few especially big, favoured trees, like the one in our little wood, but there were also little woods – called hollins – entirely comprised of holly and harvested like a crop.

Until the nineteenth century, hollins were common in many upland areas, and the Olchon Valley, just on the border with the Black Mountains, was famous for the number of hollies used in this way. But then stock management improved, turnips began to be grown for winter fodder and, perhaps most influentially, holly wood was found to be ideal for making cotton bobbins. There is a record of 100,000 hollies being cut down from Needwood Forest in Staffordshire in 1803 and sold to the burgeoning Lancashire cotton mills. The consuming maw of the Industrial Revolution had reached trees growing on remote wind-blasted hillsides.

Although holly might seem pretty prickly fare, sheep and cattle love eating the leaves and they are an important part of their diet. In fact, given the opportunity they will often eat the foliage from different trees as tree roots can access minerals, such as selenium and copper that are beyond the reach of grass roots, and animals instinctively seem to know when they need to supplement their grass diet and will go and find plants to eat as medicine. One of the reasons that you never see a young oak growing unprotected out in an open field is because it is one of the first things that any grazing animal will devour and we have found that hazel, hawthorn and willow all get enthusiastically nibbled at, even when there is lots of good grass about. But by December all these leaves have fallen and all that remains are holly, ivy, yew, a few box trees and gorse. The gorse is eaten but was traditionally cut and crushed and chopped before feeding. Yew is poisonous to all stock and box too rare to be an issue. Ivy will make fodder but is very localised and quite hard to gather so holly makes for a high-energy food that can mean the difference between life and death in a particularly harsh winter.

Our great holly has clearly been pollarded at about 5ft. This would be too low to stop cattle reaching in to eat the leaves, but high enough to deter sheep. I suspect that the eighteenth-century farmer would have had his dairy cows in the byre over winter, especially in the worst weather, and they had the best of the hay but the much less valuable sheep had to fend for themselves on the hillside.

This regular pollarding explains the density of these almost vertical branches, compared to one or two of the other very big hollies we have that have rather elegantly curving and horizontal boughs growing proportionately from the trunk.

But this one has an almost angry rash of growth erupting from its squat, massive base. The farmer would have cut the new shoots growing from the top of the trunk, loaded them onto a sledge – wheeled carts were never used on the steep hillside until well into the twentieth century – that his pony would have dragged out of the wood and down the green lane that is still there, to the waiting sheep who would have eaten the leaves first and then, when stripped bare, nibbled all the bark off the branches.

The lower leaves of a holly are extremely prickly, which is an evolutionary ploy to deter grazers. Higher up, out of reach of all but a deer on hind legs or the largest cattle, the leaves become almost completely smooth and easier to eat. This means that pollarding does not have to be done as high up on a holly trunk as on willow, ash or oak, all of which were very often pollarded 8ft to 10ft up the main trunk and needed ladders, whereas the holly could be cut with feet firmly on the ground.

It is still considered bad luck to cut down a holly tree and I have seen many laid hedges along the lanes of Herefordshire with hollies left standing above the newly canting and bound hedgerow, either harking back to the days when holly was a valuable source of winter fodder or for fear of troubling ancient gods.

Ivy

We have a tendril of ivy that is slowly spreading indoors. It starts outside on the front of the house and has worked its way up the wall and through a gap between the window frame and the casement and on across the windowsill and down the other side. We have no plans to cut it back, let alone remove it. It looks good.

Ivy gets a bad press. I receive lots of letters asking how to get rid of it and in 30 years have never had a single query about how to grow, let alone encourage, it. It is either seen as a problem, smothering trees and clinging destructively to walls, or is overlooked to the point of abandonment and not really considered a plant at all. But it is incorporated into almost every kind of Christmas decoration because there is nothing else remotely like it available for providing green tendrils at that time of year.

Well, I like ivy. I do plant it in the garden but it also appears on our walls and one or two of the trees on the farm have effectively become 'ivy trees' because the host tree has long been submerged by ivy that now has stems the thickness of my thighs and is a favoured daytime roosting place for owls.

Hedera helix, the native British ivy, is one of only five native British woody climbers (the other four are clematis, honeysuckle, woody nightshade and the dog rose). It is often assumed that it is parasitic and sucks the life out of otherwise healthy trees but in fact, it behaves like any other plant, drawing all its nourishment from its own roots and via photosynthesis. Rootlets – which only grow on the side away from the light and in response to a young shoot touching a firm surface – develop to support the ivy rather than feed it as they cannot absorb food or water. Thus, if you sever an ivy's main trunk so that no nutrients are sent up from the soil, the plant will invariably die. This also disproves the notion that ivy draws water from a wall that it clings to. The only real problem is that ivy can shade out its host's own leaves and kill it off by depriving it of light.

But it has many virtues that every gardener should nurture. It provides a green wall or surface at a time of year when green is at a premium. It will tolerate extremes of sun and cold, will grow in almost complete shade and, once established, needs very little moisture. It is self-clinging so needs no elaborate support structure and it provides vertical winter cover for birds, insects and bats. Ivy flowers appear very late in the year and are full of pollen and nectar, so are a really important source for autumnal insects, especially bees. Ivy honey crystallises very quickly and is said to have special healing properties against bronchial problems. It certainly has a very distinctive taste.

_____

Mistletoe

In the mid-1990s I planted an orchard of 40 apple trees. Herefordshire still has thousands of orchards and all of them of any age are decked with mistletoe, so I hoped – assumed – that my trees would host some too. But for a long time nothing happened. It grew in great berried balls in the hedgerows around, preferring the hawthorn, lime or poplar. But there was not a single sprig on any of my apples. Then, after fully fifteen years, I noticed a little green shoot appear and since then there are about a dozen new growths of mistletoe.

Some of the balls – it always grows as circular bundles – are now quite big and quite a few have come down along with branches that I have removed as part of the annual winter pruning. In short, my orchard is now fully and properly mistletoey. Why did it take so long? To understand that you need to know how mistletoe grows and how it is spread.

Birds – and especially the mistle thrush and the blackcap – love the berries but once properly ripe, around mid-February, the flesh that surrounds the seeds is very sticky. So to clean their beaks or, in the case of the blackcap, to avoid eating the seed, they wipe their beaks on the branches near where they have eaten and in the process deposit seeds that adhere to the bark with the glue-like flesh of the berries. The thrushes also excrete the seeds onto nearby branches. So, regardless from which end it comes, a seed is deposited amongst a blob of binding material.

It is a fallacy to think that the seed needs to be put under a flap of bark in order to germinate. In fact it needs light to trigger germination. As it puts out a tiny shoot, so the roots bore into the bark and the stem of the tree. It takes another two years for these tiny shoots to establish themselves in the tree – hence the lack of mistletoe in my orchard until the trees had become large enough to be a suitable breeding ground. But after that, mistletoe will grow fast, spreading its roots down into the centre of the branch and eventually completely filling it, like the spokes of a wheel.

Mistletoe does have green leaves so can photosynthesise but it also takes a lot of nourishment from its host tree, so is also semi-parasitic. Ultimately, this is its downfall. The roots of the mistletoe become so congested that they block off the moisture and nutrient supply to the branch that is growing beyond where the mistletoe is, so the branch dies off and the mistletoe with it.

If allowed to spread and take over its host tree, it will inevitably mean the tree's early demise. The answer is to prune it every year, taking what you need for Christmas decoration. Nothing could be easier as mistletoe wood is very brittle and simply snaps off with a tug.

For many years, no one really understood why mistletoe flourishes in the western side of the UK but not nearly so well in the east. However, this is changing and it has been observed that there is a direct correlation with the increased migration of blackcaps from Siberia, together with milder, wetter winters.

Any plant growing out of a tree and keeping its green leaves all year round, as well as producing strange white, milky berries, was bound to be associated with midwinter magic, but mistletoe only became directly connected to Christmas in the seventeenth century. The tradition of kissing under a bunch or sprig of mistletoe was only established, along with so many 'ancient' traditions, in mid-Victorian times.

———

Rookery Nook

I remember the first time I went to the tiny Castle Theatre in Farnham, Surrey, when I was aged about six or seven. It was a Christmas treat that was repeated every year but no subsequent visit matched the almost unbearable excitement of that first time. We saw a Brian Rix farce and I can see him and the stage now as I write this almost 60 years on. It was all dropped trousers and hiding in cupboards, and I was almost sick with laughter. The name of the play stayed with me as a symbol not so much of the shenanigans of theatrical farce, but of the intense excitement and smell of a real live theatre. It was *Rookery Nook*.

Until then laughter was not something I had ever associated with rooks. In fact they were scary and even persecuted. Gamekeepers hung their carcasses on barbed wire along with the rows of weasels, crows, sparrowhawks and magpies – the trophies that every gamekeeper paraded to prove their diligent protection of their master's pheasants. Rook shoots were common in my childhood, with a dozen guns hiding in the fields before dawn and blasting the birds as they took to the early-morning air. Rook pie was not unusual although I have no memory of eating it.

On the farm they are rare, far less common than either jackdaws or crows. The irony being that a bird that prefers farmland finds our upland fields, made up almost entirely of grazed pasture, too inhospitable. They are a bird of the garden edge rather than mountain and moor, rarely choosing to be above 1000ft – which is the lowest level of our land.

Nevertheless, they are almost everywhere that can accommodate their need for open, soft pasture and Britain suits them well. It hosts nearly half of Europe's rooks, which is a reflection of Britain's lack of large stretches of woodland and forest compared to the rest of Europe.

Although rooks almost invariably nest in trees, they are not woodland birds at all and it is strange to think that they did not arrive and stay in Britain until sufficient wildwood had been cut down and cleared by the early Neolithic farmers as recently as about 5000 years ago. As Oliver Rackham pointed out, more of Britain's trees have been cut and cleared with stone axes than with chainsaws.

_____

Coal Tits and Great Tits

The bird table is busy with birds eating the Christmas scraps, and none are busier than the various tits. Blue tits are easy to identify, whilst the long-tailed tits instantly present themselves in a cluster of tiny soft bodies attached to the eponymous long tail. But coal tits are shy and elusive and quite hard to identify. They are the size of a blue tit but look a bit like a great tit – until you see them next to each other and then you realise they don't look like each other at all.

Whereas blue and great tits have confidence and swagger, coal tits are all diffidence and hesitancy. The only time I really notice them is at the bird table, but there can be long intervals between their visits. When they do come to feed, they will swoop in, take a seed and almost immediately swoop away to eat – or store it for later consumption – elsewhere.

With a black cap pulled down over its eyes, white cheeks, black throat, a black Mohican blazed down the back of its head, grey wings and a noticeably slender bill, the coal tit should be distinctive for its dowdiness, but instead seems to act as a blurred recognition halfway between blue and great tits. This is not helped by the way that tits join together in winter as large, mixed-species flocks.

The coal tit's more pointed, thinner bill has evolved to enable it to get at the seeds of fir cones and it is more likely to be seen in coniferous woodland than deciduous. All in all, it is a neater, sharper bird than a great tit, the black of its feathers seemingly blacker, the white, whiter.

There is no such ambiguity about the great tit. For a start, it is bigger and, like the blue tit, has a swagger. Their colouring is clear and self-proclaiming: black head, white cheeks, black bib running down the centre of its chest against yellow breast feathers, and greeny-blue wings with a distinctive white stripe. In males, the black bib goes all the way down to its belly and tail but in females, it peters out around the belly.

The population density of great tits is greatly influenced by the availability of beech mast – the seeds of the common beech (*Fagus sylvatica*). This, like oaks and their acorns, tends to have irregular, exceptionally productive years and the great tit population booms in line with these 'mast years'.

In the breeding season, great tits look for protein, feeding themselves and their young on insects and invertebrates of all kinds and have been known to kill other small birds and, in a deliciously dark detail, peck out the brains of hibernating pipistrelle bats.

I have found great tits' nests in all kinds of places, and a few times with Nigel hairs lining the mossy cup.

NIGEL

Nigel was present in every page, every moment outside with me, and most of the time that I was writing – sleeping at my feet or, if bored, gently rolling a slobbery yellow ball across the keyboard as a gentle hint that real life was lived outside.

But he died the day after I finished writing this book. His death was completely unexpected, completely shocking.

The day before had been a glorious May day – just as there had been all spring with day after day of unseasonable sun and warmth, and the garden blossoming as never before. This was just as well because we, like the rest of the nation, were confined to the house and garden due to Covid-19. I only left to take the dogs for a daily walk in the fields, and three times between the middle of March and the end of June to check the sheep when my son was unable to do so himself.

On Sunday 3 May, Nigel seemed as well as any twelve-year-old dog could possibly be. He slept in the sunshine, walked briskly through the fields and followed me round the garden. He was affectionate, interested and sweetly gentle. His appetite was good and there was not a glimmer of illness or discomfort. He seemed especially happy.

Then, at one in the morning of 4 May, he had a major seizure. We held and calmed him but he did not appear to know who we were or where he was, and seemed to have lost his sight. The fits continued all night, one after the other, terrifying, violent and exhausting for him. After a few hours of this I confess I wanted him to die in my arms so it might stop. We rang the vet at dawn and took him to the surgery, waiting in the car park as he fitted again in the back of the car. Then, awkwardly observing the rules of social distancing, we carried him into the theatre and they tranquillised him. The vet said the prognosis was not good but they would do everything they could.

That day I was filming for the BBC and throughout the day, between takes, the surgery rang as each successive level of treatment failed. By eight that night there was nothing left that they could do, so we agreed that he should be gently put to sleep. They asked if I wanted to come and see him first. No, I said. I don't want my last memories of Nigel to be of him attached to tubes on a gurney. Let him go.

Throughout it all, the vet could not have been more kind, professional or considerate. The cause of the fits was probably a brain tumour, although we will never know.

I was filming an edition of *Gardeners' World* over the next two days, which meant we could not bury him – so they kept Nigel in their freezer. Two days later, filming done – the first without him for nine years – we collected him. The virus restrictions meant that we stayed in the car whilst he was carried out in a box to the car park, and then they retreated indoors before we collected the body. Although frozen solid, the great big bear lay sleeping, untouched, his long auburn fur ruffling in the breeze.

We buried him in the coppice with 50 yellow tennis balls, his bowl full of an extra big helping of food, lots of biscuits and a bunch of the best flowers that this May garden could provide. I have buried five dogs now and the worst bit – the outrage, the bit that rips through you – is that first shovel of soil over the body. But it was done, and a socking great stone set above him with foxgloves, anemones and primroses planted all around it.

Then there is the slow, hollow grief of losing a dear friend, and just the raw process of getting used to the expectation that he will come plodding round the corner or be lying in his bed. The emptiness.

I did not release the news of his death until the beginning of the next week. I wanted us to have time alone and also he had already been filmed for that week's programme and it was too late to change it. But it became front-page news. I did make a few television and radio appearances but turned down scores more. We received hundreds of cards of condolence. Through social media I had hundreds of thousands of messages. It was extraordinary.

But I was not wholly surprised because I knew that Nigel was really, truly loved. Everywhere I went, people would always ask 'Where's Nigel?' Even on aeroplanes, in royal palaces, hospitals, in Japan, America – even during my brief visit to Iran – everyone loved Nigel.

Every Christmas he had many more cards than the rest of the family combined. When I gave talks, I knew that people wanted to see him really, not me. *The One Show* had him as their star guest with his own dressing room, hairdresser and limousine home. The Hay Festival had an event featuring an hour-long interview with Nigel that was a sell-out. I came along as interpreter.

There was never a plan to have him on *Gardeners' World*. It just happened. He would be around – as he always was when I was outside – and cameramen and directors could not help noticing that he seemed to naturally find the perfect spot where the light was best and the composition made complete. After a while, he would come to work on a filming day as a fully signed-up member of the crew, staying close by for all ten hours, waiting for his call and then, without any prompting, striking exactly the pose in the best possible light. If he felt that things were a little slow, he would steal the scene by wandering in and placing his ball in the least opportune place and moment. Worked every time. Audiences never tired of him, never had enough Nigel. He was an undisputed Star.

There was never a dog like him and never will be again. Dear, simple, noble, beautiful Nigel just happened to find his true calling on a television gardening programme. Life is very strange – not least because no one is a star to their family. He was Nige, one of us, and was loved with the same careless irreverence that all families share. Yes, he was gloriously handsome, incredibly photogenic and his guide-dog genes meant that he was ideally suited to the patience needed for the snail-slow process of filming. But it was more than that.

I think that the genuine love and affection people felt for Nigel was based on something deeper. He had an innocence and dignity that shone out. He had life stripped down to the things that mattered to him and he pursued them with a quiet focus. He was endlessly loyal and affectionate and, for such a great big shaggy bear of a dog, very gentle. For those of us privileged to share our domestic lives with animals of any kind, we know the extra level of humanity that this brings out in us.

In an age of trivia, uncertainty, duplicity, inequality and anxiety, Nigel represented a basic decency that we all crave. He was a symbol of the goodness that matters more than any amount of wealth or worldly success. He reminded us of our better selves.

And for us, who lived with him, there is still a great big Nigel-shaped absence in our lives, in the house, in the garden and on the farm. But we feel grateful for a good life shared well. And Nellie is lying at my feet now and we have little Patti, the feisty Yorkshire terrier (who adored Nigel and often slept on his back), and I may well get another dog before long. The leaves will fall on his grave in autumn but the primroses will flower again at Easter time. Life will flow on all around him.

ACKNOWLEDGEMENTS

My agent Alexandra Henderson has been a constant support, mentor and friend throughout. At Two Roads Lisa Highton has suffered this book's shifts and stalls with calm forbearance and my editor Hilary Mandleberg has been, as ever, a delight to work with. Andrew Barron added elegance to my jumble of pictures and many thanks to Derry Moore for his wonderful cover photographs. And thank you to my son, Tom, for the photograph of Nigel in Spring.

My assistant Polly James deals brilliantly with all the worldly clutter so I have the space in which to write and without Sarah none of this would have any meaning.

INDEX

ABOUT THE AUTHOR

Monty Don OBE is a well-known gardening writer and broadcaster. He lives with his family, garden and dogs in Herefordshire. His previous books include the *Sunday Times* bestseller *Nigel*, *The Jewel Garden* with Sarah Don, and *Paradise Gardens* and *Japanese Gardens* with Derry Moore, which was shortlisted for the Edward Stanford Travel Writing Awards.

montydon.com
🐦 @themontydon
📷 themontydon